# BALLOONING
# OVER EVEREST

Handshake over Mount Everest

Expedition Team 1990/91
Michael Balson   Ian Bishop   Russell Brice   Martin Crook
Dick Dennison   Chris Dewhirst   Mandy and Leo Dickinson
Michael Dillon   Jacqui Dudley   Andy Elson   Martin Harris
Martin Hutchins   Eric Jones   Heather Martin   Peter and Sheila Mason
Mark Simmons   Glenn and Irina Singleman   Paul Tait   Lisa Young

1990
Roger Brown   Keith Goffin   Per and Helen Lindstrand   Rob Palmer
Alex Ritchie   Jules Wigdor

*by the same author*

FILMING THE IMPOSSIBLE
ANYTHING IS POSSIBLE

2   Lift off from Gokyo

# BALLOONING OVER EVEREST

# LEO DICKINSON

JONATHAN CAPE · LONDON

For Mandy

First published 1993
© Leo Dickinson 1993
Jonathan Cape, 20 Vauxhall Bridge Road, London SW1V 2SA

A CIP catalogue record for this book is available from the
British Library

ISBN 0-224-03606-8

Leo Dickinson has asserted his right under the Copyright,
Designs and Patents Act 1988 to be identified as the author of
this work

Filmset by SX Composing Ltd, Rayleigh, Essex
Printed by Butler and Tanner Ltd, Frome, Somerset

3   *over page:* Eric Shipton's Valley of Silence – the Western Cwm, with the dark
shadows of Nuptse on the right – photographed by William Thompson on the National
Geographic mapping flight

# Contents

# *Foreword*

I FIRST GOT to know Leo Dickinson in the summer of 1969. It was a suitably dramatic location – the Bonatti Pillar on the West Face of the Dru above Chamonix. I was climbing alone and passed Leo, and his partner Brian Molyneaux, who were inevitably moving more slowly. Some hours later they pulled on to a ledge to discover me sitting down and shaking – I had fallen and then been held, almost incredibly, by a fifi hook. Leo invited me to join him, but I was determined to finish the first British solo ascent. We did, however, join forces for the perils of the descent and thus began our long friendship.

Over the years we've shared many adventures. We climbed the North Face of the Eiger in 1970. It was then, when things weren't going to plan, that I first experienced Leo's skill at coming up with alternative ideas to keep things going. In 1976, during our trip down the Dudh Kosi River below Everest, the canoeists wanted to go home, leaving the film without an ending. Leo alone persuaded them to canoe the lower reaches of the river. It gave a fitting climax to a great expedition.

It was the same story with our balloon flight over Everest. Having recently read some of the correspondence that took place before we left, I know that I would have quickly abandoned the idea. Our flight lasted a matter of hours but the effort needed beforehand to get us to Nepal with two balloons, film gear, a crew and support would have discouraged most men. Despite the disappointment of our first attempt – a revolution in Nepal and the near-fatal crash of a rival Japanese team – Leo kept the project alive through his own special brand of infectious enthusiasm.

Rebuilding the team from scratch, he invited me to come along as a cameraman after persuading Star Micronics to fly a second balloon. I had been among the highest mountains on earth before, but soaring over Everest in an open wicker basket gave me a perspective that few mountaineers have the chance of seeing. Just making the flight would have satisfied most people, but, for Leo, filming the achievement was equally challenging. Anyone with a love for the world's high places will be struck by the beauty of the images he took and the determination required to get them.

ERIC JONES
*North Wales*
*August 1992*

4   Everest at dawn, as seen from Makalu by Doug Scott

# 1. *The Balloon Goes Up*

THE SMALL RED dot moved steadily towards Mount Everest. At 32,000 feet it was on course to clear the summit by a comfortable margin. It would not be long before the three-man Japanese crew could claim the first flight by a hot air balloon over the world's highest mountain. Circling above in a jet aircraft, a Japanese reporter watched their progress as the radio crackled into life.

'There is no wind. We have almost stopped.' The voice was pitched high and betrayed an edge of nervous tension.

The balloon began to drift lower. Soon it became clear that the crew had lost control as the great envelope gyrated in a terrible down-draught that sucked thin unstable air down the sheer North Face. In a matter of minutes the balloon had dropped almost 12,000 feet and then it struck the mountain – or so it seemed to the observer above, watching from the safety of his pressurised cabin. He knew how precarious would be the plight of the three men in their wicker basket if they sought an emergency landing in such an exposed position on the mountainside. He grabbed the radio. 'Kanda! Can you hear me?'

For a moment the balloon was lost from sight as the plane circled behind a ridge. When it emerged again, the balloon had vanished. Then a thin column of smoke was seen rising from some rocks at about 18,500 feet. Flames quickly consumed the basket as the reporter yelled into the radio, 'Kanda! Saito! Can you hear me? Can anyone hear me?'

The radio hissed with static, but no voice was heard.

Their expedition had set off in the spring of 1990 from the village of Yaleb, forty miles to the north-east of the mountain in Tibet. A Chinese weather balloon had given them the right wind direction before the winds dropped. The two crew, Michio Kanda and Sabu Ichiyoshi, and the cameraman, Atsushi Saito, finally became becalmed. Their take-off had been swift and their enthusiasm was unquestioned, but they were in a balloon that was too small and had too little fuel for such a long flight. The crew had been trying to nurse their craft down when it struck the mountain.

Miraculously no one was killed, but Ichiyoshi's femur was broken in the impact. Kanda and Saito cut through the envelope and pulled their friend away as the balloon caught fire. They were barely clear before the propane exploded. All their survival equipment was destroyed in the blaze and their

5, 6    Masso Masuda records the Japanese balloon being prepared for take-off in Tibet.
Its flight ended in the balloon striking the mountain and bursting into flames.

✳

situation became critical. Kanda set off for base camp to fetch help, leaving a radio with Saito who stayed to look after the injured Ichiyoshi. Without sleeping bags and at an altitude of 18,500 feet, the two men used their parachutes for shelter. Thirty-six hours after their balloon crashed, Ichiyoshi and Saito were finally rescued.

The Japanese attempt to be the first to balloon over Everest shows that the mountain's pulling power as the world's ultimate symbol remains undiminished. There are harder mountains, more beautiful or more dangerous, but there is none higher and to reach its summit is a singular achievement. No mountaineer, from the early pioneers George Mallory and Andrew Irvine to modern experts like Reinhold Messner and Chris Bonington, could resist that ultimate temptation – the highest mountain in the world. A first on Everest is something special, something beyond other experiences. George Mallory described seeing Everest for the first time in 1921 thus: 'Gradually, very gradually, we saw the great mountain sides and glaciers and arêtes, now one fragment and now another through the floating rifts of mist, until far higher in the sky than imagination had dared to suggest the white summit of Everest appeared.'

This image of an elusive summit has brought climbers back again and again to climb it from the north, from the east, up this ridge or that face, without oxygen, alone, in days or in hours. Ed Hillary and Norgay Tenzing are famous forever after making the first ascent, while Doug Scott and Dougal Haston made themselves almost as well-known in 1975 when they became the first Britons to reach the summit. In 1978, with Eric Jones, I witnessed for myself a part of this great history when Reinhold Messner and Peter Habeler became the first men to climb the mountain without oxygen. Reinhold had been impressed with my film-making, both on the North Face of the Matterhorn and canoeing the Dudh Kosi River below Everest, and he wanted me to repeat the operation on what Don Whillans affectionately called the 'Big Hill'.

Whillans and I had met for a drink shortly before my departure for Nepal when I told him of our plans. Don's face lit up and he carefully put down his beer glass. It was the signal that a 'Whillansism' was about to be launched in my direction. To hear him in true voice, the reader should adopt a dry and nasal Lancastrian accent and narrow the eyes menacingly.

'Without oxygen?' Don exclaimed. 'It'll be more than oxygen you'll need. A bloody helium balloon is more like it.'

Messner and Habeler made the summit without bottled oxygen and I made a film about it. Two years later Messner climbed Everest from the north, this time without oxygen, balloons or a partner. Don Whillans had no response to that, and neither he nor I realised at the time how prophetic he had been, for ballooning featured in my plans sooner than either of us could have guessed. The Dudh Kosi canoeing film impressed HTV as much as it had Messner and after its success the television moguls appreciated that adventure didn't necessarily mean mountaineering. When HTV were approached by a team planning a flight over the Sahara, they asked me to film it.

Before embarking on what was for me a completely new kind of adventure, I was despatched on an introductory flight over South Wales.

7, 8    Leo Dickinson, the first to cross the summit of Everest in a balloon, with Doug Scott, the first to reach the summit via the South-west Face. (Mandy Dickinson) Doug Scott on the summit, photographed in the last rays of the day's sunlight by Dougal Haston.

9       *over page:* Dougal Haston at the top of Mount Everest. To the left is the ridge of Nuptse, and hidden in the shadowed valleys beyond is the balloon launch site at Gokyo (photograph by Doug Scott).

10    Reinhold Messner, the first to climb Everest solo and the first to do it without
'bottled' oxygen, photographed on the latter ascent by Peter Habeler

The valley from which we took off sheltered the balloon from any gusts of
wind and we went up as straight as the smoke from a nearby cottage.
Looking around at the pretty countryside was delightful to begin with but I
quickly realised that ballooning largely involved going up, looking around
and coming back down again. There seemed to be little excitement involved.
It occurred to me that the most obvious way to change that would be to hop
over the edge of the basket. Just thinking about it gave me an immediate
adrenalin rush and I resolved to learn to parachute.

No one goes to the edge of a high cliff and peers over it without
experiencing the fear of taking one more step. To make a parachute jump,
you have to cross that gap, push your mind through the protective barrier of
fear, and step into the void. It is an alien thing to do and irreversible.

To a large extent, fear can be controlled and some people cope better
than others. Yet everyone is frightened, even terrified, at the prospect of the
first jump. There would be something wrong if they weren't. A person
lacking in fear ought to be restrained from sky-diving. Fear, like pain, alerts
you to impending danger. If you're not afraid, why take the parachute at all?

I remember my first jump vividly. All too soon we were on our first run,
bumping down the runway and lifting through the air. In no time at all I
heard the command – 'In the door!' Surely that didn't mean me? Suddenly
my feet were in space, scrabbling to reach the ground far below. I was dead.
A jolt on my harness stopped the horrible tumbling, and I was alive again.
The plane was gone. Silence took over. There was a pulsating green

organism stretched above my head and I laughed with relief. The fields seemed far below and there were tiny cars driving along pencil-thin roads. But I could float this way and that without hindrance. I was free.

By the time we arrived in the Sudanese Sahara these new experiences had changed forever my ideas about adventure. The local villagers seemed less sure of our plan. Who were these strange white men planning to fly in a wicker basket, driven by bottles of gas and a great big hot bag of air? Our balloon's envelope was spread out on the desert floor ready to be filled. The burner started up with the noise of a small jet engine. As the flames shot through the evening sky, the effect on scores of villagers who had gathered round to watch was dramatic — as dramatic as the sight of hundreds of scattered sandals, hopelessly abandoned as their owners fled in panic.

There is a strange ritual balloonists the world over perform. Before taking to the air they stand in a circle, all talking at once. Then someone stoops down, scoops up a handful of dirt and hurls it into the air. I assumed it was some primitive method of determining the direction the balloon might take. As I learned more about ballooning, I understood just how primitive it was.

Giles Hall, our chief pilot, was an eccentric character, dressed usually in a check shirt and pressed cravat, who might have stepped straight from the pages of a P.G. Wodehouse story. Most balloonists are con-men and Giles has no equal. His ability to charm and scrape through is legendary. Going through customs we had been stopped for some minor indiscretion

11   Eric Jones and a Sherpa climb through the Khumbu Icefall (Leo Dickinson)

concerning two guns in place of one and a hundred rounds of ammunition instead of the ten written down on the import forms. With a manic laugh Giles counted ten sets of ten.

'There you are,' he said with a flourish. 'Ten. Oh, and this gun doesn't work. Look!' He pointed the muzzle at the horrified customs official and squeezed the trigger.

By the time I had flown with Giles across miles of sandy nothingness I suddenly thought to ask him the simple question, 'How far can a balloon fly?'

'As far as your fuel lasts,' Giles replied.

'Could you go all the way round the world?' But I had the answer already and a new project was born – a balloon flight encircling the globe.

Our balloon hit the sand dune at terrifying speed. It came as a shock, for Giles had assured me that the wind always dropped off just before sunset. Foolishly I had believed him. My cameras flew everywhere, sand flew everywhere, everything flew everywhere and all control was lost. Gradually our speed decreased and we came to rest.

'Ballooning is forty minutes of sheer delight followed by forty seconds of sheer terror,' Giles said with a hearty laugh. I agreed, and made a vow never to land in another balloon.

We had flown over the Sahara Desert, floated back and forth across the Nile, and crept up on wildlife in a game park, but, with our trip coming to a close, we still lacked a climax for the film. We found an original solution to the problem. One of the team sky-dived from the balloon and was then fielded back into the basket which had been made to descend more quickly than the parachutist. It resulted in him being wrapped round my precarious camera perch at the end of a rope ladder hanging below the basket. Climaxes are never easy.

On our return from the Sahara, Giles and I set about raising half a million pounds with which to fly around the world. My credibility as adventure film-maker opened the doors and Giles's legendary charm did the rest. The plan was a sound one, though perhaps ahead of its time. It was barely two years since the Scottish engineer, Don Cameron, had set off from Newfoundland to attempt a balloon flight across the Atlantic. He had almost succeeded with his co-pilot Chris Davey, a former tank regiment major with a pronounced stutter. Legend has it that Chris never actually finished the order to f..f..f..fire until they were p..p..past the target. Later I made him the subject of a film about ballooning across the Austrian Alps. This was a hair-raising experience for his passenger Eric Jones. He was teaching Eric to fly, and told him to 'b-b-b-b-burn!' Eric burned, and kept burning, waiting for Chris to finish. 'Nooo! Too much!' he finally managed to yell out.

Cameron and Davey came down in the sea 110 miles short of the French coast. It was a hundred years since the first trans-Atlantic attempt had been made but within two weeks they were to see three Americans snatch the honour by making it all the way to France. One of them had even planned to arrive on English soil by hang glider until it was discarded in mid-Atlantic as ballast, although a 2-lb jar of peanut butter survived.

There are two kinds of people in this world: those who do things and those who talk about doing things, and it soon became obvious that our round-the-world project had far too many of the latter. I had gone to a television company with the idea for a film and this allowed Giles to bring in ICI as sponsor.

The project got off to a bad start and rapidly grew worse. At first no one could agree upon what size of balloon was needed. Then Giles was fired by his own choice of project manager and went off to form a rival team sponsored by Count Vittorio Rossi, who happens to own Martini. Not to be outdone, our hit-man went for royal patronage, but before too long the whole project collapsed. In an attempt to salvage something from the wreckage, I suggested to the TV company awaiting my film that we went instead for an attempt on the world hot air balloon altitude record. The balloonist would be Julian Nott, who not only had been involved in our round-the-world project but had held the altitude record for most of the 1970s.

At first we planned to take off in Albuquerque, New Mexico, but the wind never dropped sufficiently to launch our 375,000 cubic-foot monster. Our second choice was Longmont in Colorado, where good weather was guaranteed. While Julian would try to take the balloon up to 60,000 feet, I would be jettisoned with my parachute at 30,000 feet and leave him to it.

I climbed into the perspex dome after Julian and the door was closed. Anticipating the cold five miles up, I had dressed in mountaineering clothes and found the heat inside the capsule stifling. We lifted off, looking like two overdressed goldfish.

A thick layer of cloud had settled over Colorado that morning and Denver Air Traffic Control was not eager to see me free-fall through their air space. I would have been happy avoiding any passing jumbos, if I'd been allowed that option. Instead I was instructed to bale out before we reached the cloud at 18,000 feet.

Obediently I clambered out of the gondola, switched on the remote control cameras hanging from the lip of the balloon, gave Julian the thumbs-up and leapt backwards into space. I had just touched down in a little field at the side of a farm when a silver-haired lady wandered over.

'Ah been livin' here forty years,' she exclaimed in a lovely Mid-west drawl, 'and I never seen anythin' like you before.'

High overhead, Julian's burner went out at 53,000 feet and with liquid propane gushing everywhere he failed to relight the flame. The balloon had enough momentum to coast upwards to just above the three per cent margin of error required to set a new record. This was to be Julian's last foray into the record books, accomplished with relatively low-level technology. Waiting in the wings was the next generation who would stretch science to its limits.

Per Lindstrand was a balloonist after my own heart. When I first met him he had just taken up sky-diving and we made a few jumps together. I took to him immediately, liking his well-developed and mischievous sense of humour. He was a big kid with big toys who had spent all his adult life playing with balloons. Per had moved from his native Sweden to England in 1978 to set up a balloon building business, Thunder and Colt. It quickly became one of the world's biggest manufacturers of lighter-than-air craft and its boss led them to the fore with a series of spectacular ballooning adventures, mainly with Virgin's flamboyant boss Richard Branson. Together the two of them monopolised ballooning in the world's press for a five year period until our Everest project.

It all started when Per was in the Swedish air force in 1973. He was grounded after breaking his leg in a skiing accident and made a bet with a couple of pilots that if he couldn't walk by December he would fly across the airfield. They humoured him.

Balloons had just begun to appear in Sweden and Per had only seen pictures of them. Yet that was enough to spark him off. He was his squadron's engineering officer with time on his hands and before long he had set about making his own hot air balloon. Armed with a sewing machine and eighty surplus canopies, he went into the parachute loft and began to stitch. Next he welded up a frame and burner and plumed it to a propane tank. Despite his crutches and a total lack of balloon flying-time, Per managed to get the contraption airborne and across 400 yards of the airfield. He won his bet but he was landed with seven days house arrest for flying without permission.

His first foray into ballooning in front of the general public was a complete fiasco. The Milk Marketing Board of Great Britain had sponsored him to break the world altitude record and were keen to see a return – in terms of media coverage – on their considerable investment. Just to overturn Julian Nott's record of 53,000 feet would have been enough for a first attempt but, with the lure of a spectacular result in front of the nation's television cameras, Lindstrand felt under pressure to go straight for his greater ambition of a flight to 80,000 feet.

To reduce drag and gain that height, the balloon needed to be shaped like an arrow. It would also have to use dangerous fuels and would be extremely susceptible to even light winds. In addition, a balloon of 1.2 million cubic

feet in volume would have to be put down in water. By the end of
September the sea round Britain's coast would be too cold and the Royal
Navy's search and rescue teams killed the project for that year.

Undeterred, Per went back for a second attempt. This time his sponsors
announced 4 August for the flight to ensure the largest presence of TV and
press. When the day arrived, it became obvious that the weather conditions
were unsuitable. Per was asked to inflate the balloon for the sake of the
assembled reporters. Without the usual parachute in the top of the envelope,
to spill the air when it came into land, Lindstrand and his team could only
deflate in a high wind by having it towed forward from the top of the
envelope to force out the air from the bottom. A tractor was hitched to
perform the manoeuvre while two girls held on to the mooring rope. As Per
walked past them he suddenly heard a shout and saw them being lifted up
into the air on the end of a rope. Unable to hang on, the two anchors let go
and Per himself, who had gone to their rescue, went sailing up 50 feet into
the air. The tractor driver never looked back. Spotting the distortion in the
ring at the top of the balloon, Per knew it was going to snap and, rather than
be shot hundreds of yards across the grass, he too let go. Millions watching
on television saw him fall heavily, breaking a foot and a hand and damaging
his back.

When he had recovered, Per persuaded his milk sponsor – now joined by
a cornflakes company – to move the operation to more stable conditions in
the United States, where NASA advised Page in Arizona as the calmest
spot. In three weeks he experienced three sandstorms, one snowstorm, and
winds of never less than five knots. The sponsors pulled out.

By 1984 other balloonists were wanting a slice of the action. I received a
strange phone call from an exuberant Australian who asked if I was
interested in flying a hot air balloon over Mount Everest. 'I dream of
nothing else,' I replied as yet unaware of this former mountaineer's wicked
sense of humour and elastic optimism. Chris Dewhirst had managed to get
some of the permits necessary for the flight but not the all important one
from the Chinese to allow us into Tibet. This denied us an attempt to fly
over Everest, but didn't stop us flying near it. His film producer – another
Australian, Dick Dennison – was a charming but ruthless movie mogul
whose watchword was 'divide and rule'. We wanted to mix Tibetan myth
and modern technology in our 'Flight of the Windhorse'. Chris and I were
to fly in one balloon under the direction of an airline pilot called Aden
Wickes, while Brian Smith flew the other with the American photographer
Jan Reynolds and balloon manufacturer Phil Kavanagh.

The two balloons took off before an excited crowd in the centre of the
Nepalese capital Kathmandu. We had not reached the 29,000 feet height of
Everest before a malfunction in the oxygen system extinguished the pilot

burners and caused a fast frightening descent almost to ground level. Faced with diminishing fuel supplies, and with the valleys ahead rapidly filling with cloud, we were forced to land in the hills above a village called Khare to the south-west of the mountain. The other balloon had similar problems and landed, according to Brian, 'very carefully in a 50-foot tree'. Their basket was inverted and then caught fire in much the same way as the Japanese basket would do five years later. The crew narrowly escaped death as they fought to put out the flames with their hands.

Perhaps I should have paid more attention while Chris was reliving our flight for the *Daily Telegraph* journalist Pearson Phillips. He described in fulsome terms looking down on the summit of Gauri Sankar. It was a forgivable piece of romancing as Chris well knew our flight passed to the south of this peak, not over it. In fact, we hadn't got close to any high mountains, landing at 14,000 feet.

Dick the movie mogul was eager for us to go straight back up. We didn't see our flight as the failure he clearly did, but after resting in Kathmandu for ten days, we did make a sortie towards the Annapurna range and the sacred mountain of Machhapuchhare. Brian, who was using a leaky oxygen set, traced a wobbly course over the foothills and alongside the vast chain of the Himalayas. When the wind died after two hours, we descended early just to the south of Lamjung Himal.

If we hadn't achieved a great deal it had been enormous fun, and made us the first to attempt a Himalayan balloon flight.

Meanwhile Per Lindstrand was busy at his factory in Oswestry. Thunder and Colt were building two airliner-shaped balloons with the Virgin Airways logo on the sides, but he had his mind on grander ideas. When Huw Band, Virgin's managing director, walked unannounced into the office, his eye fell on secret plans which had been left out accidentally on Per's desk.

'What's that?' Huw asked as Per hastily rolled them up.

'Oh, I'm just thinking about an Atlantic flight,' Per said casually.

'I'm interested.'

In fact Huw Band wanted first refusal on any balloon crossing for his adventurous entrepreneur boss, Richard Branson.

It was the spring of 1986 and Branson was about to cross the Atlantic by power-boat. Three days after his boat had broken the trans-Atlantic record he was sitting down to lunch with Per Lindstrand and negotiating a deal, worth hundreds of thousands of pounds. It was settled in an hour, despite the entrepreneur knowing nothing whatever about balloons.

While Lindstrand tested all the sophisticated systems for the flight, Branson took to the skies with ballooning instructor Robin Bachelor. The pair got on famously. Eight days later he had his licence, and not long after that a lucrative contract with TVS for the privilege of promoting his own company. All that he needed now was some instruction in parachuting, and that was where I came in.

It had to be an 'accelerated' course, which doesn't mean falling faster, rather that you dispense with traditional static line jumps, in which your chute is opened automatically as you leave the aircraft, and go straight on to freefall. In this way, two instructors hold on to you as you drop through space and make sure you open your canopy correctly. Branson seemed to absorb the theory well and was relaxed about making his first jump while we were still on the ground. He kept cool on the way up and I positioned myself to film his first exit from the aircraft. Suddenly, as I hung from the handles outside the plane's door, Richard decided he needed a refresher course on correct procedure from his instructors. Then he jumped. As our celebrated charge bombed earthwards, he caused anxious moments by curling into a ball before eventually pulling the ripcord as he had been taught.

He never managed to do it again. On the next three jumps he failed to find the handle and his chute had to be deployed for him. Anxious to make up for previous failures, on the fifth jump he grabbed a handle with gusto. The main parachute appeared and then disappeared. He had pulled the cut-away pad instead of the rip-cord. Fortunately for Virgin's shareholders, the reserve chute worked perfectly. It wasn't the place for practical jokes – to which both Branson and Lindstrand were more than partial – so I kept mine for the launch day.

My plan was to dash from the crowd just as the Virgin Atlantic balloon lifted off in New England, with a large raincoat covering my parachute, harness and a climbing karabiner, and clip on to the gondola in front of the battery of television cameras. The message I would press to their window read: 'This is a hijack. Take me to Europe.' There was just one snag. When I ran from the crowd I would also be running the gauntlet of police firearms. The danger would be if they missed and hit the propane fuel tanks instead.

It is probably as well that I thought better of it because there was an unforeseen drama on the launch field anyway. As the huge craft rose into the air two cylinders of propane hanging outside the closed gondola fell twenty feet to the ground. It gave the men from the media something to report but did nothing to impede their smooth passage across the ocean. Then, as they approached the Irish coast, all contact with the balloon was lost and rumours of disaster began to spread. There couldn't have been more confusion if Orson Welles had announced that the Martians were arriving. The weather had suddenly deteriorated and a cold front lay across Northern Ireland while everything to the south of Manchester was calm and clear. Lindstrand and Branson's track would take them over Londonderry and the Mull of Kintyre, north of Glasgow, and then out over the North Sea by way of Aberdeen. They had to get down before then because the track

12    The first Himalayan balloon flight from Kathmandu in 1985, Everest in the far distance just to the left of the basket (LD)

would have taken them over Sweden that night, and then over Russia, where permission to land had been denied. There was no real choice but to come down either in Northern Ireland or in Scotland, and by this time Per had been awake for thirty-six hours.

He decided to go down low and make a practice approach over Ireland and then fly on to land in Scotland. Their best chance would be to aim for a beach since their track north of Glasgow would take them into the Highlands, where the whole region was in cloud. Coming in for the practice run they were caught in the cold front and sucked down by air currents. As Per dropped the balloon through the last 5,000 feet he found he couldn't arrest its descent.

The biggest balloon ever landed before this was the half-million-cubic-foot Heineken balloon, and Virgin Atlantic was almost five times that size. Per decided to abandon the idea of a rehearsal and to take them in for a full landing instead; the draught pulling them down would, he felt sure,

disappear just before the ground. He went to radio his intention to their support crew but discovered to his horror that the radio battery was dead. From that moment they were out of contact and confusion about their whereabouts began.

Per directed his craft towards a farm and a target field he had picked out while descending but missed it by a few hundred yards. Suddenly the weather deteriorated severely. It was quite clear that they were going to bounce up again, so Per decided to burn. They hit the ground close to a farmhouse and immediately rose up again. Soon afterwards, a woman telephoned the BBC to say that Richard Branson's balloon had landed in her back garden in Limavady, Ireland.

The balloon climbed again. With the cloud base at 500 feet Per could no longer risk continuing to Scotland since the mountains surrounding his intended landing site were about 1,200 feet high. The only option left now was to ditch in the sea, an eventuality the capsule's designers had allowed

13   Per Lindstrand and Richard Branson before take-off (Boccon Gibod)

for. They made another approach over the Irish Sea and struck the water. Per fired the explosive bolts. Nothing happened.

The basket should have separated from the envelope but another faulty battery prevented the system from working. Worse still, Per could not be sure that the bolts wouldn't go off later as the balloon rose out of the water again, perhaps dropping them hundreds of feet back into the sea. He shouted at Richard to get out of the gondola and into the water.

Per told me, 'As I threw myself into the sea I turned round and saw him still standing on top of the gondola. He hadn't taken in the urgency of our situation. In my entire life I've never seen anything worse than Richard Branson standing like Captain Ahab, grasping the rail of the world's largest balloon as it disappeared up into the murk at about 400 feet. He was gone. You can imagine my feelings. I hadn't the slightest worry about myself because I'm a strong swimmer but I thought Richard was going to die.'

It was probably the only instant decision that the entrepreneur ever failed to make.

Meanwhile, Per was in the Irish Sea with only a floating parachute for a life raft. He had been too busy flying the balloon to prepare for bailing out and had left Branson to gather up the survival gear. Richard had the lot –

the life vest, the lifeboat, the ELT radio, the survival kit, the fishhooks, the Russian roubles, and the emergency guide.

From his survival training in the Swedish air force, Per knew that he had to keep moving to maintain body temperature. He deployed his parachute for any passing aircraft to spot and, stripping off his clothes, struck out for the shore four miles away. After half an hour he realised that he had made no progress at all in the strong tide that was running against him. It was starting to get dark too. Quickly he changed course and immediately made headway. The local lifeboat missed him, despite Per waving frantically as it passed by within three hundred yards. Gradually the coast grew larger and he could clearly see a rock face above the sea. He became worried that once he reached shore he wouldn't be able to climb out. Helicopters passed overhead, searching for the stricken balloon, but failed to see the tiny figure of Lindstrand struggling through the water.

He still had a mile to swim when they found him. He had been in the chilly waters of the Irish Sea for more than two hours when out of nowhere came a Navy Lynx helicopter. It flew in quickly and then stopped dead, hovering just above him. When Per swam towards it, it moved away. He waved but the helicopter took no notice. It seemed to Per that the pilot was intent on teasing him and he began to lose his temper. As he raised his arm to shake his fist, his hand struck a dinghy that had come up silently behind him.

With its winch out of order, the helicopter had been directing the dinghy towards Per. Nor could the aircraft come down and pick him up on its skids because of the wash caused by its rotor blades. There were three local youngsters in the boat, clearly bemused at the sight of a Swedish émigré thrashing around in the water and cursing a helicopter. One of the crew leaned out and asked Per if he wanted to come aboard.

'I was so frozen I couldn't speak, he told me. 'They were obviously thinking, "Here's a funny guy. Does he want to come aboard or doesn't he?" I heaved myself out of the water and just managed to crawl aboard. Then they realised something serious had happened and a girl gave me a sweater. I had nothing on apart from my underpants and these ludicrous surgical stockings that the doctor had given us to wear so we didn't get circulation problems.'

Per sat there in his underpants and the borrowed sweater while the boat, which had a hundred horsepower Johnson engine, cut through the waves at a brisk 35 knots for the twenty-minute trip back to port. He'd spent over two hours in the water and was now being finished off by the open dinghy. He finally came into harbour wet, cold and tired only to find the press were waiting for him. They found Per's appearance hilarious and began laughing as he walked up the jetty in his support stockings. The first cameraman looked through his lens, grimaced and then turned away. A blanket was thrown across Per's shoulders to save him any further embarrassment and a big Sea King helicopter arrived to take him off.

Meanwhile, Richard Branson was left in charge of the biggest hot air balloon in the world without seeming to have any clue as to how it worked. He didn't read the analogue altimeter, although he could have made use of the transponder, which had a digital readout, if it had not been turned off. He had radios but didn't try them. There was a big red button saying ELT (Emergency Locator Transmitter beacon). All he had to do was press it and there would have been a satellite fix on the balloon within seconds. Any aircraft within thirty miles would have been there in minutes. Per later calculated that the balloon had sailed to a height of 5,000 feet, with no coaxing at all from the sole occupant.

'Surely,' I asked Per, 'the whole world must have known where the balloon was anyway?'

'With the transponder down,' Per told me, 'the radar lost us and no one knew where we were to within 15 miles. Do you know Richard wrote a letter to his wife, and another to his mother. When they were done he filled in the log book. The only thing he did fiddle with was the gondola's hatch. He took it off, looked out, and managed to replace it back to front. After a while

14   The Virgin balloon comes down in the Irish Sea after completing the first hot air Atlantic crossing. A naval destroyer goes to the rescue of Richard Branson. (Martin Hutchins)

the balloon floated seawards again and gave him a second ducking. This time a navy frigate was soon on the scene and in minutes a rescue helicopter had lifted him to safety. He was very lucky because by replacing the hatch incorrectly the gondola had started to sink.'

I asked Per whether Richard wrote any cheques during his hour of reckoning. 'No,' he said, laughing. 'But there was a funny incident about a £50 note. Richard never carries cash, as you might remember.'

I remembered very well. After his parachute training, Branson took all his instructors, Mandy and myself out for a meal. He was in top form now that he was safely on the ground and wanted to celebrate surviving his first jump. When champagne was ordered the waiter recognised him immediately. He alerted the other diners to Richard's presence by announcing, 'Mr Virgin Atlantic, I presume?'

When it came to paying the bill, Richard became embarrassed and disappeared for a moment before returning to tell me there was a telephone call for me outside. I was puzzled, sure that nobody knew I was there. I looked perplexed, but Richard insisted, so I left the table. In the lobby he explained that as he had only credit cards and the Amesbury Italian took only cash, would I lend him £200? When we left the owner whispered in my ear, 'Eet was not Meester Richard Branson after all. This man had no money.'

Something similar had taken place on the trans-Atlantic flight. Richard hadn't wanted any money, but his Virgin colleagues insisted it would be embarrassing to send him off without any cash. They spirited a wad of £50 notes into his flight bag and put it in the capsule. After it had been winched up on to the frigate later that night, the crew stuck in a hose pipe to pump out the water. Suddenly the hose went erghmmbump. The pump clogged up, slurped, and then jammed altogether. A crewman called out for a light as there seemed to be some paper stuck in the tube. It was a £50 note. Suddenly every Naval rating ran for the capsule and there were £50 notes flying everywhere. Strangely enough, none was ever recovered.

Per and Richard were re-united on the frigate and then flown to the hospital at Kilmarnock. With his legs in agony, Per had taken off his stockings and underpants, so that all he had on as he walked up the hospital steps was a blanket, while Richard appeared in a jazzy naval uniform. There seemed to be a thousand people waiting for them, and when they saw Richard, they made a rush through the barriers. 'I shut my eyes and prayed,' Per says, 'and when I opened them again I was alone. Richard was trying to make good his escape, hotly pursued by several hundred women.'

Per went to hospital for a check-up, then to a press conference, and finally to a party, wearing a jacket he had borrowed from one of the crew, some green trousers and slip-on hospital rubber shoes. He had organised probably the most ambitious balloon flight ever attempted. He had shattered the earlier hot air balloon distance record of 900 miles and established an astounding new one of 3,075 miles. He wasn't at all concerned that Richard Branson absorbed most of the media coverage. 'That's what he pays for,' he explained to me. 'I expected it and I couldn't have made the flight without his money. The ballooning world knows who did what, and that is enough for me.'

It was not the last of the Lindstrand records. For the best part of a decade Julian Nott had dominated high altitude hot air ballooning and seemed to assume that altitude records were his exclusive domain. Per was set on taking his crown. In 1988, on a flight lasting just over three hours, Per took his craft to 65,129 feet above the state of Texas, beating Julian's best by more than 11,000 feet. There was little publicity surrounding the flight, in direct contrast to his previous attempt when the world's cameras had watched him fail. He travelled 80 miles on his record attempt and managed a flawless landing with the balloon this time coming to rest the right way up. 'I went as high as you can go with normal fabric and normal burners,' he recalls. 'Any higher and you would have to use rocket fuel and really expensive materials.'

I had to admit that Per Lindstrand had achieved the ballooning equivalent of Bob Beamon clearing the long-jump pit.

# 2. *Bonington Takes Off*

WHEN I RETURNED from Nepal after our flights above the Himalaya, rumours of another attempt to fly over Everest soon began to spread and I tried, without success, to get on board. Norman Apsey, a middle-aged balloonist who had never attempted anything as ambitious before, had approached various television companies offering a film about the proposed flight, and the BBC contacted a film producer, Hasseeb Zafar, to oversee the plan. Hasseeb hired a marketing company to sell the idea to potential sponsors and among these was a computer printer manufacturer called Star Micronics UK Ltd.

Per Lindstrand agreed to pilot the balloon but didn't want the trouble of organisation because he was already heavily involved with his own plans for crossing the Pacific with Richard Branson. It was Star's general manager, Ian Smith, and his public relations team who came up with a method of prising the media's attention away from Branson and on to the Everest idea.

'Let's get Chris Bonington to open a press conference.'

Bonington was delighted to lend his name to such a worthwhile project. Shortly before the press conference he replaced Norman Apsey in the balloon.

'It would,' Chris wrote in the sponsor's brochure, 'be the culmination of a lifetime's dream – seeing Everest from the air, floating as a cloud.'

It was all good lyrical stuff. The lavishly illustrated ten-page booklet knew no bounds and Chris's celebrated talents were stretched to the full.

'For centuries Mount Everest has captured the imagination of every man,' he wrote. 'Rising like a vast three-sided pyramid, Mount Everest dominates the Himalayan range that divides Nepal from Tibet, its almost airless peak scraping the sky at 29,028 feet above sea level. For millions of years nature has sculptured this stark, majestic beauty, creating a magnificent mountain – the ultimate challenge. The venture, sponsored by the computer printer manufacturer Star Micronics UK Ltd, will push both man and machine to the limit.'

Hasseeb Zafar sought me out with some questions on our experiences ballooning in the Himalaya in 1985. He began by inquiring about the availability of helicopters in Nepal. I knew his reason for asking, but I still wanted to hear it.

'Well, there is an Allouette 3, and the King's Puma, of course.' We had used this to salvage our balloons in 1985. 'Why do you ask?'

'To film from, of course,' Hasseeb replied haughtily.

'And what altitude is the take-off site?' I asked.

'14,000 feet.' Hasseeb was becoming uneasy.

I was silent for a moment. Now it was my turn to be high-handed. 'Do you know the ceiling for an Allouette?' I asked. 'Do you know the climb-rate of an Allouette? Do you know the climb-rate of a balloon? Not many helicopters can fly above 16,000 feet and their climb-rate at altitude is a few hundred feet per minute. A large balloon can manage 2,000 feet per minute. Sorry, Hasseeb, you haven't done your sums. Why not let me come along to film from a second balloon.'

Of course, this was out of his area. I would have to speak to the sponsor. I outlined all the best reasons for having me along in a long letter to Star Micronics and waited. I had a pretty good record – more than fifty adventure films, many of them winning awards round the world, and I was also an experienced parachutist. Eventually I spoke to Ian Smith for the first time on the phone, but try as I might, I couldn't get the idea of a second balloon to be taken seriously.

Mischievously, Per called me to suggest I try to get aboard the first balloon. It seemed they had an inexperienced cameraman in mind whom Per wanted me to replace, although he didn't have any sway with the sponsor.

'Why don't you see what Bonington can do? He'll understand the PR value.'

No sooner said than done. 'Chris? I gather you are going to balloon over Everest with Per Lindstrand.'

'Yes, that's right. Per is absolutely the man for it. Got all the right qualifications. It will be tremendous to look down on the summit and take some pictures. I'll be writing a book about it, of course.'

'But will you be filming it?' I inquired.

'Well, not exactly. There could be a third cameraman in the basket.'

It should be me, I thought.

'Do me a favour, Chris, and put forward my arguments for a second balloon to the sponsor. I'll find the pilot. It's the only way we'll get any good aerial material.'

The voice on the phone cooled somewhat. 'It's not really my place. I don't know how much pull I have. It might jeopardise the whole trip.'

One might be forgiven at such a moment for seeing Chris's opening bonhomie as transparently thin. At first he had said how nice it would be to work with me but, when it came to it, he was not prepared to help. I'd long ago learnt that if you want something badly enough, you have to get it yourself.

Alternatively, of course, you can just sit back and let fate lend a hand. Per and Chris didn't get on.

'There was no actual conflict between us,' Per recalls. 'We never clashed, but we were different personalities altogether. I'm easy-going and he is not. Chris has little sense of humour and, while he is a good speaker and an excellent writer, I found the meetings about Everest very heavy going. There was no life or spirit in the project, and I don't like climbing.'

Bonington had once taken Lindstrand climbing on Mount Blanc with Independent Television news in tow to record the event. What followed was a well-publicised loss of temper.

'The television people told me to come nearer the edge of an ice overhang,' Per remembers. 'I was annoyed with them because I thought they wanted to see an accident. The camera was left running with nobody next to it so that I wouldn't know it was on. They kept telling me, "Go further. Further!" I said I wouldn't, that I didn't want to go any further. We were roped up and I sensed that they wanted to see the overhang break. Why should they film me falling, even on a rope? "Damn your pictures," I said. "I'm not going to hang on a rope just to make you happy." And they used my tantrum on TV, which I considered a cheap trick, not least because I had no idea they were filming it.'

The original plan was for Chris and Per to fly over Everest in the autumn of 1989. In the event, political disturbances in Tiananmen Square intervened, and in any case they were nowhere near ready. The reconnaissance had not been carried out properly, the permits were not to hand and much of the equipment was lost in Bombay. Per decided they could not fly that year. It was going to be organised properly or not at all. He didn't want the Skyquest fiasco all over again.

By this time Chris Bonington had decided to leave the expedition. Whether his heart was no longer in it, or the delays were interfering with other things he wanted to do, I don't know. Whatever the reason, I was the one who benefited most.

'Per here,' a very correct but slightly foreign voice said when I picked up the phone. 'Bonington's dropped out, so do you want to come in the balloon over Everest?' I was finally on board.

Not only did Per need a new balloonist, he also decided that organisation for the expedition should be put in the hands of a project manager. Peter Mason was an ex-journalist who changed from writing about to flying with hot air for a living. I had met Peter through parachuting. He had written a tongue-in-cheek article about my fictional parachuting character, Wally Gubbins, for *YOU* magazine. Wally's sky-diving adventures with several naked ladies had also been reported in the pages of *Paris Match*, *Stern* and

15  *over page:* Everest, Lhotse and Nuptse – our projected flight path – photographed by
    William Thompson (on the National Geographic mapping flight)

*Penthouse*. Peter has a stable of sponsored balloons, such as the one belonging to the *Financial Times* which resembles a rolled-up newspaper. He had impressed Per with his management of the altitude record flight, but it was made quite clear to him that Per didn't want to be sitting on top of a mountain in Nepal, waiting for the equipment to come out of customs. The problem was that Per could spare only three weeks to complete the flight, while the rest of the team prepared the balloons and monitored the weather in advance. The plan didn't leave much margin for error.

The expedition, minus Per, arrived in Kathmandu in the spring of 1990. Apart from Mandy and myself, the team included Peter Mason, my old friend Eric Jones, and Paul Head, who was a farmer from Massachusetts. He was to double as a weather man and had been sent out by Per's personal weather forecaster Bob Rice, who had predicted the weather on their trans-Atlantic flight. During the expedition Paul went down with the usual stomach ailments experienced on a trek to the monastery at Thangboche. On his return to Kathmandu he had a tee-shirt made with the slogan 'Happiness is a Dry Fart' printed on it. It was unfortunate that subsequent events should make his comment seem a fitting epitaph for the whole expedition. Martin Hutchins, Per's trans-Atlantic design engineer, had been appointed launch master and Jules Wigdor was to be Peter's management assistant. Roger Brown, a climber and sky-diver as well as being a fixed wing pilot, was to head our retrieval team in Tibet, and Per had included two engineers, Keith Goffin and Alex Ritchie.

It was not surprising to me to see border officials completely flummoxed by what kind of expedition we were, and the balloons stayed stuck in customs. We had no way of moving the most important equipment to Namche Bazar before Per arrived. Not an auspicious start.

Soon we were coping with even bigger problems. Our sponsor had paid the Chinese for a very expensive permit that would allow us into Tibet, but, unknown to us, a similar licence was issued to a rival Japanese team at the same time under the pretext that theirs was a scientific expedition which didn't conflict with our adventurous one. The difference was lost on me.

On the surface, at least, the Japanese seemed far more organised than we were. They were said to have 25 Betacam camera crews, although the precise number might have been mangled in translation. They certainly had the services of a Chinese jet aircraft from which to take video. Their television producer spoke excellent English, and she had charming eyes that I knew would open more doors than Peter's stiff upper lip. One of their pilots, it seemed, had been an Olympic athlete, although he was no mountaineer. Neither had he parachuted. He smoked rather more than I thought sensible for someone who might land high in the Himalayas.

I realised the need to acclimatise and so I hired some boots and trekked to Everest Base Camp alone. There I met Tim McCartney-Snape, who was to solo the mountain without oxygen later that spring, and his wife, Dr Ann Ward, who made me welcome. While I was away the problems grew worse. A revolution flared up in the streets of Kathmandu.

Most Westerners see Nepal as an easy-going country whose poverty seems bearable and whose people seem content. By the spring of 1990 there were plenty of reasons for discontent. Revolution had caught fire all over the world, from Central Europe to China. In Nepal political parties were banned and there was little freedom of speech or real democracy. There were fuel shortages, which made the country's position as sixth poorest in the world even worse, and censorship prevented the press from talking about it. The democracy movement had no wish to depose King Birendra, merely to change his rule from one of virtual dictatorship to that of a constitutional monarch presiding over an elected multi-party assembly. The Queen was less popular. Her connection with the deposed Rana clan, which had ruled the country until 1951, made people suspicious. As Democracy Day approached, the King appealed for calm and the democracy movement got ready to protest. The authorities imposed a curfew as tension grew.

One night the team was eating by candlelight in Helena's restaurant when a brick came crashing through the window. Peter Mason was the closest and immediately dived under the table. When fighting broke out the next day Peter went to the British Embassy, where he became trapped for the night. It all made for good stories later and turned Mandy into an instant war photographer, a role I had studiously avoided since my college days.

'I'd never experienced any hostile public situations before,' Mandy recalls, 'and it all seemed very exciting. I wanted to watch. I picked up the Canon Hi-8 video camera, rather than the Betacam which might have attracted too much attention, and made my way towards the Palace, where most of the action was taking place. Roger came with me to take stills, but we were stopped by some soldiers barricading the way. I backed away about ten feet and started filming. More soldiers wearing riot shields and wielding enormous sticks arrived in a truck. Some of them carried guns, which added to the tension. My filming deteriorated as my hands started shaking. I felt a mixture of excitement and fear, and I tried to imagine what Leo would have done in this situation.'

I can tell you I would have legged it quick.

'Although the soldiers were shouting at everyone to go back to their homes or hotels, I decided to hang around. I was told to stop filming and was moved on. I ended up with a crowd of the "rebels" who were much happier about the camera. They wanted their message to reach the outside world.'

Mandy thought the average age of the protesters was about twenty. They chanted democracy slogans and threw stones at the soldiers. They were not really threatening, and it reminded her of children playing war games. She hid behind a lamp-post in line with the rebels and facing the soldiers, who retaliated by throwing the stones back at them. Roger hid behind in a shop doorway, giving her moral support. It all seemed like harmless fun.

'This changed when suddenly there was a gunshot. I saw smoke from the barrel of a gun, which seemed to be aimed in my direction. It was then I realised that I wasn't quite thin enough to be covered by the lamp-post. The rebels became concerned for my welfare and insisted I move to a safer place. With Roger's help, I climbed up on to the roof of a garage where, hidden from the soldiers, I could go on filming.'

Soon the crowd dispersed as tear-gas bombs landed in their midst. Mandy stayed as long as she could before the smoke drove her away, her eyes streaming. On the way back to the hotel, Mandy and Roger were approached by many Nepalese who expressed sympathy for their discomfort. They were sure that her filming the demonstrations would help. When she replayed the video later, it showed a soldier firing in her general direction and a large stone hitting the lamp-post inches above her head. But this was a minor disturbance compared to what went on in front of the Palace, where two Western photographers were killed. Fortunately Mandy hadn't been able to get through the barricades to that area.

Per arrived as the fighting broke out but managed to escape into the mountains before a curfew was imposed. The gear remained in customs and now the military became nervous about our permits. While I continued to acclimatise at Everest Base Camp, Per trekked to Namche Bazar and Thangboche with his wife Helen, Eric Jones and our weatherman, Paul Head. Per had no idea what was going on, I had disappeared and the balloon was still in customs. Before leaving Britain, he had been confident that, with the rest of the team preparing the way, three weeks would be ample time to fly over Everest, but already the expedition was beginning to fall apart.

When word reached me that our team was trekking towards Thangboche, I ran down from Everest, arriving in a state of near-exhaustion at Namche Bazar the same night. There I discovered that Per and Helen were 1,000 feet higher, at the air strip of Sangboche, waiting for a plane to take them out in the morning. I staggered up the hill in the dark to the Everest View Hotel, where I found Per already in bed.

He was woken, and we immediately launched into an argument. Per had spent several days in the Khumbu, talking to Paul Head about the chances of getting the weather we needed. They had come to the conclusion that a flight from Namche Bazar in the spring was out of the question. Per was running out of time and clearly felt that there was little chance of getting the balloon into the air. After spending two and a half weeks just waiting for something to happen, it seemed inconceivable that Per wanted to go home without making an attempt.

Next morning Helen, Paul and Per flew out from Namche to Kathmandu, just missing Peter Mason, who had hired a helicopter on Per's instructions and who was not amused at spending an extra $2,000 needlessly. I returned to Kathmandu with Peter and found the rest of the team still trying to extricate the gear from the authorities. Per was arguing with almost everybody and only hours after landing in Kathmandu he was on a plane to London.

No sooner had he departed than, perversely, our balloon emerged at last from a Nepalese customs shed. We inflated it in Kathmandu, close to the spot from which we had lifted off in 1985, to test that nothing was damaged, and then took it down and packed it away again. We were left holding the pieces of an expedition jigsaw that no longer seemed to fit. Peter Mason, now a project leader without a project, was almost in shock. Martin Hutchins felt personally let down. Self-recrimination filled the day.

'I'm not criticising anyone,' said Peter Mason, 'but if Per had just blamed the weather and not criticised everything else I could have understood it.'

I didn't think the sponsor would take it so well, considering the expense they had gone to in researching the weather patterns. What interested me was whether anything could be salvaged from the expedition.

'Let's talk about the options we have,' I said, trying to lift our dejected mood. 'We can find another pilot, team up with the Japanese in some way, or, as Peter suggests, we could come back in the autumn.' I didn't like this last option because I felt sure that Star would pull out if we left at that stage.

Jules Wigdor didn't think much of the first two ideas either. 'It'll take two or three weeks to get a new pilot, and teaming up with the Japanese will cause real problems at the border, and with customs. The third option is the only viable one.'

Martin wanted to stay and wait for good weather. Peter changed his mind for the second time that day. It didn't get us round the problem of not having a pilot. Per had said as he left Kathmandu that he would come back for another six weeks another time, but I knew full well that this was just a parting gesture. We would have to find another pilot. That morning, Peter had said he would fly the balloon himself if he had to, and now I called his bluff.

'If you'll fly the balloon, Peter, I'll come with you.'

Peter suddenly looked very uncomfortable. 'I'd like to know from Paul exactly what the odds are of getting this thing across Everest at this time of year,' he said.

'At this time of year – from Sangboche – I would say the odds are about a thousand to one,' Paul told him. This was an improvement on the odds of 10,000 to 1 that he had quoted me earlier in the day, but even so Peter's enthusiasm evaporated.

'If Peter won't take an outside chance, I will. Nothing ventured, nothing gained,' I said. 'Most worthwhile achievements involve some degree of risk. My whole life has been spent taking slightly higher risks than most people accept. I can't do it on my own, but if Eric were to come with me, then we could give it a go. I also believe that Star will not put in another £100,000 for us to come back in the autumn, or next year.'

Peter was not on my wavelength. 'I take risks; I jump out of planes, I fly balloons. What you are suggesting is suicidal. You're not minimising the risks nor acknowledging the dangers, but going for it come what may. That is foolhardy.'

Peter would have none of it. It seemed our expedition was over.

Both Eric and Mandy said later that they would have gone with me. It's easy to think so now, but I believe them. Mandy is stubborn and believes she can accomplish anything I can. She's done quite a lot of extreme cave diving and became British National Skydiving Champion with her team, proving that she is most certainly better than me in at least one adventure sport. Eric has a habit of leaning further over the edge than most people, finds he likes it and asks for more. We would have been a good team. Once over Everest, we would have made a three-way sky-dive out of the balloon, then Eric could have led us out of trouble. It was a lovely dream.

If our expedition had ended abruptly, that of the Japanese finished in a far more explosive way. After taking off from Tibet rather than Nepal – the only material difference between our two expeditions – their balloon was becalmed at 32,000 feet and crashed into the mountain as they tried to land, seriously injuring one of the crew. The pilot failed to extinguish their pilot lights and their envelope caught fire, leading to the dramatic explosion witnessed by the journalist flying above in their chartered Chinese jet.

The balloon's co-pilot, Sabu Ichiyoshi, had been evacuated and flown home to Tokyo with a broken leg. It seemed that while they had massive resources and good equipment, their weather forecasting was too primitive. This meant that their balloon took off with the crew believing they would find favourable winds that didn't exist. They weren't as well-prepared as they looked.

Peter Mason and Jules Wigdor visited Sabu in hospital in Tokyo. He was waiting for a precautionary brain-scan – perhaps to ensure he wasn't planning to do it again. Peter asked him why they had overloaded the basket

16   Inflating our balloon in Kathmandu (LD)

17 Mandy's telephoto picture of the Everest summit covered in spindrift after a storm

and flown when the winds weren't right. The answer sounded disturbingly familiar.

'That was the sponsors' decision,' Sabu replied. 'Very important to carry cameraman. We thought that the size of balloon, with three people and fuel, was big enough, but the plan was based on much faster winds. In Japan, we did test-flights from 3,000 feet. In the Himalayas we took off at 15,000 feet, and were slightly heavier.'

The difference in altitude meant that the balloon had to be much hotter to generate the necessary lift. Peter was unsure if continuing with the project was a good idea and asked the Japanese if he felt it could be done. Sabu told him it could, but he would have to be patient. It also worried Peter which direction was the right one. The British were planning to fly over Everest from Nepal while the Japanese were trying to go the opposite way.

'We can't both have been right. Who was wrong?' he asked.

'There are such variations in the upper winds,' Sabu said, 'I think both are possible.'

Would he do it again, Peter wanted to know, despite their ordeal?

'Of course. We make a small mistake. It is possible to make a much better landing than we did.'

'I'm thinking,' Peter told him, 'this is more difficult and more dangerous than I first imagined.'

In the event the Japanese pulled out, and were followed shortly by Peter.

# 3 • *Getting our Fax Straight*

IT WAS A melancholy homecoming from Kathmandu, and I knew we would have to act quickly if there was to be any hope of keeping the project alive. We had hardly distinguished ourselves in the eyes of our sponsors, and only Mandy and Martin Hutchins, besides myself, still seemed to believe in the idea of ballooning over the world's highest mountain. To prevent Ian Smith of Star Micronics from losing interest altogether, I put some new proposals to him which I thought promised a much better chance of success.

For a start, I wanted there to be two pilots, one acting as reserve. With Per Lindstrand out of it while his mind was on crossing the Pacific, I suggested replacing him with Chris Dewhirst, who had piloted one of the 1985 'Windhorse' balloons, and Martin Hutchins, Per's one-time design engineer. It was essential to be better acclimatised and for everyone to have at least basic mountaineering experience. My climbing friend, Eric Jones, who had been the first Briton to solo the North Face of the Eiger, would be a more than useful person to have in the team. Nobody should be indispensable – especially after Per's uncommitted performance in Nepal. Finally, I proposed that the launch site be shifted north-west, from Namche Bazar to the village of Gokyo, which, at 16,000 feet, was much nearer the mountain. From there we would have less height to gain after take-off and Everest would be in full view for the whole of the expedition. Being upwind could also be helpful and the mountain's massive shadow would be a constant reminder of the scale of our undertaking.

Of course, Gokyo had some disadvantages as well. It is one of the highest dwelling places on earth and living there is a severe test of any European's fitness. Just getting two balloons, each weighing 400lbs, to that height by porters on foot would require a tremendous effort.

About a month after putting my ideas to Ian Smith in the summer of 1990, I had a meeting with Per Lindstrand at which we healed some of our differences. It was clear that he had not lost interest in the Everest venture and he added some useful suggestions to my own. The most important of these was to increase the size of the balloon to one of 400,000 cubic feet. The Japanese had barely scraped up to the height of the mountain using an envelope much the same in size as we had previously taken to Nepal, and Per believed that we could do better employing the valley winds to pre-position a larger balloon before popping up into the jet stream. It would mean taking more fuel because we might need to stay in the air for up to twelve hours.

In Per's view, we also needed more accurate weather forecasts. Satellite forecasting equipment at Base Camp would help, and I was anxious to be able to interpret more than one view of the conditions. Perhaps we should also monitor the weather in Tibet.

Morale seemed to be the key to everything. Peter Mason had almost entirely abandoned hope. Bewildered by the speed with which our expedition had fallen apart, he had left his meeting with the battered Japanese pilot with the feeling that the risks were simply too great. Bob Rice's pessimistic meteorological report did nothing to raise his spirits. According to him, there was no more than a five per cent chance of finding an upper level wind that would take us on the right track from a launch site in Nepal to a safe landing in Tibet. 'It's not the lift-off or the flight, it's the landing that scares me,' he said. In September despondency finally drove Peter to resign.

He was not the only controversial figure involved. Per had misgivings about Chris Dewhirst. From some things Chris had written about aerodynamics of the *Financial Times* balloon Per had reached the conclusion that he didn't have much idea about technical matters.

At that time I would hear nothing said that was critical of my choice of pilot. The more Per and Peter were against the man, the more intransigent I became about having him. I suggested to Ian Smith that he should invite Dewhirst to Britain and talk to him before finally making up his mind. It would allow him to keep his options open while he gained some facts against which to set all the negative opinions he was constantly hearing.

To Ian Smith, the question was quite simple. 'It's obvious to me that you and Per will not work together,' he said to me on the phone, 'so I am left with a choice. Either I find a new adventure cameraman or another pilot. I think it's probably easier to find another pilot.' He agreed to interview Chris who, as I expected, made a good impression. Our sponsor was persuaded to keep the project alive, but with one proviso. Ian Smith wanted Peter Mason to come back on board to manage the expedition and returned his letter of resignation.

That night Chris, Mandy and I celebrated with champagne. It was good to see Chris again after six years. He had lost none of his sparkling enthusiasm and good humour, and I was looking forward to sharing another adventure with him. The train was back on the rails and we were going to have fun with Chris. As Mandy remarked after we had seen him off at Heathrow, 'Chris is one of those people who can't have an enemy in the world.'

Chris lost no time in helping to revive our fortunes. At his suggestion,

Dick Dennison, our film producer from the 1985 Flight of the Windhorse expedition, wrote offering me a co-production with the Australian Broadcasting Corporation and perhaps a deal with National Geographic in the United States. It seemed as if the old team was coming together again. Chris also insisted that a proper test programme should be instigated in Australia to check that the balloon had the necessary climb-rate and would be capable of carrying the required load.

The tests were arranged for April 1991. Martin Hutchins was to conduct the test programme and teach Chris the secrets of high altitude flying. Mandy and I were already committed to our next film, *Dead Men's Tales*, and could not afford the time to travel to Melbourne, and so missed the opportunity to meet Dr Glenn Singleman, an adventure cameraman, and Chris's wife, Heather, both of whom were to play significant roles at a later stage.

Per Lindstrand's first attempt to achieve the double with Richard Branson by flying a hot air balloon over the Pacific as well as the Atlantic Ocean had ended in disaster before our abortive Everest trip. After an unintended splash-landing at the end of their Atlantic crossing, the Pacific balloon had been left out overnight on the launch site in Japan where it froze to the ground. The television cameramen loved it. Bits of molten material stripped off the envelope and fell to the ground as the balloon self-destructed before their very eyes. The embarrassment was compounded because Richard had prematurely organised a party at Liz Taylor's house to celebrate their success. The headlines in the next day's papers were not the kind he was used to.

Branson and Lindstrand went for a second attempt in December 1990, but due to bad weather stood down over Christmas and reassembled on 6 January 1991. Just one week later the conditions were right and they took off from Japan for North America. Unhappily for Per and Richard, the Gulf War started six hours later. Once more Richard was deprived of his headlines, this time by aerial activity over Kuwait. Per had been well aware of the imminence of war because their flight permission from the United States Air Force had been withdrawn from a specific hour. The Americans didn't want their search and rescue aircraft called out when all available manpower was needed in the Gulf.

It was a surprise to Per that Virgin didn't call the whole thing off, but after so many years of preparation, everyone was eager to finish the project. This was even more risky than their Atlantic flight. Per and Richard, without helicopter or aerial rescue possible, could find themselves out over

18    Per Lindstrand's 2,500,000 cubic feet of balloon canopy being inflated before the
      Pacific crossing (Boccon Gibod)

the middle of the Pacific with the nearest shipping lanes twenty-four hours
away. With 45-knot winds and 25-foot waves, landing in the sea would have
been very dangerous.

It was also an uncomfortable flight. The jet streams above the Pacific are
very rough and the two men were buffeted throughout the 46-hour journey,
burning continuously to maintain their height above a storm at 20,000 feet.
Per lived on a diet of Mars Bars, peanut butter and Jolt, the Cola with five
times the usual caffeine content to keep him awake.

The flight nearly ended in disaster when frozen fuel crystals formed
around the jets and a giant flaming snowball fell on top of their gondola,
setting it on fire. The blaze was extinguished only by gaining extra height.
Their situation was not enhanced by the loss of two full tanks – half their
unused fuel – which were accidentally jettisoned only ten hours into the
flight.

Per had planned to land in Santa Barbara, California, but the winds took
them off their planned track and pushed them far to the north. When finally
they came in to land, the balloon was 2,000 miles off course in northern
Alaska. 'It was a bit chilly,' Per recalls, 'over 30°c below, and blowing 30
knots. We were hundreds of miles from the nearest town.'

He landed the balloon perfectly on a frozen lake. The problem was that, while Bermuda shorts were in plentiful supply, they had no winter clothes with them.

'I had no idea of the topography,' Per told me, 'because Bob Rice had said there was no need to take maps of the North Pole! My chart ended somewhere round Edmonton in Canada. Five minutes after landing an otter came running over the snow and Richard said, "There's a dog! There must be a hunter up there." I told him it wasn't a dog. The otter trotted over and peered at Richard but decided he wasn't edible so wandered off. After such a tremendous flight Richard was a bit disappointed not to be greeted by the usual media and champagne cocktails. The otter was the only living thing we saw for six hours.'

Eventually Per made radio contact with their retrieval crew and was able to arrange for a helicopter to take them to Yellowknife. The story has it that Richard spent the flight enthusing to the pilot about their adventure and how dangerous it had been. The pilot told Richard that one of his main jobs was rescuing tourists who had come to Alaska ill-prepared for the conditions. Tourists who might not be dressed properly, for instance, or who didn't really know where they were. He also collected people who hadn't survived long enough to be rescued.

'How horrible,' Richard said.

'Yeah. Getting some stiff the shape of a Maltese Cross into my chopper

19  Lindstrand's Pacific crossing ends with the balloon crashing on the ice in Alaska
    (Per Lindstrand)

ain't easy. One time I shared my cab with three of them. If they don't fit in here though, I tie them to the skids instead.'

Richard remained silent for the rest of the trip.

✳

While Per and Richard were preparing for their journey across the Pacific, Peter Mason flew to Melbourne to meet Chris Dewhirst. He had barely landed before Chris gave him a surprise. Heather, Peter was told, had not formed a good impression of our organisation. To her way of thinking, he was cutting corners to save money at the expense of her husband's safety.

Many faxes had been exchanged concerning 'turning vents', and one in particular about a quick release deflation system. There were mixed views in ballooning circles about the use of these devices in hostile terrain. Some thought that with enough pressure from wind-sheer turbulence in the mountains, the system could come undone and the whole balloon collapse in mid-air. Peter was still strongly influenced by Per, who was vehemently opposed to these innovations on a mountain flight.

To give him his due, Peter did most of what diplomacy and friendliness required. He took the Dewhirsts out to an extremely expensive restaurant in South Yarra for dinner and, while the coffee was being served, asked Heather if she would mind him smoking. She minded very much and announced that she would take a taxi straight home if he so much as struck a match. Peter refrained, but it left the conversation strained. 'It was a Mexican stand-off,' he said, 'in which no one wanted to make the first move.'

Peter's dislike of her 'hairy armpits and her air of intellectual superiority' was not modified by her forthright demand for a job on the expedition. After Per had taken his wife, Helen, last time, Ian Smith had ruled that no wives or girlfriends would be paid for again. Peter felt he was being put into a corner and without much enthusiasm he suggested that perhaps Heather could be our communications officer. 'She certainly had a personality and a voice to suit the job,' he said afterwards. I must say I found myself warming to this formidable-sounding lady. Nobody could quite fit his description of her!

From Melbourne, Peter flew to Dallas in Texas to meet the balloonist Ed Chapman. While Chris was already the pilot for our Everest flight in my mind, Peter and Ian were still keeping their options open, and Chapman had come highly recommended by Per. Ed had been a U.S. Marines Phantom pilot and now flew airline passenger planes. He would be more expensive to hire than Chris Dewhirst, but then he had more experience even than Lindstrand, with more than 12,000 hours fixed-wing flying time and 3,000 hours in balloons to his record. He seemed a sensible and rational man and, what was more, he didn't have a wife to consider.

Peter reported back to Ian Smith, giving a scale to his recommendations, with Per Lindstrand as the market standard 'ten' by which everybody else was judged. Ed got nine, Chris a more equivocal seven, and Peter awarded himself a tongue-in-cheek one. Nobody could accuse him of promoting his own cause. But there was one flaw in his logic. I had told Ian Smith that if Chris Dewhirst wasn't going then neither would I. Chris had no idea how close he came to being pushed out of the basket.

Every expedition goes through periods of tensions and misunderstanding as egos clash and people fail to get what they personally want. The curious thing about ours was the huge distance separating the main players. This forced us to pursue arguments by fax machine because the Australians were usually asleep when we were getting angry in Britain. In the middle of December Chris fired off one fax that once again threatened the project's existence. It was a letter to Peter, thanking him for offering Heather a job on the expedition, and Chris added beneath his signature that he had sent a copy to Ian Smith. Peter, of course, had yet to clear his offer with Ian and was stunned that his boss would discover from a third party what he had done. Quickly he phoned Ian's secretary to intercept the missive but all this did was to bring it to Ian's attention. Ian looked for the letter in vain. Chris hadn't sent it at all.

It was a farce of global proportions. What made it worse was Chris innocently suggesting to Star that Chris Bonington rejoin the expedition for publicity purposes. Ian Smith did not like the idea. He was also getting nervous about the whole business of Heather joining the project and decided to give Chris an ultimatum. There was no job for Heather on the expedition and either Chris came alone or not at all.

A flurry of faxes ensued. Heather by-passed Peter, much to his chagrin, and explained the situation directly to Ian. 'I understand the very significant investment Star has made in the project and that you feel the need to eliminate any avoidable risk factors. It just comes as a shock to be cast as a risk factor at all. I ask you to trust me.'

Ian asked me for my gut-feeling. Was he being uncharitable in insisting Heather stay at home? I thought not but assured him there was no real problem and that the whole issue had been blown out of proportion. He also asked me my views on Ed Chapman and whether he was a practical replacement for Chris. I said that I would need to get to know him and there was so little time. 'I'm afraid it's Chris or a wrap,' I told him for the second time. 'I've given Chris my word.'

In my next communiqué to Chris I alluded to my conversation with Ian Smith but didn't reveal the ultimatum I had made. Instead I warned him that, due to his intervention, the situation demanded a low profile. 'I am afraid, Chris, you are going to have to reassure Ian by not taking Heather.'

Ian responded to Heather's frustration by reiterating the expedition's policy of not taking wives or girlfriends unless they had a vital role to fill. He cited Per's abrupt departure from Nepal, and offered the theory that Per's wife had been partly responsible.

'Thank you for your fax,' Heather wrote to Ian Smith. 'It has rather ensured that it will be a bleak Christmas for both of us despite your good wishes. This letter is, unashamedly, an expression of my own frustration, desolation and incredulity.'

Peter was not reassured. 'I tremble to think what the next nine months will bring, never mind what the atmosphere will be like when we finally get to Everest.' But he didn't respond to Heather's remarks. The matter was still not resolved, but the tension had certainly been defused. We had wasted a lot of time that could have been put to more valuable use, but at least the expedition was still happening.

After all the frustrations, Peter, Mandy and I left in the new year for Chateau d'Oex in Switzerland. An international ballooning meet is held there each winter and the more settled weather allows flying when conditions in Britain are too unpredictable. The trip enabled us to get shots of Star's Everest balloon against the snowy backdrop of the Alps. It was a good plan but Peter forgot to arrange any snow. From 16,000 feet we could look across to Mont Blanc, the Eiger and the Matterhorn – a flight to remember.

20 'Mandy photographs my first flight with Andy Elson at Château D'Oex in Switzerland'

It was while we were in Switzerland that Peter met a pilot called Andy Elson, who was flying a Thunder & Colt balloon, and was impressed by him. Martin Hutchins had been our original reserve pilot for Chris in Nepal, but for various reasons he had decided to settle for the role of launch master. Sensing that Andy would make a good replacement, Peter asked for my opinion. We agreed on a trial run: Peter would take the Star Flyer One and Andy would take me in his balloon so that I could film Peter. Andy is roughly my size and build and has a similar beard and glasses; he also has a very dry sense of humour which was to prove invaluable later.

On our first flight he was very matter-of-fact and flew as I instructed. I was pleased with my shots and with Andy's instinctive control of the balloon – something I hadn't experienced before. When we came to land, Peter overshot the launch field. To my amusement and great satisfaction, Andy landed right on the spot from which we had lifted off one hour earlier. It wasn't a matter of luck. Andy Elson was just the pilot we were looking for.

I also had him in mind to help with our latest film project. *Dead Men's Tales* was based on reconstructions of parachuting epics where things had gone terribly wrong but where the outcome was happy. The script required me to make a number of jumps from a balloon. Working together on that film would give me the chance to get to know Andy better. Afterwards, it seemed a good idea for him to accompany Martin Hutchins and Chris Dewhirst on the test-flights in Australia later in the spring.

In due course, Chris reported that the test-flights had gone well. Martin, Chris and Andy had flown from 15,000 to 33,000 feet with a climb rate in excess of 1,000 feet per minute. That mirrored exactly our projected flight path and our calculations for keeping the balloon aloft for four to six hours. During the months of June and July, film producer Dick Dennison firmed up his arrangement with National Geographic and Mandy and I started making final preparations. Just before our departure we met, by the strangest quirk of fate, an Everest pilot from an altogether more intrepid age.

# 4. *A Spy from Calcutta*

ON 20 MAY 1927 a young American called Charles Lindbergh made aviation history by becoming the first man to fly the Atlantic solo. With the Atlantic challenge taken, aviators began to look for new records to break. Commander Richard Byrd flew over the North Pole, and three years later turned his attention to the South. This proved more difficult. Byrd and his team had to winter in Antarctica, with their precious craft entombed in a hanger of ice. On 28 November 1929 they took off in their Ford Trimotor on a round trip of 1,600 miles. Well into their flight their fuel looked alarmingly low and they threw out everything that could be spared but after ten hours Richard Byrd reached 90° South, becoming the first man to fly over both Poles.

'Firsts' were fast running out when a British team, led by the Marquis of Clydesdale, arrived on the plains of northern India in 1933 with the intention of flying over the 'Summit of the World', Mount Everest.

The British have always regarded the mountain as their own private prestige symbol. They had established an early interest by presumptuously renaming it after Sir George Everest, the Surveyor-General of India, and then sealed the lease by giving it a heroic sacrifice in the forms of George Mallory and Andrew Irvine who disappeared forever into clouds just below the summit in 1924. Everest belonged to the British in much the same way as Nanga Parbat became German and K2 American.

By the early 1930s, very few people had flown at altitudes over 30,000 feet but setting new height records had become all the rage with the French, the Italians and the Americans. The problem was that no sooner did the record fall than another team arrived to topple the new one. What was needed was a one-off flight that would stand out as special. The French and the Germans had long considered the Everest flight and Sir Alan Cobham had attempted it for the British on his way back from Australia in 1926, but he could not get his aircraft to climb above 16,000 feet, and he abandoned the idea.

In an effort to boost British aviation and persuade the Indians of British engineering superiority, two Westland aircraft were shipped out from England for Clydesdale's adventure. They had been stripped down to their bare essentials, to make them as light as possible, and were fitted with Bristol Pegasus S3 engines which had recently powered the British to a new high altitude record of 44,000 feet. One of the planes was an experimental two-seater bomber, the PV3, which was renamed the Houston-Westland in honour of the expedition's financing committee. Unfortunately the PV3 was unique and so the expedition's second aircraft was a Westland Wallace, or 'Wally' as it was affectionately termed.

The expedition was based at Purneah, 300 miles north of Calcutta, under the executive leadership of Air Commodore Fellowes, a Great War flying ace who had won the DSO. It was a military-style affair and officers were housed in a bungalow belonging to the Maharajah of Darbhanga, with private tennis courts, a golf course and a race-track nearby. These were rather different from the conditions they expected later in the year. Other ranks had to rough it by the landing field at Lalbalu, ten miles away.

They were also using a new fuel, Tetra-ethyl, which would, it was hoped, cope with temperatures down to 60°C below. Special suits were worn with an elaborate system of heating elements throughout, including the boots and flying helmet. The flight required prodigious amounts of electricity, and so larger generators were fitted to the aircraft. Even the goggles and face mask were heated.

I wondered if any of these early pioneers were still alive. Peter Mason started imagining all manner of publicity stunts involving old-time explorers in our balloon. Unfortunately his PR company could not pick up the trail and, after exhaustive research, concluded all the expedition members were dead.

Halfway round the world, in a Melbourne pub, Chris Dewhirst was chatting to a fellow countryman. 'I'm going to fly a balloon over Mount Everest,' he said in his usual humble manner. It's the sort of conversational topic that crops up in bars anywhere.

'That's a coincidence,' said his companion. 'My dad lives in England and his next-door neighbour flew over Everest in 1933.'

When the fates offer you this big a coincidence, you have to take them up on the deal. Mandy and I drove to Newbury in Oxfordshire to track down the veteran aviator. It was a beautiful summer's day in a part of the country that is quintessentially English. Dick Ellison lives in a rose-covered cottage in a small village with mementos of his flying career and his time in India around him. He is a tall man, although a little stooped these days; it was obvious that he had been a dashing figure in his youth. He still has a glint in his eye that suggests an audacious but understated character. Apart from his adventures in the skies above Nepal, Dick and his wife, Beryl, had flown around Europe in a Puss Moth and had celebrated their golden wedding anniversary by going up in a balloon. He also admitted that he would like nothing better than to try hang-gliding and microlite flying.

'I went out to India in 1929 with 5 Squadron which, in those days, flew Bristol fighters,' he told me. 'In 1930 I was sent up to Nepal to lecture to the

21   Leo with Dick Ellison, the last remaining survivor from the first Everest flight in 1933 (MD)

Gurkhas on how aircraft can help ground forces in fighting battles. As there were no airstrips in Nepal then it was all fairly academic. They are a grand set of people. In 1930 Nepal was an independent state and the Maharaja wanted to keep it that way. There were railways running throughout the country but these stopped twenty miles short of the Indian border. From the railway station to the border you had to travel by elephant. The Maharaja did this to keep strangers away and the country from spoiling, which is what is happening with tourism today.'

We sat drinking tea in Dick's beautiful English garden, transfixed while he recreated from memory the world of exploration sixty years ago. 'Funding the expedition was hard enough because in 1932, with Ramsay MacDonald at the helm, everything was in recession and there was virtually no money around at all. This is why we had three main sponsors. Gaumont British had the film rights and *The Times* had the publication rights. Clydesdale went to see Lady Houston who had been very generous over the Schneider Trophy races because she thought a lot of the RAF.'

Lady Houston had the reputation of being a very difficult person because nobody could tell what kind of mood she was in. When Clydesdale went to see her on the day of his appointment she was in her bed and wasn't going to get up. They had to communicate with each other by passing notes under the bedroom door. She did, however, turn up trumps, providing £10,000 to support the expedition, which, in 1933, was quite a large sum of money and probably worth about £300,000 today.

'The RAF insisted,' Dick went on, 'that the pilots should be tested in a pressure chamber at Farnborough in order to make sure that we were healthy enough to go up. While you were de-pressurised they made you count peas into a pot and kept you going until you passed out. Then they gave you oxygen and you continued counting peas where you had left off. Unless you could reach the required aviation height without oxygen and enough peas then they didn't consider you suitable for flying the aircraft.'

'Did you pass the pea test?' I asked him.

'I didn't, because I was in India and was reserve pilot anyway. So I wasn't tested but was considered good enough to fly without having to count peas.

'The RAF also insisted that we had a meteorologist from the government of India and he was called Mr Gubter. He used to put up hydrogen balloons at dawn every morning although it wasn't much help as there was a lot of haze at that time of year. Unfortunately, on one occasion a hydrogen balloon exploded and Mr Gubter was badly burned. He had to be taken off to hospital. The Indian Met Office sent out some other chap from Calcutta but it didn't really delay us for long.'

Originally the plan was to make the flight after gaining some local flying experience. 'We were delayed by very high winds over the top of Everest, which during the first fortnight were never less than 100 miles per hour. Do you know how fast our planes went?' he asked me. 'Barely 110.'

'Could you have landed on the summit?' I asked Dick, jokingly.

'Worth a thought,' he mused, 'worth a thought. The winds meant the flight was completely impossible. We expected temperatures of minus 50°C at 33,000 feet but we never expected such high winds as our meteorological officer was measuring. At the same time the committee in London thought we were taking far too long in making the flight, and couldn't understand the reasons for the delay. So when the winds dropped to about 60 miles per hour, Air Commodore Fellowes, who had done a reconnaissance in the Puss Moth, decided we would have a go. The aircraft climbed straight away from Purneah, north towards Everest, but by the time they got there the winds had gained speed again, so instead of flying over the top, they were carried to the east which put them miles from the summit.'

Dick said that the local people treated the mountains as something sacred and felt that if their gods were disturbed, all sorts of queer things might happen. Bonnett, the Gaumont cameraman, would stand up to take pictures and each time he wanted to change a plate he had to get back into the cockpit.

22    The 1933 bi-plane flight over Everest

'On one occasion,' Dick continued, 'he trod on an oxygen pipe. As he stood up the pipe parted company. A piece of sticking plaster and quick thinking on his part saved him. However, after he'd been working with his camera for a little bit longer, he passed out and eventually collapsed into the bottom of the plane. The pilot couldn't do anything about it as they were in two separate cockpits. He recovered as they descended.'

Since they had not achieved what they had set out to do, Shepherd, of *The Times* newspaper, was asked not to publish anything about the first flight. They had insurance cover for two flights, and now the plan was to make another attempt to get over the top.

'Unfortunately for us,' Dick said, 'the Gaumont British laboratory had taken on an Indian to help with the film-processing work. He was a spy, in the pay of the *Calcutta News*, and when he saw that we had been near the top of Everest he sent a telegram which appeared in the paper the next day with the headline, "Flight over Everest's summit". *The Times* was furious.'

It was decided the following day, that while the wind was still low, Fellowes and Ellison would go up to get film footage for the Gaumont British producer who had moaned about the lack of coverage of Everest. Dick took Bonnett with him while Fisher, the other ciné cameraman, accompanied Fellowes.

'We took off just after dawn and I flew considerably lower than the other aircraft. I was to navigate and Fellowes was to follow. Unfortunately, by the time we had finished all our filming, the clouds had started to form around the mountain and Fellowes, who hadn't come as low, lost sight of me. I climbed back up to look for him. Nowhere could I see him.

'Previously we had arranged to make our own way back to Purneah, and I was surprised to find Fellowes wasn't there when I got back. I had only about half an hour's fuel left. We waited for Fellowes until long after his fuel would have run out, but still we hadn't heard from him. It was about six o'clock in the evening when finally we got a telegram from Fellowes. You must remember that we had no radios in the aircraft in those days and telephones in India were few and far between.

'He had mistaken his course back and gone south. Eventually he realised that he was lost. He landed in a meadow by a railway station, where he knew he would be able to send a telegraph. Of course, as soon as you landed in India in those days, swarms of people would appear from nowhere. It made it very difficult – until the police arrived – to take off again.

'Fellowes decided he hadn't got enough fuel to take off and fly back to Purneah that day, so Clydesdale went out in his Moth with pickets to tie the aircraft down for the night and it was agreed that I would go out in the Puss Moth in the morning with petrol to refuel it and bring the plane back. This was big news for the media and they published headline stories about one of the aircraft making a forced landing on its return.'

The insurance company decided that this flight, which was undertaken for photographic reasons and didn't involve flying over Nepal, counted as the second flight for the expedition's insurance cover. They argued the case but the insurers wouldn't budge. Mandy and I were now let into a dark secret. The 'second flight' flew around Kanchenjunga instead of Everest, although the pictures looked similar to the uninformed public.

Telegrams flew between the committee in London and the team in Purneah until finally instructions were sent for the flyers to return home. This they felt they shouldn't do because they hadn't flown over the summit itself on their first flight. Then Air Commodore Fellowes fell ill with a fever and the rest of the team decided that they would break the rules. Provided the wind dropped sufficiently, they would make a trip over Everest without insurance. Speaking of 'insurance', I asked Dick if they carried parachutes.

'We were controlled by the RAF and it was a rule in the air force that parachutes must be worn, though we were only carrying an emergency chute each. I don't think over the top of Everest it would have been any use at all because your rate of fall would have been too high. We only took off 300 feet above sea level, so in the foothills it probably would have been satisfactory, if an emergency had arisen.'

Mandy asked, 'Had you got any parachuting experience?'

'I personally had no parachuting experience although another of the pilots, David McIntyre, had in 602 Squadron. On the one occasion when he used his, David had been doing aerobatics but had forgotten to do up his safety belt. When the aircraft turned upside down he fell out and his parachute worked very well. But he was the only one, as far as I know, who had his life saved by a parachute.'

Their plan was for the Wally and the Houston to fly a hundred miles west and then climb due north. They hoped the wind would carry them back over the top of Everest. Dick Ellison was to do the dawn reconnaissance to see that the mountain was clear of cloud. With the wind dropping, they finally set off.

'The flight took about three and a half hours. Their climb rate was quite fast at the beginning, probably between 700 and 1,000 feet per minute, but it dropped off as they got up. The aircraft going over Everest were fitted with special air screws 14 feet in diameter in order to make the engines more efficient at high altitude. It was a complete success. They flew over the top of Everest with no trouble and we took some very good pictures of it.

'As I had flown the reconnaissance flight, I stayed out at the aerodrome

23   The Himalaya as seen from the open cockpit in 1933

waiting for the aircraft to come back. Fellowes, realising that there was nobody about at Purneah, decided something must be up. He drove out to the airport and asked me where the aircraft had gone. I told him, "They've gone to make another trip over Everest." He said nothing but looked very pleased.

'One of the objectives of our 1933 flight was to obtain pictures of the approaches to Everest so that the climbers would have them when they started off up the mountain later that year. We thought that aerial pictures would be of the greatest assistance to them, but Eric Shipton and his team didn't reach the summit. I find it very difficult to imagine being on the top in winds of 100 miles per hour and more, added to the oxygen and fatigue problems,' Dick said.

'The flight had no perceivable effect upon my life at all. I suppose I saw a lot of India flying over it. Clydesdale decided that he would far sooner return to England on the P&O ship, so he took my ticket and I flew his Moth Major home, while the others brought the two Westlands back. I was in no hurry and took ten days flying back from India. That was a very interesting trip indeed.'

We talked for a while about our balloon flight. Mandy asked Dick if he

24 Pink sunset over the summit of the world as it appears today (William Thompson)

would like to do it. 'Oh yes. I would have done in the days when I was out in India, most definitely. It would be magnificent,' he said. 'I'm getting a bit old now to strut out to Nepal and climb up mountains, but I would have done it a few years ago, if I'd had the chance. This sort of thing is tremendous fun,' he chuckled, 'especially if you come back.'

There was one final twist left in the tale of the Everest flight. Legend has it that Hitler's deputy, Rudolf Hess, contacted the Marquis of Clydesdale before his famous flight to Scotland. He wanted to give himself up to an honourable gentleman and could think of no one more honourable than the man who had flown over the highest mountain in the world.

*

In order that Dick Dennison could finalise his film deal with National Geographic, we finally persuaded Star to back a second balloon to allow us to film each other as we crossed the summit. It was the only way we could get the shots I wanted – helicopters can't fly that high and an aircraft would be too hard to organise. This second balloon would be flown by Andy Elson, with Eric Jones as cameraman.

Most of the extra paperwork landed on Peter Mason's desk and he seemed to be almost buried in it at times. The whole idea was on and off throughout June as people made and then retracted promises. Even by their standards, the Chinese military were taking an unusual interest in our expedition at the time and made the point that our permit specified one balloon and not two. Eventually, on 9 July, a deal was struck between Peter and Dick.

At this stage Dick started to cause confusion over team membership. He hadn't told me that his mountain cameraman was only available for the early part of the expedition and would thus miss the all important take-off day. Film finances were already tight but the only solution was to employ another mountain cameraman, Dr Glenn Singleman. Glenn wrote to me: 'Trust me. I'm a doctor: if all goes according to plan, you'll hardly know I'm there, but if it doesn't you'll be glad I am.'

Just when I thought things were finally sorting themselves out with the Australians, Dick detonated the most serious bombshell in months. Heather, who had tacitly withdrawn her demand for a job in the face of Ian Smith's determination not to have wives and girlfriends on the expedition, was now given a job as production assistant on the film. I started to have serious doubts about what Dick Dennison was up to. I had seen strong personalities put the expedition on the rocks before and was worried lest Star's Japanese owners pulled the plug on the whole enterprise.

Ian felt betrayed. He wasn't going to throw his weight around at this late stage, but he made his irritation known to Chris. 'We can't really refuse this but I'm very disappointed. I suspect this has been planned all along.' By offering Heather a job on the film, Dick gave the appearance of being divisive, but I didn't realise that someone was leaning on him. Much later, in Tibet, Chris admitted with a laugh that he had told Dick he would be able to show more interest in the film if Heather had some part in it.

For the sake of the project, Peter Mason decided to bite the bullet and accept Heather. Dick, who was enjoying making a drama out of a crisis, then suggested that one of Chris's ex-girlfriends, Jan Reynolds, come along as well and wait for him in Tibet as part of the retrieval crew. With Heather waving Chris off and Jan waiting to catch him back into her arms, the whole situation was turning into an Australian soap opera. I decided this was even more divisive and quite unfair to Heather. Peter and I stood firm and told Dick that Jan couldn't come as part of our team. So determined was Dick to get more of his people involved, he tried to make me feel guilty when I refused to meet his demands. Tempers were lost and new frustrations were harboured and these prompted a return to our fax machines.

'Guilt is a virtue I'm incapable of feeling, particularly regarding this project and petulance is not a virtue,' I told Dick on 25 July. Next day his response emerged from the over-heating fax machine in my office.

'We're not going to achieve anything by writing insulting faxes to each other except anger and disharmony. You know I like to keep all that for my films. I think you and Leo are dreaming up all this controversy for a book.'

'I don't need to dream up controversies. They leap off the page and bite me on the ankles every time I read a letter from you,' Peter faxed back.

Finally Heather wrote a four-page fax to Ian Smith and the matter seemed to die a natural death. She was now on the expedition and I was intrigued to meet the woman who had got under Peter's skin so badly. The problems with the finances of the second balloon provoked enough correspondence to fill a book, but we got it off the ground at last, though not without a parting fax from Peter about Dick.

'Leo, I know you were acting with the best of intentions but I rue the day Dick Dennison ever came aboard. Playing the hard man and driving a good bargain is one thing, but this man is proving to be a complete asshole. Comments, please, in a plain envelope.'

On 6 September we all arrived in Kathmandu. Flying the balloons seemed to be secondary to the undeclared war between the Australians and the British. Peter Mason and Dick Dennison approached each other like two gunslingers from the Wild West. Dr Glenn was videoing the moment and later analysed the tape. Peter appears holding his hands over his balls and Dick leans backwards throughout the confrontation. It was, Glenn explained, the classic law of the jungle. When one male gorilla is threatened by another, he must protect his private parts because he is expecting them to be kicked at any second. Dick was leaning backwards to avoid an expected fist in the face. All this was locked away in their subconsciousness. The analysis delighted the rest of the team. Our doctor was going to be a lot of fun.

Heather was not at all as I expected, although after all the faxes I wasn't quite sure what that was. With long skirts and plaited hair, she reminded Mandy of Olive Oil in Popeye. My question was – would Heather let me share that balloon with Chris? Only time would tell.

# 5. *The Wind in the Willows*

IN KATHMANDU, WHILE waiting for the balloons to clear customs and dividing the other gear into loads, team members who had so far only communicated by fax got to know each other properly. Dick Dennison, despite being the adventure equivalent of Cecil B De Mille, made some thoughtful entries in his diary.

'Peter should have been an actor. He has this wonderfully imperious Shakespearean voice with no vestige of his Australian background. Although he's a con man and all show, he's a good con man and it's a good show. I realised that he was a complete pussy cat. He likes to keep the adrenaline flowing and does it by generating hysterical activity around him whereas I prefer everything to be smooth and practical.

'There is a lot of bad blood between Heather and Peter, probably because Heather isn't quite what Peter expects from a woman. She is a lawyer and a fighter and meticulous about details. She and Chris do a lot of laughing. Chris has also got a streak of the exhibitionist in him. That is what motivates so many balloonists; they want to get up there where people can see them. His chosen career, making balloon flights over Melbourne, is very fulfilling for someone with an anarchistic mind because you can go anywhere and land in anyone's back yard. He is the same Chris Dewhirst as he was in Nepal six years ago, but he is now really focused on Heather. Chris's loyalty is divided between the balloon flight and his wife, and that shouldn't happen on an expedition. There are a few strands of grey in his jolly beard, he is more settled, more confident but still bent on mischief. I sometimes forget the outrageous streak that lurks behind that charming exterior.'

On the plane over from Sydney, Dick had spent a long time talking to Glenn Singleman, our doctor and cameraman. I was looking forward to knowing Glenn. During the high altitude test programme in Australia, he had found that there was no room in the balloon basket for him as well as Chris and the sky-diver Nick Feteras, who was there to set a new Australian altitude jump record. So Glenn rigged a suspended seat on to the outside of the envelope, added a cylinder of oxygen, a parachute and a video camera and followed them up to 35,000 feet, from where Nick claimed his new record. Glenn videoed this in spectacular style as the cold air meeting the hot balloon caused a white cloud to collect round the bottom of the envelope.

Later, Glenn taught Nick to climb. By combining skills the intrepid pair reached the top of Great Trango Tower (20,640 feet) in the Karakoram and skydived down its vertical 1,800-foot wall. They fell for nine seconds before opening their parachutes and scared the living daylights out of Mandy and me. We prefer being in among the action to acting as passive voyeurs, and on our ballooning trip Glenn restricted his activities to those of cameraman and doctor.

Dr Singleman took his medical role seriously on our expedition. 'When I arrived in Kathmandu I found that there were eighteen very different people going into a hostile environment. Because of this, I asked everyone for a fairly detailed medical background. Naturally there were a few arseholes who didn't bother – Leo, Mandy and Dick, for instance – but Martin Harris more than made up for it with his extended medical history. My first impression of Peter, who smokes and drinks a lot, was that this guy was going to die in the Himalayas.'

As an Australian, Dick noticed the reserve of the British contingent. 'The other recruits are Andy Elson, a quiet character with a beard who Leo tries to organise. Andy's ambition is to float off the planet on a bubble of hot air. If he could get hold of a space suit, he would set a new altitude record. He was once weighing cylinders and floated off across the English Channel while he sat in the basket, measuring. Andy doesn't see that the flight here is dangerous but then he hasn't been to the Himalayas before.'

Dick saw Eric Jones as a hero of the old school. 'At the age of fifty he took up BASE jumping, and now ballooning. Eric is a great mountaineer, quiet but confident, tough but humble and greatly respected by Leo. Although he was brought up a Welsh Baptist, Eric says he is probably an agnostic and lives from day to day. Despite having a young wife and two daughters, he is addicted to adrenaline and acknowledges that this love of danger is probably a substitute for the fighting instinct. Then there is the Kiwi Russell Brice, a full-blown adrenaline freak who has been given the very stressful jobs of trying to get all the permissions together and organise transport.'

The wealth of our expedition and the poverty all around us in Kathmandu was something Dick couldn't avoid comparing. 'As we watched the beautiful children begging in the filth of Baktapur and I realised how short many of their lives will be, the thought slides across my mind of just how extravagant is a $2.5 million balloon trip over Mount Everest. How can the Goddess Mother of Earth condone it while her babies are dying? People here have it all worked out; the quicker you travel through a miserable life, the sooner you will be free, so this timeless old rabbit warren has contentment, harmony and a beauty which takes your breath away. By making the film and exposing the beauty of the country, we will bring money and tourism here, and this is my justification for spending the money. I know the power of the media and, at the same time, I know that if you gave the money directly to some sort of fund for children it wouldn't end up there. It would be just a drop in the ocean. It needs real fundamental action at government level.

'Chris woke this morning in a sweat. He had dreamt he was teaching in a school and on the wall was a plaque in memory of Chris Dewhirst. He decides to dress his balloon in prayer flags, as a courtesy to Everest and the people who worship her. This is just an insurance, and we discuss the importance of fear, the emotion the body produces to protect itself. Only fools would deny their fear.'

Dick saw me in a different light. 'Leo is tired of ordinary adventure, but being the film-maker he is, he keeps coming back to it. He says serious people do not approve of adventure, which only happens when exploration gets out of control. The most dangerous sport, in terms of fatalities for the number of people playing it, is bowls.'

Chris had his own views on how things were progressing. 'Leo is like a dog with a bone. He buries it, digs it up, buries it again, digs it up, gnaws at it. He doesn't like unfinished business. It's his nature to keep going with a project like this, and good on him, too, because he's stayed with it, and he got back on the wagon when it started rolling again. I guess it's appropriate that this is a British expedition; they were the first to die on Everest and the first to fly over Everest in 1933.' Chris might have added that it was the British who organised the first ascent.

Our gear was still in customs and echoes from the previous expedition came back to haunt me. It also meant that various power struggles were waged to fill the void of inactivity.

'This is a huge game of chance,' Dick wrote, 'and I'm certain that, at some stage, survival will be on the line. It's a case of men trying to turn themselves into legends. There are much stronger egos than mine at work here in trying to be the first to balloon over Mount Everest.'

The same film crew was here as Dick had for Flight of the Windhorse in 1985. Among them were some strong individuals who had their own views of their mercurial director. The film's editor was Mike Balson who, to justify coming along on the trip, doubled as sound recordist. Mike is quite different from Dick and avoids conflict at almost any cost. He is a large and cuddly middle-aged hippie who interprets the spiritual side to each and every issue. Dick on the other hand met problems head on. Paul Tait was Dick's chief ground cameraman and, being something of a diplomat, he complemented his boss. He was also a first-rate professional and dealt well with the hardships of filming in the Himalaya.

It was becoming obvious that the second balloon, for which I had fought so hard, had not been well-received with the Chinese authorities. Peter Mason introduced us to Stanley Wong, the representative in Kathmandu for the Chinese tourist agency, and we were told that he didn't want to apply for permission to fly the second balloon into Tibet because it might jeopardise the existing permission and could cost another $250,000. It was decided that the second balloon would land on the Nepalese side of Everest and thus avoid the problem.

The deal for the second balloon was complicated. The money came partly from National Geographic and partly from Star Japan and Australia. Dick's contract insisted that payment only be handed over when the balloon was delivered. Peter was nursing a large overdraft and wanted the debt cleared. Dick argued that the balloon might well be in Kathmandu but it was still unobtainable in the customs shed.

'This is the most intense expedition in terms of logistics and planning,' Dick said in his diary. 'It took Martin Harris fifty-five minutes to explain the meteorological gear in the simplest terms. Every minute was fascinating. People don't realise how intense the expedition has become.'

One of the unsung heroes was Ian Bishop, usually referred to as Bish. His role was the shortest but for me the most important on the whole trip. Bish was going to rig and hang my four suspended cameras from the edge of the balloon in the five minute period between it being stood up and our departure. The timing was critical – I knew the pilot would not want to wait.

During the first few days in Kathmandu there were many menial tasks to accomplish. One of these was decanting oxygen into small cylinders for the flight. While this was being carried out, there was suddenly a tremendous bang, which I took to be a car backfiring. Five minutes later I wandered across the lawn and noticed that Bish was completely covered in what appeared to be tomato sauce. Dick was filming, and I assumed he was inventing some drama as little else had happened that day.

'It's blood, Leo, not sauce,' someone said, reading my mind. 'An oxygen regulator blew out its glass as it exploded.' There was a round red mark on Bish's upper chest surrounded by hundreds of smaller cuts from which blood was leaking.

'Where's Dr Glenn?'

'Filming the monkey temple.'

Bish was standing up with a disarming smile that seemed to say everything was fine. He didn't look fine, but more horrifying was the thought of how close to his eyes the splinters of glass had flown. It didn't bear thinking about.

When Glenn returned he examined Bish and decided he needed a stitch. The procedure was turned into a medical briefing for the whole team. Andy, who hates the sight of blood, refused to watch. I asked him what would happen if Eric were injured. 'Leave him there to die I suppose,' Andy replied. I suggested that we might be able to find a less squeamish pilot.

25, 26 Ian Bishop survives the over-inflated pressure gauge which imprints itself on his chest. (LD) Peter Mason washing his smalls at Namche Bazar. (MD)

Eric eventually persuaded Andy to observe, but he wasn't happy about it. Tempers were beginning to get short.

'Chris is a little edgy,' Dick observed. 'He sees the whole expedition as a promotional stunt for Star, with none of the dangers of real mountaineering. "A piece of cake" is his description. I feel he is tempting fate too much. Eric's view is that he has put aside all the dangerous scenarios so he can sleep at night. It is obvious to me that, while some people are able to suppress their fear, it will come out in the end and in one big rush.'

By the middle of September we were almost ready to go. Loads were finalised and assigned on specific flights to the airstrip at Lukla near Namche Bazar, the village from which we had planned to take off the previous year. 'It's like the night before Christmas,' was how Dick saw it. His festive spirit extended to renaming us as characters from *The Wind in the Willows*. I was Toad, because of my love for new gadgets and wild ideas. Eric was Badger, highly respected by everybody, wise and something of a recluse. Andy was Mole – he actually looked like him. Chris was a perfect Ratty, always talking, always cracking jokes and making up poems.

All four of us had parachuted. Mandy, as a former British sky-diving champion, was first reserve for a place in the baskets. With the exception of her, I was the most experienced, with 2,500 jumps, Eric was next, with 500, Chris had completed an accelerated free-fall course and Andy 'half of one'. But, try as she would, Mandy could not sneak a place on board. Eric and I were very careful to use the Nepalese cook as a food taster. He never did understand why we took so much interest in his food.

With our preparations almost complete the Chinese finally gave us a permit for the second balloon to land in Tibet and for the sum of only $5,000. On 21 September we started for Gokyo.

'Like coiled springs set free,' Dick recalled, 'we were catapulted by helicopter out of Kathmandu this morning after a fortnight of waiting. It was like the evacuation of Saigon. Chris and Leo looked down at the spot where they had landed during the Flight of the Windhorse. I filmed the Puma helicopter shuttling gear around, Chris and Heather left the group to go trekking on their own, creating bad feelings among the others.'

I had been so many times to the little airstrip carved out of a hillside at Lukla. I looked down at the Dudh Kosi, the river of milk that flows from Everest, which had been a turning point in my film-making career. Memories flooded back like the white water itself. In my mind I saw Mike Jones try again and again to drag Mick Hopkinson from the torrent. That time he was successful and his act of heroism made my film. I had been 'lucky' enough to have been in the right place at the right time with my cameras. 'Luck,' as Ken Wilson, ex-editor of *Mountain Magazine*, said, 'was my hallmark.' I'd happened to have the camera rolling as Cliff Phillips fell 200 feet down the North Face of the Eiger. The same with Mike and his canoe. Eric Jones fell a hundred feet in an avalanche down the Matterhorn and my camera was there to record it.

I was back in the valley below Everest that I'd visited first with Mike Jones in 1975, with Reinhold Messner in 1978, and then with Chris Dewhirst in a balloon in 1985. Now I was going up again to make our ballooning dream come true and, for once, I hoped I wouldn't be coming back here.

The spartan conditions and high altitude began to test the patience of some expedition members. Martin Harris complained about the lack of organisation; his personal equipment had not arrived and his tent was soaking wet. Peter Mason felt exhausted. He had not walked so far for years. He was tired just walking down the hill from Lukla to our first night's stop in Phakding. All he wanted was a drink of chocolate and sleep; he even passed up the offer of a wee dram of duty free, so I knew how far gone he was. While still complaining about his gear, Martin added that his two assistants, students from his meteorology department at the Polytechnic of North London, were cold. Lisa Young and Jacqui Dudley, both in their early twenties and involved in an expedition like this for the first time, were also very pretty – so if they really had been cold there would have been several offers to warm them up. Lisa now told Martin to stand up for himself against Peter. At the expedition meeting that night in Phakding he dropped his bombshell: either Peter went or he did. Martin actually had no

intention of leaving. He just wanted to take the wind out of Peter's sails a
bit, but he managed to send the rest of us into a panic.

Later that evening, Mandy told Martin he was wrong to have a go at Peter
in front of everyone. Martin was surprised she wasn't supporting him, but
Mandy pointed out that he had backed Peter into a corner and the only way
out for him was to retaliate. She also told him that she was surprised that
the work Martin had come to do at Gokyo, with so much equipment, meant
so little to him that he could pack up and go home. His answer was that the
girls and Martin Hutchins could do his job – he had planned to leave early
anyway. Mandy felt he had no intention of going and just wanted some
attention.

When I heard about Martin's outburst, I characteristically went in with all
guns blazing. I told Paul Tait, Dick Dennison's cameraman, that I would
pay for Martin's fare home. Most of the others wanted him to stay because
they thought the flight couldn't be made without him, but I wasn't going to
be manipulated. Paul agreed. 'I'll go halves with you on the ticket, mate,' he
added. 'Peter's right on this occasion.'

Next day I promised Peter that I would stay with him on the gruelling and
relentless climb from Phakding to the Sherpa capital of Namche Bazar, a
height gain of a few thousand feet. He could have avoided the physical
punishment of trekking to Gokyo by staying in Kathmandu to handle the
press, but Peter wanted to see things through to a conclusion.

27   Putting a sock in it: Chris and Heather in their tent (LD)

We had all day to talk. Peter, it seemed, harboured a secret desire to do the flight. 'If I had known how things would turn out with Chris and Heather, I would have taken eighteen months off to learn how to climb,' he told me. Bravado made him say it, but none the less I admired his determination.

At Namche Chris took up Martin's cause. 'Peter's got to apologise to Martin or otherwise he'll go home.' Chris was sounding off with only half the facts absorbed – a favourite technique of mine. Seeing a mirror image of how I could behave was a salutary experience. If the argument seemed crazy to those inside the expedition, I can't imagine how it seemed to outsiders who watched it.

'Two Sherpa ladies spinning and knitting outside their little shop in Namche couldn't believe what they were hearing,' Dick wrote in his diary. 'Chris and Leo were involved in a noisy debate over Chris leaving the expedition to walk up the hill with Heather. It sounded as if Chris and Leo were having a lovers' tiff; certainly the argument was about loyalty. As two men in one basket, their lives are intertwined and both of them have strong egos. Meanwhile in the tea-house overlooking the path where the two were arguing, their women were apologising to each other for their men's behaviour. It was a very funny situation.'

A young English climber, Joe Simpson, heard the ruckus and said he was glad he wasn't on our expedition. I was glad he wasn't on our expedition but for different reasons. For a start, he had a broken leg – apart from the ruined knee for which he had become famous after writing an award-winning account of his excrutiating crawl down Siula Grande in Peru. Joe told me next day that he intended climbing Pumori with his leg in a cast. He'd sustained this second injury earlier in the year on Pachermo when his companion, Mal Duff, suffered a broken crampon which precipitated both men 400 feet down the mountain. While Joe had smashed his leg and wrecked his face, Mal was uninjured and helped Joe back to Base Camp. How many lives could he have left?

Joe thought that our expedition was 'too bloody dangerous'. I was speechless. The pot calling the kettle black had nothing on this. Joe had endured the most dreadful mountaineering epic of all time but still had the gall to say our expedition was too dangerous. I shook my head as he hobbled off on his crutches in the direction of Pumori with the firm belief that he was going to climb it. In the event, he did manage – God knows how – to get above 19,000 feet.

As I watched Joe's back rocking stiffly down the path, I thought of all those Jeremiahs in England with their knives out. 'Told you so,' they seemed to say. 'Far too dangerous. You're out of control.' We had to succeed. I turned and walked back to Namche for a brew.

*

28  The rebuilt monastery at Thangboche (MD)

The monastery of Thangboche lies at over 12,000 feet, a day's march from Namche Bazar. It is built on a grassy slope below Ama Dablam and Kantega, with the Dudh Kosi buried deep in the valley to the south. Burnt down a few years before, the monastery was now virtually restored, and remains one of the most important centres of Buddhism in the Himalaya. It is a regular spiritual staging-post for all Everest-bound climbers. I went with Chris and Eric to be blessed by the monks and to seek protection on our flight over the home of their gods. Andy stayed behind because, as Dick put it, his god is the spanner carried in the bottom of his rucksack.

'The three balloonists lined up in front of the stupah,' Dick wrote afterwards. 'Eight monks sat sipping tea behind them. Everest was shrouded in cloud. The monks intoned a chant, some rice was thrown and the prayer flags were blessed. Silk scarves were then tied around the balloonists' necks, reminding me of the bandannas worn by Kamikaze pilots. We should have brought Andy's spanners and got those blessed instead. At that moment Everest lifted her veil and the storm clouds vanished. The blessing cost 3,000 rupees and the scarves were 30 rupees each.'

Dick paid for it all. I think it was to make up for lacking insurance against not completing the film on time. The last laugh, however, was on me. After denying my belief in God, I twisted my knee on the way back from the blessing.

We retraced our steps to Kunde, where we had digressed from our trail, we discussed emergency plans with Russell Brice who would soon be leaving for Tibet to organise our retrieval. Russell had been the first to climb the infamous pinnacles on the North-east Ridge of Everest in 1988, where Joe Tasker and Pete Boardman had lost their lives six years before. It was one of the most technical pieces of climbing ever done at this altitude. Russell and his partner Harry Taylor were unable to continue along the ridge to the summit so his name is not carved in stone as an Everest summiteer, although I'm sure it will be one day.

Russell punishes himself in the mountains like nobody I've ever seen. While everyone else was resting for midday tea, he would suddenly pick up

29 Receiving a blessing at Thangboche (MD)

30 *over page:* 'Our objective in sight on the skyline, Everest and Lhotse, as the yaks labour up the mountainside' (MD)

his rucksack and run back to Lukla for the afternoon and return later. Before disappearing into Tibet, he offered us some last minute advice. 'At 24,000 feet on Makalu there is a perfect landing area on the glacier. It's nice and snowy, but don't climb down on the Tibetan side; there are very steep ice and rock falls. If you do have to land there, head for Nepal. If you crash above 23,000 feet, you're on your own. I won't be able to reach you quickly. If you land on the East Rongbuk Glacier, there won't be a problem. There are a lot of climbers on the Kangshung Glacier at the moment. Just don't land high.'

We knew that our radio messages would be accessible to anyone with a receiver, so Peter worked out a secret six stage code covering minor mishaps to complete disaster. Stage six involved possible fatalities. It was his job to notify next-of-kin if the worst happened.

'There's no point telling my wife until you've found the body,' Andy remarked. 'She'll only get excited about the insurance money.' Peter comforted him with the thought that our insurers, Lloyds of London, rated this morbid eventuality at just under two per cent.

As everyone would be wondering which of us had crashed, we decided to refer to Chris's balloon as Charlie and Andy's as Alpha. Major and minor

The blessing of the team was an opportunity to demonstrate the effectiveness of the Widelux camera

would refer to pilot and co-pilot. Heather, perhaps thinking with her lawyer's hat on, mused that she and Mandy should be told first as they would be most affected.

'Surely,' Andy suggested, 'the people in the basket would be most affected.' Everybody laughed, and Heather said, 'Sure Andy, but if it's you, you'll have nothing to worry about.'

Death is rarely taken seriously in situations like this. It occurred to me that if we bailed out near Everest, Russell could end up chasing an empty balloon across Tibet, Bhutan and right into China. I suggested we left a tape recorder in the basket with the message: 'Back in Kathmandu, drinking chang.'

Later, in Kunde, we were all given blood oxygen tests for research into acclimatisation at the hospital founded by Ed Hillary. 'I am about average,' Dick wrote, 'and there are lots of competitive comparisons to see who's best. Heather wins, which she always likes to do. I found a sit-down 'dunny' at the back of the hospital, luxurious bliss, but, alas, I was constipated. I like Peter Mason's description of the Sherpa toilets; 'Not the sort of place to drop your false teeth.'

# 6 • *Approach of the Yeti*

NEXT MORNING WE left Kunde. 'The mountain of pain has begun for the two hundred porters and thirty odd yaks who will carry our gear to the mountain base camp at Gokyo,' Dick wrote in his diary. 'It requires eleven porters just to move the 400lb balloon. The scene at Dole tonight is one of freezing people, huddling in down jackets and trying to be jolly. One more camp and we are there. Glad to get to bed, despite greaseballing.' This quaint Australian slang means getting into bed without a bath or shower.

On the road to Macherma next day, a yak suddenly slipped and rolled down a hillside. Inside one of its damaged boxes were a 16mm film camera, my video camera and two stills cameras. These were to have hung from the balloon's envelope and been remotely controlled from the basket. With some trepidation I brought out the box in question. The 16mm lens resembled a shattered car windscreen but the camera still worked. I was in a state of shock. All sorts of 'what if's were flashing through my mind.

'A dead lens is quite pretty in a strange sort of way, isn't it?' I mused.

'I'll just get a couple of close up shots of Leo looking through it,' said Paul Tait.

'Did you get him holding it up to his eye?' Dick was more concerned about getting the shot than my cameras and it provoked a chaotic argument. The altitude was getting to us.

'Yes,' said Paul patiently, 'I've got heaps of him doing that, but I'll film some more for you, Dick.'

'Leo, hold it up for the director. Rolling! Hold it to your eye.'

'No . . . into the sun, get it in the sun!'

Paul assumed Dick was talking to him. 'Here, do you want to film it?'

'Look, just do it,' Dick snapped.

'I am doing it,' Paul snapped back.

'I'm giving directions to Leo, not you. Just hold it into the sun.'

'Fucking hell, Dick, you couldn't direct a stream of piss.'

'Cut!'

The sign at the Macherma Hotel read 'Scene of Famous Yeti sighting'. In July 1974 a nineteen-year-old Sherpani named Lhaupa Dolma sat watching over her parents' yak herd. It was monsoon time and raining heavily. Lhaupa was sheltering underneath her cape with her mind on Everest, where her brother was a climbing Sherpa, when she heard a whistle. Suddenly, without warning, she was flung into the stream.

31  One of the yaks carrying camera boxes later slipped from the high track and
fell down the mountainside (MD)

In front of her was a full grown yeti. It grabbed one of her yaks and killed
it by simply twisting its neck. Then, after ripping open its stomach, it started
to devour the yak's innards. The Sherpani watched in terror as a baby yak
came to investigate. The yeti hurled it to the ground, where it too was killed.
Then the great hairy monster hid one of the carcasses under an overhang
and scampered off up the valley.

Lhaupa Dolma ran back to Macherma and collapsed into the arms of a
yak herder. At first she was unable to speak, but then, after assurances that
whatever demon was chasing her had disappeared, she told her story. The
beast was seven feet tall and had shaggy brown hair and a long pointy head.
The yak herder went to see for himself and the Khumjumg lama was
brought in to perform a powerful pujah to exorcise the spell of the yeti.
According to Stan Armington, who told the tale in his book *Trekking in
Nepal*, the 1974 incident at Macherma was the most credible yeti sighting
ever recorded. So be watchful, if ever you visit this region.

I remember asking Doug Scott, the seasoned Himalayan traveller and the
first Englishman to climb Mount Everest, what he thought about yetis. 'I
think yetis appear to people when they are ready to see them,' he told me.
'The whole yeti business is interesting. It probably symbolises all that's

hidden from us. There's a lot going on that we see only in rare moments, when we are allowed to, when the veil is pulled back and we get a glimpse of a different reality. It's almost as if the yeti is a symbol of that.'

We passed the place without incident, travelling with our train of porters and yaks. Eric and Chris were behind me and Dick Dennison and his film crew up ahead. At a narrow gorge our trek met another one coming down the valley. I remember thinking it was the perfect place for the Indians to ambush the U.S. cavalry. All it needed was a bit of tumbleweed and John Wayne would come galloping around the corner.

Everyone was eager to know when our lunch stop would be, such was the combination of strenuous up hill walking and thin mountain air. Lobsang, our sirdar, and two other Sherpas were having a chinwag and a few minutes' rest. With the sign outside the Macherma Hotel still fresh in my mind, I asked Lobsang if he believed in yetis. He was a little embarrassed and grinned, 'No, of course not.' Did his friends believe in yetis? A discussion ensued between the three of them for a few moments before Lobsang turned to tell me that 'No, my friends also do not believe in yetis.'

At this they picked up their loads and turned towards the path. Suddenly Lobsang was transfixed, his foot hanging in space as he forgot to finish the next step. I too stopped. He turned towards the nearest Sherpa and breathed one word that will remain with me forever.

'Yeti!'

32   The damaged cameras after the yak fall (MD)

My eyes followed the direction of his gaze up a steep hillside to a pile of boulders. I tried to focus my eyes on something brown that was moving near the skyline and then was gone. The spell on Lobsang broke and he turned towards me. 'What you see?'

'I don't know,' I said slowly. 'I saw something brown leap over the skyline. What did you see?'

Lobsang was silent for a moment and then looked straight at me. 'I see yeti,' he said.

I wasn't sure what I had seen. 'Are you sure?' I asked.

'Definitely,' Lobsang replied firmly. 'Definitely yeti.'

'What did it look like?'

'About five feet and more high, much wider than man. Orange brown fur. Walk on four legs.' I asked if his friend had seen it. A quick conversation and translation followed. Yes, one of his friends had seen it but not the other. Lobsang asked me again what I had seen.

'Well, I'm not sure. There was something moving, perhaps it was a deer,' I suggested doubtfully.

'No deer,' Lobsang insisted. 'That is yeti.'

Perplexed, the three Sherpas set off to catch up with the main expedition. Twenty minutes passed before I caught up with Dick Dennison who was filming Eric climbing a bracken-covered, Welsh-looking hillside.

'Lobsang has seen a yeti,' Chris told Dick. At first he just continued filming and then his eyes suddenly darted round, trying to catch whoever was sharing the joke.

'No joke, Dick. Leo saw it too,' Chris added.

His eyes met mine and held me with a fierce stare. I gazed back. Whatever Dick was looking for wasn't there. He glanced at Lobsang, who totally believed in what he had seen. The tape recorder was switched on and the camera whirred. Lobsang recounted his story, then the cameras were turned on me. Dick's blue-grey eyes met mine once more.

'What did *you* see, Leo?'

'I'm not sure, I saw something brownish. It might have been a deer.'

'Perhaps it was a yeti?' he pushed.

'It might have been, but there again it might not,' I added, trying to be as helpful as possible.

Eric observed that Dick was fascinated but wary at the same time. He was defensive and thought that somebody might be winding him up. When he spoke to Lobsang and his mate he knew it was genuine because they had actually seen it. Then Dick became very enthusiastic and said, 'Let's go and see if we can catch it on film.' So the whole film crew traipsed back up the hill with Lobsang, his friend and me.

'We went to the place where they saw it but could find no trace,' Dick

33   Dick Dennison hearing the news of a yeti at large from Chris Dewhirst (LD)

wrote in his diary. 'This wasn't surprising. Legend has it that if the yeti is pursued it disappears. I found it hard to believe, except that Leo caught a glimpse of it and he would never have allowed us to shoot film if there wasn't some shred of a possibility that it existed.'

Search as we might, we found no evidence. Lobsang even found the boulder from which it had jumped, but the ground was hard and stony. Dick was satisfied. He left our group to be on his own and wandered across the hillside on a higher path than the main track. I thought he was very brave. Dick's down-to-earth intellectual pragmatism was battling with his Irish roots which told him that Leprechauns and suchlike only show themselves to the chosen few. Dick wanted to be chosen.

A lunch of tea, biscuits and cheese was spread out on a mat and all the team rested. Dick took my Betacam video and interviewed almost every member of the expedition. What did they think of the yeti? Did it exist? Did they believe Lobsang? Fifteen people had given their views before suddenly I had another theory. Perhaps it was an elaborate joke.

'Dick,' I called turning the camera on him, 'there's no question of you giving Lobsang a backhander, is there?'

'No! Definitely not. Scout's honour. Cross my heart. I asked Lobsang to make a drawing of what he had seen. It was a small, muscular, furry creature with big shoulders. It looked like a male chimpanzee, but when we went back, there wasn't any trace, no spoor, no footprints. Though, as we know from Sherpa mythology, the yeti doesn't leave any traces. They say it's a saint which, I guess in translation means spirit. I really feel they've seen *something*. I'm convinced of it.'

\*

How seventeen people kept their faces straight I will never know – it only needed one nod or mistimed wink and . . .

Dick fell for the yeti, hook, line and sinker. He even offered $100,000 to anyone who got convincing film footage of one. Like most romantics, he wanted to believe that the folklore was truth. Dick was prime yeti bait, but we wanted to catch Peter Mason as well, although separately, of course, so that they would feed off each other's imaginations. It had been a gamble all along, for enough people had to know so as to help the plot, though with each conspirator there was a risk.

Our expedition had seventeen actors and actresses who each deserved an Oscar. Nobody ever let on and Dick remained convinced until the end. There was just one person he didn't interview – Bish – and by rights he would have been the most likely to crack. Ian Bishop, sky-diver, pilot, River Severn bridge builder, was now the most authenticated yeti in history.

Seconds before Lobsang and the Sherpas spotted him, I had seen Bish jumping up and down, bellowing with impatience. There were probably forty people all told in the gorge at the time, as well as dozens of yaks. Bish was standing on the hillside with Martin Hutchins, his minder, in radio contact with Eric who was behind me. The reason for our yeti's apparent

34, 35, 36   The yeti scalp (since stolen) in the monastery at Pangboche. A yeti out in the evening sunlight.

annoyance was that nobody, least of all Dick Dennison, was taking the slightest bit of notice. To Eric and to me, it looked too obviously like Bish dressed up in an orangey-brown suit and having a tantrum.

I apologise to Lobsang now. It was a joke designed to trap a film director and not a Sherpa. Come nightfall, Dick noticed that Lobsang had pitched his tent right in the middle of the group; clearly he was taking no chances.

I remembered how gullible Peter Mason had been while preparing for our last trip to Everest. Keeping a deadpan face, Per Lindstrand had read from his blackboard where he had been writing a list of things we needed: 'Swiss chocolate, Mars bars, glucose tablets, tea, Scotch, freeze dried water, matches . . .'

'What's freeze dried water?' asked a puzzled Peter.

'It's new. It comes in packets. Mountain House probably make it but that's for you to find out.' Peter wrote it down and Per continued reading the list. Later Peter went through his notes and was clearly uneasy.

'Where do I get this freeze dried water from?' he asked.

'I don't know,' Per replied sternly, 'America, I should think, but that's your job. Do you want me to do everything?'

'No, I don't want you to do everything. I've never heard of it, that's all. How does it work?'

'You mix it with water,' Per told him.

'Water? I thought it was already freeze dried,' Peter said limply.

'Yes, but obviously you must mix it with something. You can't drink powder, can you?'

'No, I suppose not,' said Peter.

'It makes more water,' Per added helpfully.

'I see,' said Peter, not really seeing at all. 'I'll inquire.' At this we let him out of his misery and fell about laughing. Peter claimed he had only been stringing us along. Well, he would say that, wouldn't he?

The yeti idea was also born around this time. Wouldn't it be fun, we thought, if one night high up in the Himalayas, with the tents illuminated by moonlight and the mess tent full of song, Peter went out for a leak and saw the silent figure of that most elusive creature creeping along a ridge. The trick was that no one else should see it. Would Peter quickly lose interest in our balloon expedition and try to persuade the world that he, Peter Mason, had absolutely, definitely, without the shadow of a doubt, seen a yeti? Few would believe him.

Mandy bought some brown hairy material, we found an ape mask and gorilla feet and hands. Sky-diving friends sewed it up as a jump suit. We had our yeti kit. It didn't convince anybody at close range but from a distance it was quite another matter. The first wry smile came not from Nepal but from an HTV journalist who interviewed me at home.

'And what are the chances of seeing that most elusive of Himalayan creatures, the yeti?'

I suggested that, as they hadn't been exposed to balloons before, there was a good chance of one coming out to see what all the fuss was about. I smiled as I did the interview, partly at the absurdity of the questions, but mainly because the HTV interviewer was sitting on the bag containing the yeti mask and suit.

I had trekked that year to Everest Base Camp to acclimatise. Ann Ward and her husband, Tim McCartney-Snape, made me welcome and in return I offered them gifts of food and little luxuries. I also entertained them with as many Whillans stories as I could remember, and these brought beams of delight to Ann's oriental face so that, at times, I thought it would split. On my second day, when I ran out of Whillans jokes, I decided it was the moment to test one of my own.

'I'm thinking of filming a yeti this morning,' I said airily at breakfast to no one in particular.

'A yeti?' Ann asked in astonishment. 'And where are you going to find one of those?'

'There's one in the icefall,' I replied confidently.

'How can you be so sure?'

'Look, I know there's one there because we brought it with us,' I explained with mock offence. 'It's the one from London Zoo. You must have heard of it.'

Ann cracked up. 'When can we see it?'

'Well, we've got to be careful.'

The Nepalese Army camp was just over the rise and, while I was sure that they didn't have guns, it would have been tempting providence to let them get close. A headline in *The Times* reporting on Mallory's expedition in 1924 came back to me. 'FINCH SHOT ON EVEREST' is rather disturbing when one remembers that George Finch was an expedition member, although the paper was actually referring to a captured bullfinch. Imagine the furore caused by 'YETI SHOT ON EVEREST: ENGLISHMAN DIES'.

We set up our studio among the towering pinnacles that form the lower part of the Khumbu Icefall. I wanted fleeting glimpses of yetis on film – yetis running away, yetis peering around, and finally a world exclusive: a yeti interview.

Ann readily agreed to be the Japanese interviewer and a list of questions was prepared. Back in Kathmandu I had taken the precaution of having a few tee-shirts embroidered for our yeti to wear. 'Read National Enquirer,' read one. 'Save Bigfoot,' was another. 'Yetis get it higher,' was perhaps more modern, but the best was 'Bonington a Hoax?' Chris Bonington had

37   The first interview ever recorded with a live yeti – by Dr Ann Ward of the
     Australian Institute for Yeti Research (MD)

organised a yeti hunting expedition a couple of years before, and Eric and I
had laid plans at the time to stalk their trek and lay false footprints before
filming from afar the resulting mayhem.

Our interview went well. Colonel C.B. Gurung from the Nepalese Army
did not shoot us, and the yeti video remained under wraps until we returned
eighteen months later, waiting for our first victim, Dick Dennison.

＊

We arrived at Gokyo on the 28 September. Dick had a filming field day.
The place reminded him of his forebears in Ireland, and his pen hardly
stopped writing.

'For the Hindus, Gokyo is a sacred place. When Shiva was creating the
world, he drove his trident into the ground and created its three lakes. The
Sherpas also believe in the magic of Gokyo. A plunge into the lake is said to
bring lasting fertility.' Judging by the temperature, I would have thought the
opposite was true.

We had to set up an environment in which not only to live and survive,
but also to operate sophisticated scientific equipment with some degree of
comfort. Gokyo would become, for a short time, the world's highest
meteorological station. Martin Harris had brought in two tons of equipment
packed in 18 steel boxes.

'We've got satellite pictures, radio sondes, weather faxes and charts such as people have never seen out here,' Martin told me, 'all for checking how the jet stream is developing to the north and how the monsoon is going away to the south. What we're doing is looking at a wild animal in the skies. If the wild animal wags its tail or sneezes, we've got to make sure we know about it, because it might be significant.'

Memex 91, the Mount Everest Meteorological Expedition, comprising Martin, Lisa and Jacqui, would not only be able to provide information for mountaineers but also collect data on the vertical structure of the atmosphere around Mount Everest for research on global warming. Every day twelve satellites would pump information down to our weather station. Later, weather balloons would set off at dawn at 5.45 a.m. and again at 5.45 in the evening to lock us into the grid of information sent from the Bracknell weather centre in Britain. We would also add to the thousands of readings from helium balloons set off every day all over the globe to forecast the world's weather. We were looking for the right winds at 30,000 feet but we also had to bring the local weather into the equation.

Martin moved into a new hut that wasn't quite finished and customised it for his gear. Antennae were erected to catch passing satellite signals and observe the mood of Sagamartha. During the erection of our aerials the Sherpas organised their own ceremony and a local lama was brought in to

38  The balloon sausage finally arriving at Gokyo (LD)

bless the whole team. It was a good excuse to test the local chang and eat the goodies that the Sherpanis prepared. Dick wrote in his diary: 'It was a wonderful communion of people and, whether or not they realised it, was a blessing for them all. They all say silly things, except Eric, who is always honest and simple and says it was a beautiful and moving ceremony.'

Peter Mason was beginning to be affected by the altitude. Because of his smoking and drinking, Peter didn't have a good pre-morbid condition, Glenn later explained. He certainly wasn't very fit. At 15,000 feet atmospheric pressure is exactly half that at sea level and at 30,000 feet it halves again. Walking uphill over rough terrain at these altitudes is severe exercise for most people. Nepal also has other serious environmental hazards, such as one of the highest rates of gastro-enteritis in the world, a high rate of rabies, tuberculosis and infectious disease. Apart from all this, we expected a number of high altitude disorders, from simple acute mountain sickness to high altitude cerebral or pulmonary oedema.

'As well as being high, it's also very cold,' Glenn said, 'and cold injury is very common, ranging from chilblains and frostbite to hypothermia. There are also nutritional problems. We didn't have a very rounded diet and all these things can add up. Prevention is better than cure. Everybody who goes to altitude gets some degree of mountain sickness, headaches, shortness of breath or slight nausea but you normally get over these in a couple of days. If you don't, then it is best to descend. Altitude sickness is usually the product of ignorance or poor planning, so it was very useful to have Russell there because he had a good understanding of altitude disorders and had planned a very sensible schedule for the trek.'

Peter had gone through what Glenn thought were the most likely places for him to get acute mountain sickness and so, when he began to experience headaches in Gokyo that would not settle down, we had only one option and that was to descend. Rather than go for a long walk down, which would have taken out Russell, Glenn and Peter, it seemed a lot more sensible to simulate descent by putting Peter in the Gamow bag, an airtight and portable body-sized bag that can be pressurised.

We pressured Peter back down 3,000 feet and it worked very well. He said he felt like Lazarus, and apart from Peter's condition, there was a great feeling of optimism. Over the next few days, Dick recorded growing team confidence in his diary. 'More people have arrived at the camp. Lisa, Jacqui and Andy, who has been chaperoning them in his quiet way, and Glenn's wife Irina. There has been a dramatic improvement in morale today. Everyone is busy building their little empires. Martin has now transformed

39   Gokyo village, with three weather balloons starting their ascent. The two hot air
      balloons in their red bags lie in the field at the bottom of the picture. (MD)

40   Jacqui preparing to release a weather balloon above the misty lakes of Gokyo (MD)

his observatory with plastic double-glazing. Aerials are being erected. The set is under construction.'

There were four families living permanently in this tiny village. Eastern Nepal is the most remote place in winter in the snow and also one of the most wildly pretty, with its opaque turquoise lake and a never-changing mountain scene.

A Sherpa woman was playing with her baby outside. The baby suffered from eczema but her mother had nothing with which to treat it. Glenn gave her a bottle of oil. There were fifteen babies in the village of Gokyo, all suffering from some minor infection or other. Glenn was kept busy trying to help them.

Heather opened her box of goodies and the blue vein cheese smell stayed with us although the Sherpa ladies sprayed it with deodorant. Her fruitcake went down very well with my cognac. A Welsh couple reported seeing porters emptying gas out of an 170lb. helium cylinder to make them lighter. The porters were last heard speaking in high voices.

Dick wrote: 'I watch the flags the Sherpas put up and the aerials we put up, each talking to very different Gods, the technical versus the mythological. Prayer flags flutter towards the mountains, aerials aim stiffly at Kathmandu and the satellite pictures track the moods of Everest. We found nine more porters struggling up the rocky waterfall stooped under the big balloon basket. It was cruel but they earned 70,000 rupees, more than twice as much as they would earn for an average job. I felt very sorry for these men that they work so hard for so small a living. When their struggle was

41   Dr Glenn treating Sherpa children in Gokyo (MD)

42 The balloon basket is carried with great difficulty up the waterfalls towards Gokyo
   (Peter Mason)

over, there wasn't anyone there to meet them. I gave them $120 for the shot
we took of them carrying their load.'

＊

As September wore on the upper winds remained weak and from the wrong
direction, but the air mass was dryer now, giving a better chance for the
pilots to land in Tibet. Eric, Bish, Mandy and I climbed the Black Mountain
behind the moraine, over 2,000 feet above our camp, to find a new filming
platform. The effort nearly knocked us out.

   Glenn's wife Irina, a charming Russian girl, had not been feeling too
well until three members of the Russian Cho Oyu expedition came to town
to buy rum. She was delighted to pick up some gossip from home. Peter
pulled out a bottle of red wine and we each had a mouthful. 'After so long,'

Dick confided in his diary, 'it lingered like love on my palate.'

We were really playing waiting games as the weather remained stubbornly uncooperative and Martin played with his instruments. Highlights included boomerang-throwing over the lake, speed stepping-stone crossings beside the lake, marmot watching, water-skiing, funny voices, flight sweepstakes, dictionary games, barrel rolling and hunt the salami. By the first day of October, we were glad to be on the move again.

'The people of Gokyo,' Dick recalled, 'gathered around this morning to show the balloon basket to their babies before it was carried down the main street and over a few walls to the paddock where it will be launched. Standing in the basket, Chris and Leo discuss the possibilities of burner failure, bailing out and emergency situations. Eric came up with the idea of flying over Mount Everest in a barrel attached to the outside of the basket.'

Dick filled in the days by filming the difficulties faced by the more permanent inhabitants. 'The town of Gokyo with its 15 adults and 15 children has adjusted well to the invasion and they have made a little money from our presence. In her tiny house a Sherpa woman choreographed her pots and pans over the mud brick fire fuelled by yak dung. It is a beautiful but deadly scene. Many Sherpa people die at an early age due to smoke-filled and badly ventilated houses.'

Paul and Dick had a small argument about the lighting of this scene. It was an example of how the waiting was getting on our nerves and all we could do was to try and bring some of the luxuries of home to our camp. 'I had the pleasure of having my hair washed by Heather,' Dick wrote on 4 October, 'and I washed Lisa's hair. It was a nice friendly attempt to jolly each other along with the waiting.'

At lunch we introduced 'The Seven Deadly Sins Game'. A lot of lustful men were contemplating two swims a day in the lake because, as Dick explains, 'having the two weather goddesses around is bad for the hormones and there has to be an outlet. Everything I see is tormenting me. Even the balloons look like floating sperm.'

We also introduced a 'vulgarity points table'. Peter lost five points for using 'fuck' on the satellite fax, Martin Harris lost two points for playing pocket billiards, Dick lost three points for engineering an argument, Jacqui lost five points for reading *Lolita* in public, and Martin Hutchins lost three points for not remembering who played the male lead in the film of *Lolita*. Lisa then lost four points for a Sherpa ladies' joke, but when asked what she missed most, replied without thinking 'my pussy'. Bish lost five points for offering to stroke Lisa's pussy, and Eric also lost five for laughing at Bish.

By 6 October, four weeks into the expedition, the preliminary filming was complete and thirty-eight rolls of film had been shot, which, at ten minutes a roll, made over six and a half hours' worth. Martin Harris still had to get the weather station operating fully. The previous night there had been a wind of over 16 knots at 30,000 feet. This was not considered sufficient for a flight as the balloon might be becalmed. '*Kissing the Void*,' Dick mused, 'could be a good title for the book.'

If we had been lacking enough excitement, suddenly we had too much. Lisa contracted pulmonary oedema. 'High altitude pulmonary oedema, or HAPE as the Americans call it, is a catastrophic event in your lungs,' Dr Glenn told me. 'What happens is that the pressure in the circulatory system to the heart goes up, which is a product of less oxygen at altitude. Most people handle that increase in pressure without a problem, but those who get HAPE experience a change in the structure of the lungs so that they fill up and you begin to drown in your own fluids. Once that happens, your ability to get oxygen into your blood is lowered even further, and it becomes a vicious cycle.'

Lisa had climbed from Gokyo at 16,000 feet up to the ridge at 18,000 feet. There she complained of being short of breath, of tightness in her chest and extreme anxiety. This was reported by Paul on the radio to Glenn, who hurried across the glacier. 'When I saw her, it was obvious she was extremely sick. She was sitting there breathing twice as fast as anyone else. Her pulse rate was about 160. I listened to her lungs and could hear the fluid bubbling over at least two thirds of her lung fields.'

Glenn explained that people who get pulmonary oedema are graded one to four. Lisa, it seemed, was four and so had a one in two chance of dying. Something had to be done immediately. The patient had to be moved to lower altitude without delay, and from Gokyo you can't easily get much lower than Phortse. At 11,000 feet, this is still at a significant altitude. From there it's up hill again to Namche, and many people have died there due to it not being low enough.

Even better than physical descent was to put Lisa in a hyperbaric chamber: the Gamow Bag. This would restore the barometric pressure around the patient to about 5,000 feet lower in a matter of two minutes, simply by pumping it up. But Lisa was so short of breath that at first it was difficult to get her into the bag. Once in, she stayed there for about four hours, with someone working the foot pump between ten and fifteen times per minute. Glenn's reaction sounded cool but the whole team seemed to bend their wills to Lisa's survival.

'It is almost impossible,' Dick wrote the next day, 'to discuss the feeling of love that everyone experienced last night as they sat around the hut in silence focusing every tiny particle of their being on Lisa's survival. One by one we took it in turns to operate the foot pump that brought pressure into the plastic sarcophagus that entombed her in another world thousands of feet below. Inside, her arms crossed, her eyes closed, she looked as if she had flown this life. There was such beauty in her serene face that it was hard to conceive what a huge struggle was going on within her lovely frame. Mike Balson called her the sleeping beauty. I thought she looked like Ingrid Bergman. Everybody was there and for those hours the expedition was over, yet it was possibly at its most real. We have become such a tight family. It is not going to be easy for everyone to deal with the separation that comes when the balloon takes off.'

After four hours Lisa's condition had improved dramatically. Her respiratory rate had dropped to 22, her pulse was 118 and she felt much better. More important, Glenn could no longer hear any fluid at all in her lungs.

Why she became sick in the first place was an interesting question for when we were at the hospital in Kunde, at about 12,000 feet, Glenn had put her through a finger pulse oxymetry test, which involves shining a light through a finger nail. A machine then measures the amount of oxygen available in your blood stream. Lisa had a very high amount of oxygen, higher, in fact, than most of the rest of us – usually an indication that acclimatisation is progressing well. The fact that we had had a very comprehensive acclimatisation programme made her illness all the more unexpected.

Now that she was better, Glenn had to decide what to do next. There was a choice, either of taking her down or of letting her stay at Gokyo. 'She felt well,' Glenn said, 'and so I opted for the latter, although there was obviously a restriction on her going any higher so that there was no repeat of her HAPE. I continued to monitor her condition. Through the whole of the next day she showed no sign of recurrence. She was cured. It was the first time I'd conducted an active treatment for this condition, and I was greatly relieved.'

Thirteen years earlier, on Messner's Everest trip, I had met in Base Camp at 17,500 feet an Indian journalist who the day before had been in Bombay at sea level. The helicopter that brought him in for his scoop returned to the hospital at Kunde with a badly injured Sherpa. Then the clouds rolled in and the helicopter did not return. The journalist very quickly developed acute mountain sickness. Gamow bags hadn't been invented in those days, and the three Austrian doctors did what they could by putting him on a drip feed and giving him oxygen. Fortunately the helicopter managed to return before he died. A similar thing had happened on a trek Chris was leading, when one of his charges died before he could be evacuated. He was cremated at Namche. I gave thanks for Lisa's sake that technology had found a solution.

# 7. *Rehearsals and Rows*

ON OUR NINTH day at Gokyo, Andy and Martin cancelled the planned rehearsal of the balloon launch because of a monsoon storm over Kathmandu. They expected a heavy fog but it turned out to be a beautifully clear morning. Dick wrote in his diary that Chris had become almost hysterical with impatience and began to make a great deal of noise after seeing a few clouds blown off Cho Oyu. A meteorological balloon was released from which Martin recorded a wind of over 27 knots from the west at 35,000 feet. It was not a flying day and Chris quietened down after being proved wrong. It was turning into a long wait.

After breakfast we filmed a re-enactment of Lisa's agony in the Gamow bag. There were some wonderful performances and I climbed inside to get a patient's eye view. The problem was keeping the 16 mm Aaton camera far enough away from the plastic window of the bag while I operated it on my back inside. As the pressure increased, so the humidity level also rose and the camera fogged. But I got the shot I wanted on my 3.5 mm fisheye lens. All was going well and I could see our doctor performing his duties and other concerned faces at the window. It was a strange experience, being back down 5,000 feet. I felt very warm and sticky, almost as if I were going back into the womb. Perhaps that is the idea of the Gamow, to relax in harmony.

Suddenly I snapped out of my dream as I noticed two rather strange things. My actors were struggling to keep smiles off their sympathetic faces and I found myself speaking in a strange voice. It echoed, was far too high, and squeaked. The audience cracked up laughing but only, it seemed, when I spoke. Then I detected a hissing noise. Something was being fed into my bag. Helium. The bastards! I was squeaking compressed helium. I wondered who the joker was – either Glenn or Andy, I guessed, although Eric looked as if he was in on it. The end result was that Toad sounded more like Mickey Mouse.

Dick started shooting some cultural footage. 'The lady with the six children brought her baby over today with a cut hand. I thought it would be a good idea to film her tiny cottage, to try to bring some social conscious-ness into an otherwise gung-ho film. It took me a while to realise that she didn't want to be filmed because her sixth child had died and a lama had told her it was because she had been photographed too many times. We finally convinced her that more films would mean more doctors and more medicine, and she allowed me to pay her 1,000 rupees.'

Glenn gave us all a final medical briefing which was brief and to the point. It covered burns, amputations, and death. Glenn made it quite clear we were on our own and going into a war zone. From now on it would be survival of the fittest. As a last thought, Glenn asked me if I knew the best cut of meat off the human body.

'No. What?' I asked.

'A steak right off Chris's backside.'

'But I'm vegetarian.'

Glenn smiled. 'You'll change.'

For the postponed rehearsal we were up at 5 a.m. and found the generator not functioning. Everyone was anxious to get going and eventually the balloons were inflated. After the test, I had something to ask Chris about the balloon. We walked away from the launch-field for a brew and breakfast and I put to him a straightforward question about the turning vents, which he had had modified in Australia. No sooner had the words rolled off my lips than the answer came, not from Chris, but from Heather. Throughout the waiting period, I had felt a gradual breakdown in my understanding. Whereas I wanted to enjoy the experience with Chris as a two-man team, I felt unable to do so. The more I wanted the bonding process to start, the more Heather seemed determined to keep all of him to herself. There simply wasn't room for both of us and it was inevitable that something would snap.

'I didn't know you were an expert in ballooning, Heather.' I didn't conceal the note of sarcasm. 'When I want your opinion you will be the first to know.'

It all spilled out. While I was annoyed with myself for losing my rag, at the same time I couldn't understand her logic. If she were so possessive of her man, it made more rather than less sense that Chris and I should talk through 'what if' scenarios. I was the one who had fought to keep Chris on board and now I was losing faith in him.

The real problem was that in the last few days I had come to believe that Chris was not the right person to be flying the balloon. Eric confided to me that he thought Chris had let me down by bringing Heather. It seemed almost as if she had cast a spell on him. I told Mandy I wasn't happy about going with Chris while I was so unsure of his ability to loosen his bond with Heather. It was an uncomfortable situation, but I decided, come what may, I would fly in that balloon over Everest. If, for whatever reason, Chris felt that he couldn't be the pilot, then as a contingency I would fly the balloon myself and Glenn, our mountaineering doctor and cameraman, could film it. I had already talked this through weeks earlier with Martin Hutchins, just in case Chris had been unavailable to fly. Mentally, I was ready to go without him.

It wasn't quite as stupid as it appeared. Martin was to inflate the balloon anyway, and get all the oxygen and navigational systems working. After that I could duplicate Andy's actions as I followed him and Eric. When Andy burnt, so would I. Whenever he came down, so would we. The Pronav satellite navigational system would plot our course to within 150 feet, so locating our position in Tibet would be child's play. In a balloon going from 16,000 feet to 29,000 feet and over, there is only one knob to turn and that is up. Once past Everest we would have a choice – either continue or go down. This plan, of course, would fail completely if Andy's burners went out, but then foresight was one thing I couldn't organise.

Taking off as pilot to fly over Mount Everest did not hold any demons, and there is part of me to this day that wishes I had taken the option. I love parachuting from most kinds of aircraft, so jumping out of a balloon that was not going to make it held no real fears. It was almost as if I had been programmed throughout my whole life for this event. The only problem in this scenario was that Glenn would have stiff competition from Mandy, who had been told that she was first reserve if anything happened to Eric or me as cameramen. I confided my plan to Eric, Andy, Martin, Glenn and, of course, Mandy. All of them considered it an option that could be made to work.

As time wore on, Dick became more concerned about his responsibilities at home and finally decided he would not wait for the balloon flight itself. He had filmed all the shots he needed from the ground and could leave the aerial work to Eric and me. All the same, I tried to stay his departure for at least one more day. I felt it was Dick's place to be there, to see it through to the end, but he was in danger of losing money from other projects and it was worrying him. This was an altogether different kind of altitude sickness. I felt it was a bad decision and one he might regret. Little did I know how much. Dick had a very clear idea of what the flight lift-off would entail and could certainly have calmed Chris down, interviewing his 'hero' to the last. An expedition has been likened to a house of cards. Each element supports it but it's a fragile construction and it takes only one player to pull out and the whole thing can collapse.

It was difficult for me to understand Dick's sense of priorities. He had pushed so hard to join the team and now seemed to want to desert us at the crucial hour. Another fleeting glimpse of the yeti might change his mind. We would have one more go at getting Dick to look at Homo Bishop. Mike wore my radio mike to capture the moment while Bish and I climbed up on to the skyline to await their return from a walk up the valley. As they came into view, I signalled to Bish to adopt his stoop position and then

43   Take-off rehearsal at the Lake near Gokyo, with Cho Oyu behind (MD)

stride off. There was no response. Dick was now heavily engaged in conversation with Mike. I yelled to Bish to go again. Still nothing; we had failed miserably. If there was one thing I learned in Nepal that year, it was that yetis could easily exist. Here was a life-sized and mobile primate only 1,000 feet above the witnesses and it produced absolutely no response. Perhaps we are surrounded by brown furry creatures that we choose to ignore.

Suddenly Mike tilted his head upwards. He, at least, seemed to have noticed something. Dick glanced up and then quickly returned his gaze. Mike told me later he had seen the yeti, and so had Dick, but they didn't take in the furry detail and dismissed it as a trekker. And that, after all, was exactly what it was. Perhaps Dick had cleverly seen through it all and was playing a double bluff. As it was, Dick was too preoccupied with his decision to leave.

'What I can't get over to anyone is that my departure makes me feel inside that I am devaluing the expedition,' he wrote, 'but I have to get on with other important films. I am going to miss 'the family'. Mike, Glenn and Leo went up the mountain to film Andy being taught mountaineering by Eric. It is as much a bonding exercise as anything else. I made up my mind to go back to Kathmandu and made a big announcement at dinner. I paid Kunge the money I owe for staying in her trekking lodge for nine days and borrowed 40,000 rupees from Peter, who has now taken over in my place. I then had a final party with the Russians from the Cho Oyu expedition.'

44   The Russian climbers from Cho Oyu join us in Gokyo (LD)

45   Eric Jones teaching Andy Elson to climb ice (MD)

Next morning Dick was ready to go, but he postponed his departure as he reviewed his decision to leave. Watching Dick do battle with his conscience was always good value. Inevitably, pragmatism would overrule romanticism. 'We are now into serious waiting time,' he wrote. 'I did a final interview with Chris in which he expounded his theory about a slower flight over Everest and his differences with Andy who wants a fast long distance flight. Chris is concerned that the balloons will become too separated to photograph on such a fast flight.'

Afterwards Dick recorded the other point of view by filming an interview with Andy, who, as usual, was very funny. Sometimes Andy the Mole is grumpy but he can laugh at himself and his quick temper. According to Dick, 'He always seems reluctant to be interviewed but when it happens he enjoys it. He believes he is one of the best balloonists in the world and loves long passage flights. Andy carries the burden of self-consciousness and perhaps a class consciousness as well. He is tenacious and mechanically brilliant.'

It was hard to quarrel with any of Dick's succinct character sketches I found later in his diary.

'Eric Jones now has his children and his responsibilities as a reason for survival. He has taken on the most challenging of climbs, the Eiger and the Matterhorn, and every time the going got tough he smiled wider and longer. Eric believes his hard childhood has been responsible for his tough nature.

'Leo is a tough little bloke who in some ways has never grown up. He has personal demons about some women and a chip on his shoulder about people like Chris who are loquacious, lyrical and lucky. Leo has had to work hard for everything and he doesn't have the mental freedom to expand his world in a harmonious way. He gets very temperamental under pressure, perhaps using his anger as a device to get things done. He is very imaginative, and is capable of doing incredibly dangerous and complex things, just to prove they can be done. Mandy is a real anchor for Leo, consistently supportive, sane and logical.

'Peter Mason is doing it for the money – a professional PR man serving an obsessed managing director. Peter is trying to repress his hysterically dramatic nature but it keeps popping up. He's marvellously theatrical but not really the tough manager type that he appears. Everyone knows Peter's weaknesses and teases him, but he takes it well most of the time. He is now caught between time and money running out and the weather not co-operating.

'Martin Harris is afraid of the freedom that Chris has managed to create in his life. He measures every little increment of the future, is cautious and conservative, while Chris is flamboyant and brash. Martin would like to have been the silk-scarved Battle of Britain pilot but ended up in the met briefing office. In the early morning the weather man scratched the ice from the windows and peered out into the frosty dawn; another day of waiting.'

Dick Dennison left the expedition and returned to Kathmandu where he met up with Dick Smith, publisher of *Australian Geographic* magazine. Peter Mason had managed to include both men on our permit to overfly Everest in Smith's personal jet. Dick Dennison went armed with a movie camera, and the shots he took at 400 mph are memorable. The mountain doesn't exactly flash past their windows, and one gains an impression of just how massive Everest, Lhotse and Makalu really are.

46 'Everest as Dick Smith saw it a week before I photographed it' – Leo Dickinson

From 500 feet above Everest, Dick Dennison and Dick Smith claimed they saw footprints in the snow and tents at Base Camp. They suffered turbulence on the lee side of the mountain and the two men wondered what this would do to the balloons. 'I cannot describe this vast panorama but I will never forget it,' Dennison told me later. 'It was one of those pristine, unrepeatable moments in life.'

Back in Gokyo, the debate about when we should fly was hotting up. Chris wanted to go as soon as possible, but Andy was more cautious. The first day chosen – some days after Dick's return to Kathmandu – was fraught with dissent. Andy refused to talk to Chris and would walk out of any attempted meeting. On one occasion I asked Eric to chase after him and try to get him to see reason. To my astonishment, he wouldn't. Eric is very good at talking sense into people, particularly me, and I took this refusal badly.

'I couldn't work out which one was right,' Eric recalls. 'I had more confidence in Andy, so I tended to side with him. Chris was becoming more excited, and wanted to go when the conditions were not quite right. Maybe he was too psyched up. If you become hyped up and nervous about something, you just want to do it and get it over.'

Later on that evening Peter came out with the view that we should have flown two days earlier. This was not helpful, though his nervousness was understandable. If the weather got worse we might not be able to go at all. It was the finest of lines. Chris said that Peter would have moved Everest if he could. The two pilots worked out a flight plan based upon the wind directions at known altitudes from the radio sonde. It showed us five to seven miles to the south of Everest. This wasn't nearly close enough.

'I would say,' Peter announced in the trekking hut that evening 'that if the situation doesn't deteriorate from what we've got now, we should go with it.'

I put it to him: 'So you're saying that you would be happy for us to miss Everest by five or six miles?'

'I'm not happy about it,' Peter said, 'but if we don't have an alternative, and the indications are that the weather is going to get worse, we should consider how much more time we can spend just waiting here.'

'The goal has always been to fly over Mount Everest. Anything else is totally unacceptable,' I said.

The problem was obvious. We were fast running out of time and we all knew that the window would soon close for the year. We had no one else's experience to draw on and only one round in the chamber. An aborted flight was all too real a possibility. There would be no time to retrieve the balloon for a second attempt from the moraine glacier across from our camp, let alone from the Khumbu Valley. We decided that the next day, 20 October, could be launch date but it was not a harmonious decision.

Only twelve hours before our tentative lift-off, Chris was the only one who still wanted to go. My reluctance was a gut-reaction rather than a considered one. I couldn't explain it. I asked Eric. 'I don't know – but my feeling is to wait another day,' he said.

At three in the morning we all got up to check the latest radio sonde and came to the conclusion that we wouldn't go. Andy said there was nothing to be lost by waiting another twenty-four hours. Chris was getting rattled at finding that his opinions still weren't shared by the others.

We all went to bed. The next radio sonde in the morning confirmed that we would have got 1,000 feet closer to Lhotse than we had anticipated the night before, but this was still four or five miles too far south. It wasn't sufficiently close to call it a flight over Everest. The launch would be an accumulation of nearly one million pounds' worth of effort and I don't think I have ever been so sure about anything in my life as I was when we postponed the launch for yet another day.

We would go the next day, 21 October. The radio sondes were showing

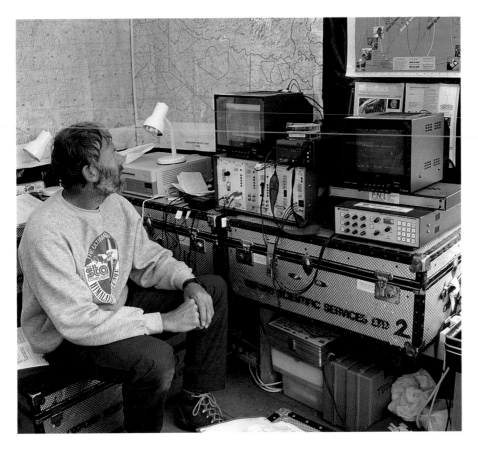

47 Martin Hutchins with the meteorological equipment (MD)

an improving situation, although immediately behind this there appeared to be ten days of bad weather, and we might not be able to wait for it to clear. I think we were all tired of Gokyo, despite it being one of the most beautiful places in the world. Everyone wanted the balloons up and to get back to the luxuries of Kathmandu. As the evening drew in, I recorded my thoughts on tape.

'It's five past seven in the evening and both Andy and Chris are working hard with their projected flight plans based on the latest weather balloon. Glenn, Irina and three Sherpas are up on Black Mountain, waiting for our 3 a.m. radio call to tell them we are going. They will then climb to the summit in the dark, armed with an Aaton, a Hi-8, and three stills cameras, including my 500mm lens which I have given Irina a crash course in using. They have been up there for two days, and we sent up more food today. According to

48 *over page:* The difficulties of landing a balloon in the high Himalayas are all too apparent in this photograph by William Thompson

Lobsang, the Sherpas have had enough of camping on this exposed ridge, although it's not a difficult mountain. Some Sherpas are obviously tougher than others.

'Today a friend of Eric's called Alan arrived. He had been with Joe Simpson on Pumori. An Icelandic climber fell 5,000 feet down to the glacier. They think he was hit by a falling cornice while on a fixed rope. His body was found in four pieces the day after.

'I'm waiting outside the met office which is illuminated by floodlights for the film. We are surrounded by bristling antennae and all the latest high-tech gear that Martin Harris was able to scrounge. The mist has come down, so I'm quite warm because of this inversion layer. Glenn and Irina are thousands of feet above. Glenn's cameras will be in danger of freezing up there. High above me is a tethered helium balloon with silver foil attached to the line, which is glittering in the evening light. It's to act as a wind sock in the morning.

'Everyone is more relaxed than they were last night but still on tenterhooks as to whether we will go. We have waited so long. I'm feeling very glad and positive tomorrow's the day. I feel an inner calm. The die is about to be cast, but the question remains, are the cast about to die?'

Peter brought out beers and some cooking rum. It was rather premature to be celebrating before we met in the trekker's hut to come to a final decision. The flyers abstained.

We gathered in the cramped building with an air of expectancy hanging over us. 'The 6 p.m. radio sonde is a good one,' Chris began. 'It lets us plot a trajectory right over the summit of Everest. Andy and I have just spent twenty minutes with our maps. I put our balloon about half a mile south of Everest and Andy has put his half a mile north, so there is a little bit of flexibility on the current figures for us to fly either side of the summit. The next radio sonde comes through at two in the morning. We will do a final plot at three, but at the moment, if this holds, we will have a very good flight.'

'I'll know when I see the three o'clock sonde in the morning,' added Andy.

Mike Balson asked everyone's feelings. 'Happy,' I said. 'Excited,' Eric added. Peter replied that, with hindsight, he was glad they had not flown the night before because it looked as if they would be lucky and have a better flight path today. Updating hindsight is always sensible, unless there happens to be a film crew recording everything.

I went to bed and slept peacefully.

Five hours later I dressed in my duvet and down trousers and went to the launch field. After packing my sleeping bag into my emergency bail-out rucksack, I picked it up. It was quite heavy, probably over 50lbs. Could I parachute out with so much weight? I would just have to wait and see. The temperature was 15° above what we expected and this meant the balloon would be overweight. Chris said we might have to dump some fuel. The tape recorder was put away for our landing in Tibet.

For Eric, 'the one and a half hours before lift-off was chaos. Andy had too much to do and hadn't organised himself properly. My oxygen cylinder was only half full and it ran out. Andy wasn't pre-breathing oxygen at all. I didn't know much about pre-breathing but had been told that it was necessary to avoid the bends. At the same time I was lugging a cylinder around I was also trying to strap one into our balloon. We were also trying to put a video camera up on the basket. The whole thing was utterly confused. In direct contrast, Chris was sitting down quietly with his face-mask on, as all four of us should have been.'

Chris said, 'I knew the moment I stepped into the basket, I would focus, but that hour prior to take off was very frightening. We were launching so close to Everest, and I knew that there was no turning back once we'd got off the ground. In the half an hour pre-breathing oxygen, I was really trying to keep calm, organised and together, but there was a moment when I thought maybe I shouldn't do this. Heather was getting on with her job. I don't think she realised just how worried I was.'

49   The team that was to fly – Chris, Andy, Leo and Eric (MD)

# 8. *Over the Top*

THE SKY WAS still dark, with a faint pink glow in the east, as we readied the balloons. Chris had left his basket in a tent to keep the frost from it and this was pulled out while the Sherpas rushed round, taking the envelopes from their bags and collecting the wires and karabiners from which to suspend the baskets. The inflation fan, a three foot wooden propeller surrounded by a cage and powered by a specially adjusted petrol engine, was fired up and began to fill the envelopes.

With all our equipment left in the take-off field, it had seemed sensible to arrange some security. Nobody could walk off with a balloon but there were other smaller temptations lying around. Lobsang had posted two of his Sherpa cooks in a tent right in the middle of the field to guard against anything disappearing back down the valley, but he hadn't thought to tell the guards that they were sleeping in the middle of an airport. As the fans inflated the balloons, their tent was overwhelmed.

The inhabitants quickly pulled on their clothes and the yellow dome shuffled sideways like an oversized tortoise until it was free of the balloon. As the huge nylon envelopes swelled against the deep blue sky, illuminated by our bright filming lights, three Brahmini ducks were startled into flight across the lake. The yaks stopped chewing their cud to gaze at us disdainfully. The loads they had carried up on their backs were preparing to fly.

Peter Mason lit the burners and blue flames roared across the field that still lay buried in the shadow of Everest. In my bulky duvet jacket and oxygen gear, I felt like an astronaut preparing for a journey into space. Mission control was a confusion of bright lights, scattered equipment and scurrying helpers, with Martin Hutchins at the centre directing operations. Martin Harris's latest report predicted a flight right over the summit. He'd done well to find us the right winds and I was glad he had stayed.

Mandy gave me a kiss and a hug and said, 'Be careful. Don't do anything I wouldn't do.' I clearly had a lot of room for manoeuvre. When she pulled away there was a tear in her eye, but she smiled bravely. It was all, of course, for the film. Now she picked up her cameras and got on with the job. Afterwards she recorded, 'If anything ever happens to Leo, it was meant to happen, and there's nothing I can do to change it. It's fate.'

Chris was worried that the temperature gauge, or thermister, attached to the top of our envelope was reading too high. As Chris watched the

50   Inside the balloon, the three nightwatchmen oversleep

51, 52   Leo pre-breathing, taking in oxygen at one end and wondering what is inflating his duvet trousers at the other. It could be a case of high altitude anticipation. Paul Tait films last minute preparations as Chris fires the burners. (MD)

needle go off the scale, he began to fear the worst. The warmer it is outside, the hotter you've got to make your balloon if you're going to get it off the ground. Chris thought we probably had a little too much weight on board as well.

'I had a balloon that was operating so hot that we were in danger of losing it,' he said. 'We either had to abort or go. If we went, I had to coax this balloon over Everest without it falling apart. I made that decision right on take off.'

Andy was more relaxed. He wandered about, checking he had all his gear, and brought us a spare oxygen bottle. He gave me a hug and shook Chris's hand. Then Andy told Martin Hutchins he would be ready in five or ten minutes and climbed into his basket to sort out his equipment and fix the radio. His burners were switched off and he still had to make his pre-flight checks.

Chris was becoming more concerned that, due to the extreme temperature inside the envelope, our balloon might fall to pieces at any moment. In reality, a simple fault in the gauge was all that was wrong, and if he had asked Martin Hutchins, or Andy, they would have reassured him that all was well. The three men had made several simulated flight profiles together in Australia, to assess the climb rate of a balloon from 16,000 feet. 'What was the point of doing them if he didn't learn from the experience?' asked Martin as he watched our balloon disappearing into the sky with our formation flying plan torn to ribbons.

We had agreed upon a twenty second interval, with the others going ahead, but Chris wouldn't wait. He had asked me if I was ready to go, and I assumed he meant when our turn came. I had my 16mm Aaton camera on its basket-mounted tripod aimed towards Chris and running, but because of the noise from the burners I didn't hear it jam. By the time I realised the problem, and had turned to ask Paul Tait if he could help, we were 50 feet off the ground. So, instead of stepping off my platform, I waved to the others as the chaos below gently receded. It was 6.40 a.m. For months I'd counted on having Eric's balloon in my sights as we skimmed the summit of Everest. Now nothing seemed to be going according to plan.

To make matters worse Andy didn't follow us into the air. I was thrown into a filming panic and assumed that something had gone wrong with his balloon. It didn't help that our balloon's intercom wasn't working and I couldn't talk to Chris. If I had been able to do that, I could have slowed him down. Andy had not yet realised we were airborne.

'The last time I saw Andy,' Chris said later, 'was two minutes after take off. I looked down and he'd left. I just felt, "Oh well, he'll be here shortly," and that was the last I thought of the other balloon.'

This would have been fine if Chris had hovered at a couple of hundred feet, but Glenn's film from Black Mountain shows a steadily increasing rate of climb away from Andy who assumed, wrongly, that we were just above waiting for him. There are three men who will probably never forgive Chris for rushing into the air like that. It was all such a waste of time having two balloons; a unique filming opportunity was lost.

When at last Andy realised what was going on, he hesitated to follow us immediately. In the back of his mind was a scene from the film of our 1985 Himalayan flights which featured a terrible collision between the two balloons just after take off. Andy didn't want to repeat the performance and so increased his climb rate only gradually.

Just after the balloons lifted off, Peter became quite emotional and shed a tear or two. 'Three years and God knows how many weeks waiting here. Isn't that beautiful?' he said. Then he recited the balloonist's prayer. 'May the winds welcome you with softness. May the sun bless you with his warm hands. May you fly so high and so well, that God will join you in your laughter and set you gently back in the loving arms of mother earth. Good luck guys, good luck.'

53, 54   The moment of take-off, Leo on his camera platform, the suspended camera
bag recording the action (MD)

55   Rising above the lake at Gokyo (Irina Singleman)

As we rose, the ground climbed with us towards Cho Oyu at the head of the valley. The Russian expedition on the mountain was to lose their doctor that day, when at 26,000 feet a tug on the rope unexpectedly released a huge loose rock. We'd visited them in their base camp, getting stuck into the medicinal spirit when the vodka ran out. They had invited us to visit Siberia, which sounded a whole lot better than being *sent* there. Choice was their new-found doctrine, and we drank to the downfall of all politicians.

As dusk fell I explained that I wanted sunset shots of Everest from a ridge overlooking their camp. We climbed up for about an hour until I had impressive views of Cho Oyu, Kantega, Everest and Lhotse. I wanted to wait for the soft warm tones of twilight, just before the day was lost forever. Cameras should be left in your rucksack until such moments. After sitting around for half an hour, the temperature had dropped to 25°c below. I've often noticed that when I'm filming I don't feel the cold, but now it was starting to get more than just cold. One of the Russians offered me his gloves. His English wasn't good but he seemed to be offering to shake my hand. 'Look,' I thought he was saying, 'I don't need them.' Not being proud, I took his hand. It was quite warm, like a mug of tea.

'Where do you come from?' I asked.

'Siberia!' He laughed. They were great guys and I loved them all. They could see us from their ridge on Cho Oyu and stopped to watch the huge balloons rise silently through the thin air.

Black Mountain dropped away beneath us. The name was ours, for at 19,000 feet it wasn't high enough to merit mention on the map. It held no snow. Glenn and his wife Irina were just below us down there, armed with an array of cameras to record our passing.

For all the times I'd been trekking and climbing in the Himalayas, nothing had prepared me for the immensity of the view from our basket. The highest mountains on earth massed around me. The soft breeze rocked the basket gently. I felt as if I had left my body behind, allowing my mind to float unencumbered through space. If it wasn't an out of body experience, it was certainly an out of basket one.

To give me a clearer view for filming, I had erected a platform on the outside of the basket, free from flying wires and gas tanks. The plywood had cost me 200 rupees (£4) in Kathmandu, and in it I had drilled four holes and threaded them with climbing tape, so as to suspend the contraption from the basket.

I had boarded my eyrie for take off, only to discover that the basket itself was not quite level under its two ton payload. Although I was clipped on with a short length of climbing rope and wore my parachute, my position, hanging out from the basket 3,000 feet above the roof of the world, felt most insecure. None the less I stayed there as we approached the towering black pyramid of Mount Everest. It was difficult to concentrate on my work.

In the film, Chris, as usual, is lyrical. 'Mount Everest is like a huge shark's fin. I wonder if that's my unconscious, just poking a little shark's fin of doubt through to the here and now. The pyramid increased dramatically in size as we flew directly towards the summit; it was enormous. My instruments were saying that we were going to clear the top, but my instincts told me otherwise. It was almost as if I were being driven towards it by an unresolved demon somewhere in my soul. I wanted to look down on Everest, and scour the summit for the remains of Mallory and Irvine, to look for all the climbers that have been lost on the mountain.'

There was nothing to stop him nipping out to take a look.

Nuptse, at just under 26,000 feet, loomed up, but we cleared it easily. I looked straight down into the Western Cwm, with the summit of Everest rising up ahead of us, Nuptse now to my left. If I leant back a little, I could also get Lhotse in the viewfinder. The balloon was at 33,000 feet, the South-west Face stretched down for 6,000 feet, and Base Camp lay a further 6,000 feet below that – altogether 16,000 feet below our basket.

56   *over page:* Looking back to Gokyo from the leading balloon, Andy's balloon following, Cho Oyu on the right (Leo Dickinson and Quantel)

57   Leo climbing back into the basket from his filming platform (LD)

I wondered if anyone down there was looking up at us.

From Glenn's camera position we would be the merest speck, and only a zoom lens could link us with the mountain which more than filled his frame. It was a difficult shot, not helped by the minus 25°c he was experiencing. To add to his frustration, his film snapped and then tore at its sprocket holes as he reloaded. Even though our early morning radio sonde predicted termperatures of minus 56°c, I had none of these problems because of the hot air spilling from our envelope. The cameras hanging from the balloon show me taking off my gloves only minutes into the flight. I never found the need to put them back on. The Siberian would have been proud. Poor Glenn! If I had known of his discomfort I could have dropped them down to him as we passed overhead.

The Western Cwm, Eric Shipton's valley of silence, flowed by beneath us, a huge sweep of the world's highest mountains with the Khumbu Glacier tumbling from its base. I had last seen it with Eric, when Reinhold Messner climbed Everest without oxygen. Now I was doing Everest without Messner – and suddenly without oxygen either. A four inch ball of ice encased my oxygen regulator and stopped the life-nourishing flow. I ran a finger across my throat to give Chris the out of air signal that divers use.

'Leo turned to me as we passed above the slopes of Everest at 34,000 feet indicating he was out of air. I knew he wasn't, so obviously he had hypoxia. I wanted to know how bad it was, so I asked him what his date of birth was. When he said 'Leo', I knew it was pretty serious. Why was he giving me his star sign?'

Instead of doing what I wanted him to do, which was to give me more air, Chris asked me my name. I wondered why he wanted to know my name? He ought to know who I am by now. I thought, Chris must be hypoxic. I carried on filming. The video shows me overworking with all my cameras in all directions, and I think it was this that gave me hypoxia. I realised that Chris was also overloaded as he didn't even suggest the emergency oxygen supply. I really wanted to come lower, where the air was thicker and where the mountains looked bigger through my lenses.

As we crossed the summit itself, I pointed downwards, looking first at Chris and then towards the suspended camera hanging from the crown. Chris followed my finger in a slow, dream-like manner. I grabbed his hand and shook it. It felt limp, and I was left unsure about my pilot's condition. Chris then seemed to snap back into consciousness and put out a radio call. 'All stations, do you read me? This is Star Flyer One. We are just crossing Mount Everest, does anyone copy?' The radio just crackled with static.

Afterwards, when we came to narrate the film, Chris improved the scene

58   From Black Mountain, Glenn Singleman records the passage over the summit of the world

with traditional Aussie understatement. 'We crossed Everest and enjoyed our moment of splendour, that incredible, magical moment we will never see again. Leo insisted on shaking hands in true British style, and I naturally complied. As we flashed over the summit at 60 miles an hour, I looked back to the Hillary Step, on to the summit itself, and it became a totally different mountain. All was white and crystalline. It was like rowing across the River Styx, coming from the underworld to the real world. We had floated from the dark, black, forbidding area of the western side to this beautiful, illuminated summit of a fluted mountain. It was a phenomenal feeling.'

It must have been at this stage that Chris thought he saw footprints leading to the summit – a truly remarkable observation from 4,000 feet above it. None of the rest of us saw them even though I looked down through a 300mm lens and took close-ups right on to the top. No climbers had been on Everest for at least ten days due to the high winds that were now whisking us so merrily along. So where had the footsteps come from? Two weeks earlier Dick Smith had flown in his jet with Dick Dennison over the summit. They cleared the peak by only 400 feet and radioed back to our base camp that they had seen climbers on the mountain and footsteps in the snow. It was Chris who took the call.

The winds blew at 58 knots as we flew over the summit ridge and continued into Tibet. Through the 300mm lens I could just make out a tiny speck floating across the landscape. In that insignificant dot had rested all my hopes of filming one another soaring over the roof of the world. It was Eric and Andy in their balloon, and we must have looked just as insignificant to them.

✳

With the plan wrecked, and fearful of colliding with Chris, Eric and Andy had approached low over Black Mountain, and were then forced to rise steeply to clear Nuptse, the Western Cwm and the black rocks of Everest itself. 'I spotted the balloon, a tiny dot already several miles away,' Andy said. 'We drifted over the moraine wall next to the glacier but I couldn't think of any way in which we could catch up, even by climbing very fast.'

Andy continued towards Black Mountain, to allow Glenn to get some shots of his balloon and then concentrated on getting over Nuptse. Eric was glued to his camera, determined to finish the job.

'My whole world came through the viewfinder,' he said. 'I was trying to remember what shots were needed. We came out of the Gokyo valley into a breathtaking panorama but I felt insulated from it while trying to get the cameras working – the stills camera battery had gone flat. After we cleared the claustrophobic atmosphere of the valley, the 360° panorama made more impression on me than looking down on the apparently flat summit of

59 Looking straight down on to the summit of Lhotse (LD)

Everest. I wasn't aware that Chris and Leo had gone so far and kept peering out, searching around the sky for them. Once I spotted them, all my concentration went on getting their balloon, now the tiniest dot, and Everest together in the frame.'

Eric was enjoying himself in his role of cameraman, strapped to the outside of the basket in a plastic barrel, zooming in with Everest big in his lens. Suddenly the deafening roar of the balloon burners gave way to a discomforting silence. They had all blown out. His film stock shows the precise moment as Eric's zoom into the summit ends abruptly. Andy thought it more important to stay alive than film their deaths.

'We were somewhere over the Khumbu Valley,' Eric recalled, 'when with no warning the burners failed. Andy broke the silence by yelling, "Help me!" He had grabbed one of the strikers and was trying to relight the burners. I pulled myself out of the barrel by the burner frame and reached for the other striker which was hanging on a cord. I was perched on the edge of the basket and Andy was sitting on the side. I was desperately pressing the flint striker when Andy managed to get the burners to fire. I breathed a sigh of relief but it was short-lived. As we flew over the Khumbu Icefall, the burners went out again.'

Andy immediately scrambled on top of the basket again with a flint striker

60   Looking south east into Nepal, Ama Dablam – one of the five daughters of
     Everest – nestling in the middle right of the picture (LD)

61   The first balloon passing over Everest (LD)

in his hand, yelling to Eric to do the same. 'When the burners went out, the mountain just kept growing and growing as we sank towards it,' Eric recalled. 'I have climbed on Everest and flown around it in a plane, but looking down from the confines of a barrel was truly incredible.' Eric had been told that when the wind blows upward through the wicker basket you know you are descending fast, but inside his barrel, he could not feel this danger signal.

It's one thing to crash into Everest in a barrel strapped to the side of a large wicker basket, but quite another to see a flying frog hovering around your head at 33,000 feet. When it soared above the burners, Eric knew something was very wrong. Kermit was carrying a radio sonde to track their passage and should have been six metres below on a cord. Their downward descent had pulled the little green fellow up above their heads. It was an unforgettable moment. As Andy observed, frogs don't fly, but when they do, it's really bad news.

Eric had never felt so out of his depth. When things go wrong in climbing, you feel you still have some control over your destiny. Here Eric thought they had lost all control and prepared to jump. Andy remembers the moment well. 'As I slid down into the basket having lit the burners for the third time, I looked at the altimeter and saw it reading somewhere around 26,000 feet. By now we were well past Nuptse and over the Western Cwm. The big mass of Everest was getting bigger all the time, but I knew that at some point it must stop getting bigger. I looked at the mountain approaching and had the distinct feeling that Eric was getting ready to leave.'

On the Tibetan side of Everest we had our own problems. So bright and so totally different from the Nepalese side was the view that, for a few moments, I thought we had lost the mountain. Chris was more worried

62    *over page:* Makalu, the fifth highest mountain in the world. 'The 24,000-foot plateau where Russell Brice suggested we might land, is clearly visible on the left.' (LD)

63    *over two pages:* 'As the balloon plunged earthwards, the frog flew upwards. In his desperate attempt to avoid crashing into the mountain, Andy burnt through seven of the twenty-eight wires holding the basket to the balloon.' (LD and Quantel)

64    *over again:* Looking down into the Western Cwm, Everest on the right, Lhotse on the left, Nuptse at the top. 'Eric and Andy were too busy saving their lives to appreciate the stupendous view.' (LD and Quantel)

65    *over again:* Andy, having relit his burners, manages to limp over Everest between the South Col and the summit (LD and Quantel)

about the balloon. 'You really don't want to operate above 140°c for any length of time,' he explained later. 'The temperature in our balloon was over 160°, probably closer to 170. It was hard to be sure because the needle went off the end of the dial. At any moment we could have lost the top of the balloon.'

Mercifully he kept this gloomy forecast to himself and in blissful ignorance I continued snapping away. If I could have shared Chris's thoughts I might have been more interested in parachuting out of the basket. I filmed the top of the balloon which looked perfectly normal to me. If his imagination was overactive, Chris's eyesight now started playing tricks as well. He claimed that the top was disintegrating and blue sky was appearing through the holes. He could see nylon melting and falling.

We ran unexpectedly into cloud – or that's what I thought until I realised it was the result of our hot air meeting the cold atmosphere. The temperature difference of more than 180°c produced – when viewed from the ground – a vapour trail similar to that of a jet aircraft flying at altitude.

The dramatic sweep of the Kangshung Face of Everest with its ice-flutings and huge seracs drifted into view. A good friend of mine, Dan Reid, – or 'that mad American' as Whillans affectionately called him – had been involved in its first ascent. When I looked down on it, his route seemed long and dangerous. Such hazards would attract rather than deter Dan, who had been on three tours of Vietnam with the Green Berets. His first route in Yosemite was an ascent of the North America Wall on the huge granite sweep of El Capitan. He was not a man who would easily tolerate failure.

I couldn't know that Dan was dead. He had fallen down the Ice Window on Mount Kenya with his wife Barbara three days before our flight. They both died. When I first met him in Patagonia, Dan had plaited hair tied up in a band and wore circular John Lennon glasses long before they had become popular. He had a foolish smile, spoke with a hill-billy twang and was acting as doctor with a trekking group. I was unimpressed. The following year he wrote asking me if he could join our Torre Egger trip, and I agreed. He was to be our doctor, paying his own way. As Eric takes great delight in reminding me, never have I been so wrong about anybody. Weeks later on our siege of Torre Egger, battling fierce winds and dodging the giant mushrooms of ice that constantly bombarded our route, I revised my opinion. The team was severely depleted; Mick Coffey had sore ribs after falling into a crevasse and Eric had torn a ligament in his knee. I, too, was ill.

66   The 6,000-foot high Kangshung face of Everest, with Lhotse on the left. Eric and Andy in their balloon are now flying at 36,000 feet. (LD)

67   *over page:* Chomolomo rising from the mists, with the second balloon now safely over Everest and in Tibet (LD and Quantel)

68   Looking towards Kangchenjunga, Makalu in the shadows on the right (LD)

But danger is only a perceived state. Vietnam had clearly tuned Dan Reid into another wavelength. Rick Sylvester was his unfortunate rope mate and Dan wasn't turning back. But after three days in the firing line, with ropes wearing thin and the chances of survival looking even thinner, Dan decided that enough was enough.

Now here we were, flying over Dan Reid's route on Everest. He would have approved. Dan arrived at his Base Camp dressed in a kilt, blowing his ancestral bagpipes, which scared the living daylights out of their yaks. No

one was surprised when he climbed the Kangshung Face, although nobody
remembers whether he got there in his kilt. Messner might have been faster,
but they didn't come tougher than Dan Reid.

Communication with Chris had been difficult from the start of the flight
because our intercom wasn't working. Both of us had been left to our own
thoughts, but Chris seemed to be getting more and more agitated. He knew
we were running out of fuel. We had planned on four tanks to get us over
Everest and four to land safely. Now we were down to our last one. We had

to find somewhere to put down quickly, but we were above the Tibetan plateau and had very few options open to us.

I would jump in an emergency, and felt no qualms about it. Earlier I had thought about parachuting into Tibet anyway. It would be a good story to tell in the pub and a good one for the log book. In the end I decided to jump only in a real emergency or if everything was under complete control and our retrieval was in view. Neither quite happened, so I climbed off my platform and back into the basket.

I should have jumped, but I was lulled into thinking of the balloon as friendly, spilling its heat down on to us like an invisible blanket. Even at minus 56°c, I felt strangely secure, and so elected to stay. It was a big mistake. In the next few seconds the balloon would be out of control.

69   Running short of fuel, the first balloon begins its descent over Ama Drime. Everest is about 80 miles away. (LD)

We were descending far too fast. For a moment I saw my suspended cameras still intact and running. I should have brought them in but there was now no time. The balloon hit a moraine ridge at a speed of 20 miles per hour. My world was now horizontal and fast becoming a drag. Boulders were scooped up in our basket, my camera fending them off. Fabric tore from the envelope, leaking in the sky.

I fell to the bottom of the basket, with Chris on top of me. I don't like being a cushion and yelled to him to get off. The film shows balloon and basket dragging horizontally across the moraine. The chaos and noise lasted for five seconds and was followed by silence as we took off again. The pendulum action of the balloon swung us across the valley a hundred feet above the ground. I was sure my time had come. The basket brushed the bank of moraine on the far side, then swung drunkenly back.

'Light the burners!' I yelled.

70, 71, 72, 73   'As we came down at 2,000 feet per minute, spinning violently, the
suspended camera recorded the last moments of our crash landing.' (LD)

I didn't want that happening again. Although Chris frantically pressed the
jet-fighter spark plug, we remained on a relentlessly downward curve. The
gas would never lift us now and a basket fire was a serious possibility. We
were facing the same fate as the Japanese suffered one year before, when
their gas exploded and their basket burst into flames.

We hit the ground again. The basket collided with a boulder the size of a
small car and stopped, but only for a moment. I, on the other hand, kept
going, catapulted forwards and outwards, the movie camera still in my hand.
Three of the remote cameras disintegrated on impact, though one somehow
kept running. It was the Canon Hi-8 video, and the last thing it did was
flash up the date before shattering in a thousand pieces.

I fell beneath the basket as it dropped; blue, black, black, blue, the sky
and the basket, the basket and sky. Another boulder hit my chest and
snapped a rib. The monster lifted again and lurched forward, taking Chris
with it. Something was badly wrong. I was still being dragged along, trapped
underneath the basket by my left boot which had caught in a line. There is
always panic, and sometimes it works. I panicked. I pulled and tugged and
twisted at my leg until the foot came free of its boot. I fell away and all
motion ceased.

I was glad to be out. I had had enough.

# 9. *On a Rib and a Prayer*

ANDY HAD MANAGED to relight his burners, but their problems were far from over. Twice more they went out and each time Eric prepared himself to jump. The question was, where to? A parachute flies into the wind at 20 miles per hour; the wind was pushing their balloon towards Everest at 60 miles per hour. Eric would travel backwards straight into the mountain at a perilous speed. If he were lucky enough to squeeze over the South Col, then the Kangshung Face would rush to meet him. And that was without allowing for the turbulence caused by Everest itself. Eric would have to avoid the mountain by a horizontal distance of not less than three times its height to escape this, and then allow an extra thousand feet of clearance for every 15 knots of wind. Parachuting out was not a comfortable option.

'I felt as if we were going into a blind alley,' Eric said. 'We couldn't go back, we couldn't go down by parachute, so we had to get up and over.'

With all five burners blazing, Andy and Eric limped towards the South-east Ridge with the barest margin of safety, only to be confronted by a noise even more sinister than the ominous silence of blown burners. One loud twang was followed by another, and then another. Seven steel flying wires, a quarter of the complement anchoring basket to balloon, had parted to hang uselessly down the side of the basket. Six wires had detached from one corner alone, leaving one solitary strand which mercifully held. If that one remaining wire had come away, the weight of the basket would probably have been too much for the wires on the next corner, leaving the basket and burners at right angles to the balloon. With the basket dangling, the envelope would have split into two and streamered itself into the ground. Too much heat had been focused into the mouth of the balloon. Andy had had no option – it was either that or lose height and crash into the South-west Face. In his mind, he prepared for the long fall down the world's highest mountain, recalling the familiar climbing pictures of Everest's 'Hard Way'. Was it really that steep?

'I was just thinking we were out of trouble when this happened,' Andy told me. 'I wasn't sure whether to rotate the balloon and direct the heat away from the weaker wires or to throttle back on the burners. Both options would lose us lift and I was convinced that we needed every bit of upward momentum to clear the South Col.'

Eric had no idea of this danger. He was more concerned with the faltering burners. Knowing that if they failed again he would have to jump,

74  Pam Mobb's painting of the crash landing, showing Leo hanging from the basket
by his trapped left boot

he checked that the rucksack with his survival gear was close to hand. Andy
would have to go first as Eric's greater experience could more or less
guarantee he would be able to land where Andy did. The odds of surviving
such a jump were growing longer, since the two men were barely the height
of Everest and losing altitude. Once out of the basket, they would have little
room for manoeuvre. Andy was reluctant to leave the balloon anyway, and
directed his burners away from the damaged wires into the side of the
envelope. Molten nylon swirled round their heads as the bottom of the
envelope melted. Slowly they gained precious height and the basket
remained connected to the balloon.

'As we cleared the mountain,' said Eric, 'I thought we were over the
worst. Just at that moment we hit turbulence.' They were not high enough
to escape the wind rotors swirling round the ridge running between the
north and south sides of Everest and the basket shuddered from the force.
Chris and I had a margin of 4,000 feet, but Eric and Andy were less than
2,000 feet above the ground.

Andy was relieved to find that his rate of climb had been sufficient to get
them over the top and he throttled back a little. Provided the turbulence
that was shaking them around didn't suck away the basket, they would
survive. He decided to let the balloon continue its climb and see if he

could catch up with Chris by flying much higher in the faster jet streams.

The whole of the Arun valley on the Tibetan side was covered with low cloud and mist, and only after they had crossed another range of much lower mountains did it clear enough for Andy to see the level brown desert of the Tibetan plateau. They were halfway between Everest and Ama Drime when the radio burst into life. 'Running short of fuel – landing shortly,' the voice said. It was the only time during the entire flight that the radio functioned.

✳

The old Tibetan stared intently. Something had gone terribly wrong. That much he could see even though he had never set eyes on such a monster craft. I wished I hadn't either. My chest hurt. The sun burned down from a deep blue sky. Feathers danced in the dazzling bright air. The man seemed to speak to a child. Or was he addressing me? I turned my head slowly and painfully in his direction. A small child was blowing into a pink toy balloon. Where the hell was I? And where was Chris? And where, for that matter, was the damned balloon?

The child looked as if it had never washed in its life; hands black, dried snot hanging from its nose. I couldn't tell if it was a boy or a girl. Some Chinese arrived, their rounder faces grinning down at me, and pushed the child aside. I tried to grin back but only managed a scowl. As I struggled to stand the broken rib speared my side and I fell back, gasping with pain. That at least was real, and I hung on to it to keep me from sliding into unconsciousness.

I found my plastic mountaineering boot. By coming off so easily it had saved my life. I struggled to get it back on my foot. Where had these Tibetans and Chinese sprung from? The place was desolate – sand, stones, sky, and nothing else. St Exupery would have loved it. The old man was mimicking my actions, rubbing his ribs and grimacing in sympathy. I drank some water. I hadn't had anything since an early breakfast in Gokyo. Our in-flight entertainment didn't run to refreshments, just a stupefying 360° panorama. A feast for the eyes while the stomach waited.

I began to piece together the final moments of our flight. After crashing into the moraine wall, I had been dragged along by my foot, sandwiched between the basket and the boulder-strewn ground. I had thought I was dead. Chris tried to grab me as I went underneath and then fell out himself. The balloon bounced across the featureless, rock-strewn plateau like a giant ping-pong ball. Star Flyer One had only just held together.

At first Chris thought he had broken his leg but he tested it, stood up and discovered it was sound. He offered me some morphine to relieve the pain in my chest. I told him I would think about it. I didn't want to lose my senses again just yet. Already my mind was fuzzy and I was only dimly aware of Chris chasing after the stricken balloon which was carving a passage across the Tibetan landscape.

I sneezed suddenly. The violent action in my chest made me faint and I collapsed back on the ground. 'Where is that bloody Australian?' I muttered to myself. 'I could be dying here.' My hands were clamped around my lower stomach as I remembered Dr Glenn's last briefing. 'If one of you has a pain in the guts,' he had advised, 'the other should stand on him – hard. That'll stop the bleeding. Then call me on the radio. And don't forget, nobody's dead until I say so.' Okay. But the one thing you didn't tell us, smart arse, was what to do if we got separated from the balloon and the radio. Here I was with a pain in the guts and nobody to do the honours.

My rucksack, with all the medical gear in it, had been ripped off by the first impact about 600 feet away. I struggled over to it. We had packed ten days survival food and a SABE radio beacon that would tell the world to within ten metres where we were, or where it was if we lost it. We had even been supplied with enough local currency to buy half a yak. When I first switched on the radio I heard somebody saying, 'We are coming, we are coming,' but then it fell silent. I didn't recognise who it was. The voice sounded foreign. I could only assume it was one of our Chinese retrieval crew.

I also found my parachute. In the final seconds before impact I had taken it off, along with my oxygen mask. Having decided to stay in the basket, I had thought I no longer needed either. The chute was lying not far from my left boot and its position raised an interesting question. How does an item

75   In the high plains of Tibet, the balloon disappeared over the horizon, carving a
     furrow in this desolate landscape (LD)

weighing 30 lbs, and last seen on the floor of the basket, manage to fall out? If you have a 2lb bag of sugar at the bottom of your shopping basket, the only way to tip it out is by completely inverting the basket for a couple of seconds.

The same thing must have happened here. Our basket must have been upside down for a brief period, facing the ground. In ballooning jargon, this is 'dogboning'. No other explanation fitted. Chris must have been ejected at the same moment as my parachute fell to earth.

Chris eventually caught up with the balloon, still dragging across the desert like a wounded beast. It had crossed a small river and ploughed a trail up the opposite bank. The basket had snagged on large boulders which had held it for a few seconds before the wind filled the envelope and pushed aside the rocks with contemptuous ease. Some of these boulders were several feet across. A bulldozer would have trouble repeating the feat, such was the energy still stored in our stricken monster. Chris had to jump on top of the basket and pull the rip-line out. The balloon deflated and he rolled it up before retracing his steps along the furrow the balloon had dug. Littered along the route were bits of camera and other items of equipment.

A small crowd had gathered from nowhere and stood around in a semi-circle at a respectful distance. No one said anything I could understand. I stood up again but could barely walk due to the pain burning through my ribs. I motioned to the fellow I took to be the Tibetan head man that I would like him to carry my camera. He happily agreed and I gave him a present. He could probably have carried me as well but that might have hurt too much and my ego wouldn't allow it. If I were going anywhere, I was walking on my own two feet, however long it took. We'd all the time in the world in Tibet. Time here moves at a slower rate, although I felt as if I had aged considerably in the last hour.

Eric and Andy decided to follow us down despite still having half their fuel. There had been some debate earlier as to whether they should fly over Kangchenjunga into Sikkim and then land in outlying Tibet, but with the damaged flying wires it didn't seem a good idea. It was more logical to land as close as possible to Star Flyer One to make retrieval easier.

They had climbed to 38,000 feet, to try to catch up with us in the higher and faster winds, while we in Star Flyer One spiralled down at 2,000 feet a minute over snow-topped mountains, short of fuel and looking for somewhere to land quickly. Andy chased after us. The fact that he had so much fuel left indicated a considerable difference in technique between the two balloonists. I just wish that Eric and I had been able to knock some

sense into their heads. How much better it would have been if they had discussed the flight and worked as a team.

In his mortally wounded flying machine, Andy dared not match our rate of descent. Eric filmed our balloon dragging along the ground, pilotless and out of control. He hadn't realised yet that we had been dumped three miles to the east.

'We flew level until Ama Drime,' Andy told me, 'where I dropped the balloon down quite quickly by allowing it to cool. This caused a fast rotation and I was worried that the remaining flying wires might snap under the centrifugal load. Chris seemed to be going for the road and then changed direction for the lake. I saw marks on the ground that suggested the basket had dragged up the side of a slope but didn't pay any more attention to them as I was concentrating on getting down into Leo's valley. As it turned out I couldn't manage this without dangerously increasing the descent rate, so I flew into the next valley instead. I was surprised at the amount of heat needed to slow us down. We came down cautiously at 1,200 feet per minute and changed to a full tank to give maximum power for landing. Turning on two burners had so little effect that I turned on two more. I was worried that we might hit a bit hard, but managed to level out about 100 feet above the plateau.'

With his rip-line burnt out, Andy had no way of releasing air from the top of the balloon. They went back up to around 700 feet. Their forward speed gradually slowed and eventually they started to track back down the valley towards our balloon. They bounced three times on touching down and then came to a halt, remaining upright in zero wind. Their approach was in complete contrast to our headlong rush.

'Our landing was very gentle,' Andy said, 'and I assumed that the other balloon had done likewise. After a few minutes I spoke to Gokyo on the radio and told them that I thought both balloons were down safely. Some Tibetans arrived, but kept their distance as we packed up the envelope.'

By the time Andy returned from radioing the retrieval crew from a nearby hill, Eric had a brew going and they feasted on cheese and salami. The Tibetans, who up to then had just stood watching, now surrounded the balloon. All remained friendly while the balloon was upright and Andy was firing the burners to keep the envelope inflated. When they approached to within 200 yards, Eric went out to meet them.

'This was probably the worst thing I could have done,' he told me. 'It would have been better to stay at arm's length. They had beautiful smiles and looked like pictures of the Sherpas from olden days. I handed out

76   Chris and the Tibetan who carried Leo's cameras (LD)

77   The smashed-up basket finally comes to rest (LD)

78   The Tibetan child with his first balloon (LD)

pieces of chocolate but they were more interested in our climbing rope. I gave them odd bits until they got more cheeky and little kids tried to carry off navigational aids worth $5,000.'

The wind began to blow fiercely at midday and the Tibetans withdrew. It was then that Eric realised he had left behind their tent in Gokyo during the rush to get launched. The lapse could have cost them their lives. He put everything into the basket and built the propane tanks into a windbreak. While Andy was away making contact with Russell, Eric settled down in the mouth of his shelter to cook. It was almost dusk when, suddenly, the Tibetans came pouring over the horizon. Were they coming back under cover of night to take what they could? Eric pulled on his boots and pushed everything of value into the back of the basket. He then grabbed two ice axes and switched on his torch. The Tibetans' mood had changed. Now there was aggression where before there had been just curiosity and friendliness.

Eric showed them our Chinese permit but immediately doubted the wisdom of the move. He knew of the atrocities the Chinese had carried out in Tibet and was worried lest the Tibetans assumed we were in league with their overlords. He was a sitting duck; one man, even with two ice axes, couldn't fend off a dozen determined Tibetans. He grew more nervous as their number increased. They seemed to be on the point of jumping him when there came the sound of a truck entering the valley. It was Andy and Russ. They bundled what gear they could manage into the truck and left the rest with two Tibetan guards.

Russell returned later that night and managed to rescue the envelope and the basket. The Tibetans had taken all the rope on the envelope and had even unthreaded the handles on the basket. There would have been little to retrieve if he had waited until the following morning.

*

79   Andy and Eric at their landing site, 10 miles further into Tibet (Andy Elson)

I had ceased caring about anything now that we were safe and no longer being dragged across Tibet. I would have been happy to spend a week stuck out on the brown and lifeless plateau. When Russ had left to find Eric and Andy we spent a very amusing afternoon watching the Tibetans scavenge bits of rope. They were very polite and always asked if they could take what they wanted. As far as I was concerned they could have the lot.

Russ returned for us with his usual energetic gusto. Soon we were tucking into eggs and chips and cracking open cans of beer. It was the best meal I've ever had.

His camp was set in a valley next to a cold meltwater river and in sight of a huge and distant mountain that seemed isolated from the others around it.

'What's that?' I asked him.

'You flew over it this morning,' he replied. 'It's called Everest.' None of us had seen Chomolungma from this angle before. It looked like a huge beached whale on the edge of an ocean of sky.

We were on our way back to civilisation. After recovering that night at Russell's camp, Chris and I headed for Lhasa with the exposed video tapes and film. A three star military general wanted to inspect our material. The Chinese authorities were suspicious of the video.

'Where is the film you also took,' the general asked.

80  Everest from Russell's camp in Tibet where he had waited three weeks for our
    arrival (LD)

81   Leo with smashed cameras and smashed ribs (Eric Jones)

'That will be processed in the UK. You can't do it here,' I replied with more authority than I felt. 'Besides, it only shows exactly what you've seen on the video.' To my relief, they were convinced.

Later that day we were interviewed for Tibetan television. I didn't think many would be watching as most of the Tibetans we had met made the poverty line look like something to aim for. The following evening our flight was the lead item on the Chinese evening news.

'How many people watch this?' I asked our interpreter.

'Oh, anything between 500 and 700 million viewers.' I started working out with Chris how many of this potential fan club were eligible women. Elton John's Peking concert didn't get that big an audience. Figuratively speaking, we'd made it.

'How did you get here from Nepal, Mr Dewhirst?' inquired the interviewer.

'In a hot air balloon. We flew over Mount Everest on the way,' Chris added.

'It's the first time Mr Leo has been to Tibet. How did you arrive?' she asked me.

'On a rib,' I replied. But the joke was lost.

Back in our hotel room, the telephone rang. It was Mandy, calling from

Kathmandu. I could hear a party going on in the background. Our Mountain Travel agent, Liza Chogyll, had laid on a celebration. Prompted by Liza, Mandy asked if flying over Everest was the best thing I'd ever done. 'Yes,' I replied, and, in a rare moment of sentiment, I added, 'apart from meeting you.'

Chris and I enjoyed a few days exploring Lhasa as simple tourists. The easy atmosphere of our trip six years before, when Chris had bubbled with enthusiasm and I had shared his dreams, returned. It was the one time during the whole expedition that I felt warmth towards him. We were alone with our success. For a short while I forgot the discomfort caused by my rib and was grateful and happy he had accompanied me to Lhasa.

We flew back to Kathmandu in an airliner. Through the windows the passengers gaped at Mount Everest. From 36,000 feet the mountain looked remote and forbidding. I overhead one man say to his wife, 'Somebody flew a balloon over Everest last week.'

I sat back in my seat and said nothing.

✳

Six months after we flew over Everest, Mandy and I were sitting on Dick Dennison's verandah in Sydney, looking at the famous bridge through the pouring rain. I asked Dick what he thought of our performance. 'You should have nailed Chris down, not let him go before Andy. You should have had an iron hand.' I changed the subject to new projects rather than old. It was a little rich when you remember that Dick had disappeared.

'We're going to do it again. What do you think about that?'

'You are going to do it again?' Dick repeated with some astonishment.

'We're going right across the whole of the Himalayas. West to east, all the way across Kangchenjunga to Shanghai. We'll also have to overnight in hammocks suspended from the balloon.'

Dreams don't die, they just change.

# Epilogue: Taken for a Ride

BALLOON FLIGHTS OVER Everest are not easy to arrange. We had one chance, and one chance only, to make a success of all those years of effort, all that money spent and all the support given. While I was glad that we had achieved the principal aim of getting a hot air balloon over the summit, I was deeply upset that my struggle to get a second balloon over had been a waste of time. Eight miles apart was just too far to be of practical use in the filming.

While still in Tibet the team members had decided that, in the interests of the sponsor, to whom we owed so much, we would agree the details of the flight so as to present a consistent story to the press. Back in Kathmandu Mike Balson interviewed us as a team and then individually. Chris said that, looking back on it, the flight had been much more dangerous than he had anticipated.

'Being cast adrift in a balloon over the highest mountains on earth, in winds of one hundred kilometres per hour creating all manner of turbulence, was more than an act of faith, it was an act of great danger. Quite a number of small things didn't work and there were a few surprises. The first problem was the high atmospheric temperature, which increased the rate of fuel usage by probably four times the normal. The other cause for concern was the temperature of the envelope. It was 40° to 50° higher than I expected, and so at least 40° higher than the maximum recommended temperature of the manufacturer. When we took off, the temperature was 75°c, and I almost aborted the flight at that point. I was suddenly very fearful that the balloon would be well outside its capacity, or alternatively I would have to climb so slowly that we would have no chance of getting over Everest. I am absolutely convinced that during the flight ours was well over 160°. The needle went off the end of the dial. I was incredibly worried that we would lose the top of the balloon at any stage. I cranked up the temperature and I cranked the climb rate out to 400 feet per minute.

'We had an envelope that was too small for the job on the day, and I think we were overweight. The ambient temperature was too high and I guess from that moment I almost forgot about the other balloon. We either aborted or we went. I thought about dumping two tanks of fuel on the ground, to save weight, but then I decided I'd hang on to them for the first ten minutes. It was lucky I did. By the time we got to 25,000 feet we had

82 Looking back to the Everest Massif, with the Himalayan chain stretching to the west. The Kangshung face is in bright sunlight, Lhotse is to the left, and Ama Dablam is beyond that. To the right of Everest is Cho Oyu, and in the far distance further right lie Annapurna and Dhaulagiri. (LD)

gone through a quarter of our fuel. As we flew over the summit after only twenty minutes in the air we'd used half of it.

'There were a number of reasons for this. If you watch the video of the flight, you can see us spinning dramatically. This is mostly due to the hanging camera which created a dramatic amount of rotation and helped cool the balloon down so we used a lot more gas and that could have accounted for half of our fuel usage. No one has done enough research in hot air balloons and fuel consumption to give me any answers to this. The second reason was the windsheer which always takes a lot of fuel to punch through. Finally, the balloon was operating at a very high temperature, and for every 10°c you need a hundred per cent more fuel. We had a large increase in ambient temperature so we had a horrendous increase in fuel

consumption, and all of these things were coming home to me as we climbed.

'Mostly I was concentrating on whether the top of the balloon was falling out. I watched the changing colour in the envelope and saw whole areas of transparency forming which again increases the fuel usage. Then I saw holes appearing in the fabric. I was more interested in my balloon staying together rather than where Andy was. It was no longer a concern to me keeping the two balloons together.

'I dropped the balloon into the valley at 2,000 feet a minute, so we descended something in the order of 20,000 feet in ten minutes. It was the hanging camera which distorted the balloon and created a spinning top effect as we went into the valley. I slowed the descent rate down to 300 feet a minute at about 300 feet above the ground and scooted into a ground surface wind of about 30 knots, which is too fast to land in safety.

I could not agree with all of this, but maybe my view was coloured by being so close to events. To my way of thinking, Chris had ignored one or two facts, and some of his theories about the reasons for our difficulties seemed to me to be open to question. To begin with, he had suggested that he took off prematurely because of a thumbs-up sign from Eric, who was only twenty yards away in the other balloon. Having agreed that Andy would take off first, why should he assume this was a signal for him to go from Eric who in fact was waving to Jacqui? If Chris had needed to look to anyone for instructions, it should have been the launch master, Martin Hutchins.

When he said that the balloon was badly overheating, I felt bound to ask why, after so many exhaustive tests in Australia, had he accepted the notoriously unreliable thermister in his basket without consulting the more experienced Hutch? When Andy afterwards examined the temperature probes in the top of the balloon, which change colour according to temperature, he discovered that ours never exceeded 125° – a perfectly acceptable limit.

More surprising was his observation that the balloon was disintegrating in front of his eyes, that blue sky was appearing in the top of the envelope and that nylon pieces were falling down on top of him. Examining the envelope later in Kathmandu, we could find no holes at all in the fabric. If he had shared his worry with me at the time, I could have reassured him, just by looking. However, it was a gripping story and it sounded good on the film, although it seemed a pity to exaggerate what was in any case a great story.

Neither Hutch nor Andy thought my camera bag was likely to make the balloon spin. Indeed, my camera bag had been on over a dozen different balloons, including Chris's first Himalayan balloon. No one had complained before that my cameras had caused balloons to rotate.

The video shows that once over Everest we turn full circle every 52 seconds. I suggested that maybe one of the turning vents had been left open. That would certainly cause the loss of hot air, and of lift, and consequently lead to higher fuel consumption. Chris would not accept this: according to him, the balloon was too small for the job. It has to be said that both balloons were exactly the same size: 240,000 cubic feet. We had a heavier basket and more camera equipment aboard, but only about 200lbs more. This should have given Andy a slight increase in performance and flight duration. In the event he landed with almost four full tanks. Chris told me that we had just eight minutes of fuel left when we came down, but when Andy checked later, he found that we were left with about twenty minutes flying time.

83   'The balloon and basket finally come to rest on a flat sandy area three miles from
     where we first struck' (LD)

Our hard crash landing in Tibet appeared to be unavoidable. I didn't
blame Chris for it although some balloonists, who have seen the film, seem
to think he came down too fast. Perhaps he felt there was too little fuel left
to burn off downward momentum. Andy admits that the amount of heat
needed to stop his balloon took him by surprise. To add to his problems,
Chris had to cope with a 15-knot wind that pushed us back up the valley
during the last few seconds before impact. In the film, you can see an
Australian flag, which Heather had tied to the bottom of the basket, blowing
fiercely. It was Andy who wondered why the video pictures show our basket
moving quickly from left to right while Heather's flag is clearly blowing from
right to left. Surely, Andy said, if you were suddenly hit by an up valley wind
that shifted a ten ton balloon, then the flag ought to be blowing in the same
direction as the balloon is moving left to right. Only a few miles away, Andy
landed gently and stood up his balloon in almost no wind. Russell Brîce,
who had waited for 23 days in Tibet as our retrieve, told us that the wind
never really got up until mid-morning. We crashed at 7.30 a.m.
    Making mistakes is human, and we all made them on this trip. Eric forgot
to take the survival tent and Andy, as always, left things until the last minute.
After I arrived in Tibet I wrote down a list of all the mistakes I had made in
my filming preparations and execution. There were more than fifty. Chris

didn't want to admit to making any. His extrovert go-for-it personality was what I had always wanted so how could I complain if in the end his will to win overrode the team spirit.

But what are mates for if they can't have a joke at your expense? I'm sure Chris won't mind if I have the last laugh on him.

Eric's theory was that Chris always intended to go first and leave Andy behind. Dick, too, felt that one of the pilots would go ballistic. At the end of his interview, Chris said, 'I never felt as though we were in a race, but there was no way I was going to let Andy beat me over Everest, that's for sure.' These are the last words in our television film. He must have forgotten me asking him to keep the balloon from spinning as we actually crossed the summit, so that I could get a steady film shot of the top. The balloon was turned so that I was in front travelling towards the mountain. I can safely state that my arse went over the summit first. Chris might as well have waited for Andy and Eric after all.

# *Appendix: On Photography*

I TOOK MORE cameras to Nepal than I have ever taken on an expedition before. My problem was anticipating every eventuality. Having cameramen on Pumori, Ama Dablam, Nuptse, Lhotse, Makalu and Everest would have been a start, not to mention cameras throughout Tibet and Sikkim. But that was impossible to arrange.

Chris Elworthy at Canon UK came to my rescue for stills by lending me six EOS 600s with 28-70mm and 100-300mm lenses. Mandy had her own kit on the launch field. Glenn and Irina had another on Black Mountain to photograph the Star Flyers as we passed them on the way to Everest. Glenn had my Canon 500mm f4.5, with a 2x converter in case he was short-sighted. Russell Brice and Martin Crook in Tibet each had a Canon kit along with a Hi-8 video recorder. In Andy's basket Eric had the two zooms with which he just managed to record us bolting over Everest.

The main film was shot on Super 16mm format which, like the cinema, is wide screen and will allow us, when we get high definition television, to see an even better version of our flight than is currently available. The cameras were four Aatons with an array of lenses. Peter Bryant of IC Equipment lent me his personal lightweight Aaton for Eric to use in the second balloon and I used my own with my favourite Canon 8-64mm zoom lens. Unfortunately, this was one of the casualties of the crash in Tibet.

Suspended from our balloon was my famous camera bag, designed by Nigel Gifford of Camera Care Systems in Bristol. This had an electrical heater to keep the cameras' morale high in the minus 55 degrees we expected. All four cameras were remotely operated. There were two Canon T70s with 24mm and 35mm lenses in the bag aimed at ourselves and our basket. Alongside this was the real genie of the expedition, a Canon A2 Hi-8 video. Canon modified this so that I could control it from the basket. Finally, the bag contained a Photosonic IVN 16mm cine camera with a 10mm lens, which held only four minutes of film and so I had to be very selective with my shots. The real workhorse was the Canon Hi-8 which, apart from recording on to its own tape, had a feed into a SP Betacam recorder tucked away safely in our basket. I changed the half-hour tapes three times during the flight and missed very little of the action over Everest. The wiring loom would have been a nightmare had I not given the problem to my old electronics friend, Ian Phillips who made a simple remote box that fastened into the basket, along with several batteries packed away in yet more Camera Care bags to keep them warm. He wired a small TV monitor in the basket which showed what the Hi-8 and Beta were seeing as well as giving a good indication for the two T70s and the cine camera.

I also borrowed Per Lindstrand's old Widelux camera, which takes two 35mm frames as one picture. My only difficulty with it was keeping my fingers out of shot as the lens rotated. There is one very satisfying example earlier in the book. Film I used was, naturally, Kodachrome 25 or 64. There was no point in making a flight over Everest and not using the best film to record it. Even on the 28mm Widelux and at 8 miles range, Andy's balloon can be seen as one sharp grain of red. On the 300mm it is clearly visible.

Now we come to an admission of guilt. My dream was to take photos of a balloon flying over Mount Everest less than 1,500 feet away from me in Star Flyer One. The reader knows that this 1,500 feet turned out to be eight miles. What was I to do? I phoned up Mike Giles at Quantel, a wholly British success story in the cut-throat world of computer graphics and television special-effects. Quantel make the Graphic Paint-box, used for high-quality image manipulation of stills and for the even more complicated world of television special effects.

Mike appreciated my loss and wanted to help. There were two separate areas in which he came to my rescue. The first and easiest was to freeze, from the many millions of video images throughout the flight, certain moments of dramatic interest such as the crash in Tibet. Because of the

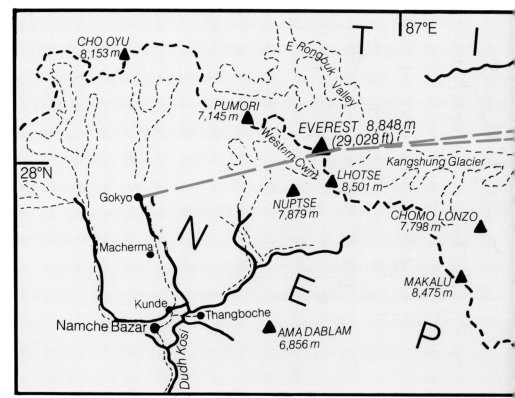

sheer scale, I wanted both ends of Glenn's zoom from Black Mountain encapsulated into one picture. Quantel took the pictures off Betacam and put them into Paint-box where they were manipulated to their best effect. These were returned to me as 35mm slides.

Next came the really clever stuff. My background pictures did have Andy's balloon in almost every frame, but so tiny was it that it hurt your eyes looking for it. We rigged up the balloon in Britain exactly as it took off from Nepal, with the dawn sun shining from the same angle, and took the close ups that had eluded me. Darren Barber carefully scanned both pictures and these were fed into the Quantel Graphic Paint-box for image manipulation. My pictures were retouched and then montaged together seamlessly. The front cover of this book and four double spreads were 'created' in this way. John Murrell, Quantel's senior graphic artist, spent three hours perfecting the front cover from three slides. The Everest background I took at about 31,000 feet, coming over the ridge of Nuptse. Andy's balloon and basket didn't actually get to this crazy angle but would have done had that one final flying wire snapped off. Finally the burner flame was pushed sideways by the strong winds that Andy and Eric encountered. If we had been close I like to think that I could have taken something very similar to this masterpiece.

In the end, Steve Parish of Visual Network turned these montage images back into colour slides. At last I had the pictures of my dreams.

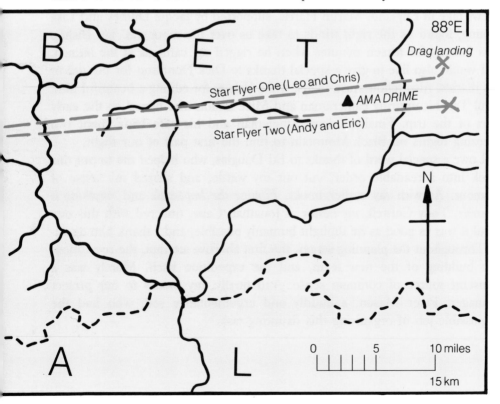

# BUILDING TO SCALE

## A Manual for Model Home Construction

*Prentice-Hall International, Inc., London*
*Prentice-Hall of Australia, Pty., Ltd., Sydney*
*Prentice-Hall of Canada, Ltd., Toronto*
*Prentice-Hall of India Private Ltd., New Delhi*
*Prentice-Hall of Japan, Inc., Tokyo*

JACKIE LEE SMITH AND THEODORE HOPPE, JR.

*Small Sales Company, Overland Park, Kansas*

# BUILDING TO SCALE

# A Manual for Model
# Home Construction

*PRENTICE-HALL, INC.* *Englewood Cliffs, New Jersey*

*To Mark, Lee, and Scot*

# PREFACE

We have noted for many years that the literature in architectural modeling indicates a universal reluctance of authors to get into the details of actual model construction. Therefore we have gathered and presented these details in this book.

In building the model home, the student will be demonstrating the concept of learning by doing. We hope that while the photographs of student and professional scale models will stimulate the interest and imagination of the student and while the discussion of building theories will develop his intellectual skills, the book will be an eminently practical guide to scale model building. We suspect that most craftsmen, while willing to learn by experience, and therefore, by their own mistakes, will be grateful to be shown the fundamental procedures of model construction. The book is intended to make model building provocative and productive, but it is intended first to make model building by the beginner possible.

Many challenges can be found in the building process itself. Should the teacher wish to provide additional incentive, he could have the students compete in teams within the school, or he could have them work on actual projects within their own community.

A town that plans a new civic building may well benefit from a contest among students to "build ideas" in the form of models of the project. The students may, in any case, enjoy a classroom competition to suggest not only the form of the building but the building site as well. Study on this very relevant level has great student appeal, for students then are talking about a real place and real problems and possibilities involved in building on it.

We began our work on this project by observing and recording the actual building of a model home by a talented, prize-winning, architectural-drafting student. Our special thanks go, therefore, to Art Elliott, who built the home, and whose talent and careful explanation largely contributed to the preparation of this book.

Jack and Helen Ashmore offered invaluable assistance during the organizing and editing of the material; and others whose consultations and talent we enlisted include: Judy Clifford and Orlan Voth, who assisted with the photographs; Chauncey Gorsage and L. D. Seymour, and their students. Photographs not otherwise identified are by coauthor T. Hoppe or by Art Elliott.

J. L. SMITH, T. HOPPE

# NOTE TO THE TEACHER

*Building to Scale* is intended to be used in the classroom by the student who undertakes the construction of his first model home. Unlike other architectural model books available, it is intended to be a book of instruction, a teaching aid, a description of the fundamentals of model-building. *Building to Scale* will guide the student in converting his two-dimensional plan into a three-dimensional reality.

Through our presentation of model home building, and the accompanying class work, we hope to (1) acquaint the student with the fundamentals of house construction; (2) stimulate his initiative to undertake independent study; and (3) provide him with the sense of responsibility and the patience necessary for the successful completion of the project.

It is important for the teacher to recognize the abilities of his students, for both the average and the superior student benefit from model home building. In the case of the average student, model building often provides a challenge that he can meet—something his other classes may not offer him. The teacher may emphasize student attention to interior design, to external detail, or to any aspect of construction that seems to enlist the particular skills or abilities of the individual student. While helping his students to discover their own facts and "truths," the teacher will find much of his reward in seeing what they produce on their own. The student who displays unusual talent and interest will find many and varied opportunities in model building to test his ingenuity and ability.

Students will be motivated if a spirit of competition is introduced into the model building activity. Class competitions and citywide competitions sponsored by local architects' and contractors' associations are excellent for increasing student interest. As a teacher, you realize that student enthusiasm and involvement are prerequisite to excellence in the finished product. And excellence in student performance is very much what makes teaching worthwhile.

# CONTENTS

# BUILDING TO SCALE

## A Manual for Model Home Construction

*Chapter 1*

## USES OF ARCHITECTURAL MODELS

If you have visited the San Francisco Maritime Museum, you will remember the models—made with infinite care and precision—of 19th and early 20th century sailing vessels: whalers, five-masted coal and grain freighters, packets, warships, and noble clipper ships. Many of the models are as old as the ships they were modeled after, and display actual shipyard construction methods and materials, including rigging with miniature pulleys, turnbuckles handmade of brass, and decks scale-planked with mahogany or teak. It would be a dull man indeed who could see one of these—for example, Donald McKay's "Flying Cloud" —without being fascinated by its beauty and its suggestive likeness to the actual ship.

This fascination man feel for models is not merely idle, not even strictly aesthetic; it is essentially functional. The fundamental reason we stare longingly at some models is that they almost seem to be the object that they represent.

Many of the great architects have been dedicated model builders and users. Men, or should we say *names*, like Le Corbusier, Saarinen, Gaudi, Nervi, Christopher Wren, and Palladio all built and used models throughout their illustrious careers. Futurists and dreamers, men whose vision was so remote from the

1

known architecture of their time that their ideas were impossible to conceptualize, used models to make their ideas concrete realities.

Model making has in recent years gained such increased favor among architects that today, typically, a competent architect does not even consider doing an important job without the aid of a working scale model. It is an invaluable aid to him in the design stages of production and in selling his "idea"—illustrated by the model—to his prospective client.

The working model represents the finished product; it is a concrete representation of the architect's ideas. A client who is not familiar with architectural plan drawing cannot "read" plans, and, therefore, cannot see what the architect envisions for him. Such a client, confronted with a set of drawings, even perspective renderings, may remain confused and unconvinced. But give him the replica—the thing itself as it will look when it is finished—and he will be able to judge the architect's project. He can see what it will look like on the landscaped, completed site; he can see how it is designed for people to work or live in it.

And if the model can be said to be useful in selling and convincing the client, its usefulness increases geometrically if the harassed architect must explain his plans to a group or a committee of baffled laymen.

It is easy to understand how a model is handy at the conference table, when the time has come to sell, but how does an architect use models to help him create? Why have great architects from Palladio to Saarinen used models, and why should you use them?

The working model affords the architect a means of efficient experimentation. That is, using miniature representations, he can experiment efficiently (1) with different materials and methods, (2) with the distribution of major architectural masses, and (3) with the use of color and natural and artificial light in his design.

Also, he can experiment with the essential features of home design: living space, privacy, mobility, and accessibility. A scale model helps the designer/architect to see the correlation of all the parts, and it enables him to discover alternate solutions to design conflicts.

Although not all architects build their own models, it is still essential that the architect know how to build a model, and most architectural degree programs require model building as a part of the student's education. We might add here that not only architects learn to build models in school; building tradesmen, contractors, engineers, and men in the social sciences of urban development and city planning all may be exposed to model building in the course of their studies. While they do not all attain professional competence in model building, they are certainly helped by being able to instruct a professional model builder about the job they want done. The extent to which the architect understands model-building methods often determines the extent of his success in communicating with the model builder, and, consequently, in getting the model built as he designed it.

Model building in the drafting class complements the drawing of plans; it makes the plans live and tests their validity. Model building encourages what Janke calls "spatial thinking," an activity most students cannot perform without building a model. Bernhard Hoesli comments on the use of spatial exercises in a classroom project in which the students were given an architectural problem to solve.

The solution was immediately arrived at spatially by means of a model (scale 1:20) without previous study or recourse to sketches. The results were remarkable in that, scarcely a month after the beginning of the first term of architectural study, projects with very interesting spatial qualities were produced. Had the students worked in the abstract from plan and section, no such architecturally and spatially logical forms, evolving naturally from the essence of the brief, would have appeared.

Student imagination and ability to think in spatial terms are greatly helped by practice in translating two-dimensional presentations into three-dimensional presentations, and vice versa. A student who has mastered "spatial thinking" even though he does not intend to become an architect or contractor, is yet a student with a new interest, a sensitivity to form and an immensely pleasurable hobby. Whether or not he uses his model-building skill in his vocation, he has a vocation or hobby that will provide fascination for his family and his friends as well as for himself.

*Chapter  2*


## *TOOLS AND MATERIALS*


You can build a model home with tools available in the average home workshop. However, the demands of working with small scale are better met with the more precise instruments. The list below has been assembled to show some of the suitable tools available.

*Cutting Knife*

X-Acto knives (the best buy) are available in a variety of handle sizes with a large assortment of interchangeable blades to fit the exact cutting needs of the student.

*Razor Saw*

Fine-toothed saw blades, interchangeable in X-Acto number 5 and 6 handles, are ideal for use with a miter box.

*Miter Box*

A miter box may be constructed by the modeler or purchased from Small Sales Company, Olathe, Kansas. The miter box will be sufficient for most 90° cuts and all 45° cuts except those in the roof. The interior width of the miter box is 2″, or eight scale feet, at ¼″ to 1′–0″ scale. Eight scale feet is precisely the height of most walls in the model used for illustration in this book. Before use, the miter box should be checked for angularity of the saw slots in the sides. Due to possible misalignment during manufacture, some miter boxes may not produce true angles. Proper angles may be recut with the razor saw and combination square as shown.

### Architect's Scale

The measuring face of the scale that indicates ¼″ to 1′–0″ is, of course, the scale, or linear conversion factor most used by architects when drawing floor plans and elevations for clients and builders. It is the same scale to which plans for model houses (including the example house in this book) are drawn. Most students in architectural drafting classes will have purchased a scale previously.

### Metal Straightedge

The straightedge is used for drawing and cutting. Do not purchase a wooden straightedge, as it will be ruined by a knife after very few uses. When cutting along a straight line with aid of a straightedge, keep a constant pressure against the straightedge, and against the material. Begin at the far end and continue to the close end, drawing the blade beyond the close end of the material. Keep your blade at a right angle, so that the cut will be perpendicular to the surface. You must practice before you can expect expert results.

### Steel or Wood Square

The square is essential for erecting perpendicular walls, lining crosscuts on wall material, lining window and door cutouts, and truing all 90° angles in the plan aspect of the house.

### Combination Square

The combination square is a two-piece adjustable steel square that will measure 45° and 90° angles, check mitres, and usually, with a level in body, ascertain levels.

*C-Clamps*

Small clamps are necessary to hold various sections together while their adhesive dries. Cardboard padding between the clamp and the material prevents pressure marks on soft materials.

*Planer*

Block planes may be used for retouching when measurements prove inaccurate or when a rough cut surface needs finishing.

*Coping Saw*

The coping saw is useful for inside cuts for windows, and may be used with a fine-toothed blade in place of a razor saw.

*Tweezer*

Tweezers are used for holding pieces for soldering or for placing small pieces of material for gluing.

*Needle File*

A fine-pointed file for detail work is especially helpful with scale furniture construction.

In addition to the hand tools above, the modeler will find that a supply of fine-grain sandpaper, rubber bands, glue, tacks, carbon paper, and tracing paper are essential. The more experienced modeler, especially while shaping details, will find discarded dental and jeweler's tools useful. While not essential to a perfect model, the following tools will speed the student's work.

*Power Saws*

An electric table saw or jigsaw will be useful for cutting baseboards and heavier materials. The jigsaw, however, is more useful to the modeler than the table saw.

*Styrofoam Cutter*

The Model Maker, an electric wire element on a base, similar to a jigsaw, is now available for the precise and expeditious cutting of styrofoam. Useful in making furniture and detail cuts, this instrument is also helpful in making scale block structures for site studies.

*Airbrush*

Use the airbrush paint spray guns for fine surfacing. They are excellent for close control in small areas, preventing brush marks that often destroy scale illusion. Airbrushes give even coverage with minimum filling, and thereby allow for texture.

*Soldering*

The beginner should use rosin-core solder with extra flux. This will insure a good bond until the beginner develops soldering judgment. A convenient product is liquid solder with flux mixed in.

TIP. When fixing a light piece to a heavy piece, allow the heat to travel through the heavy piece to the light piece. Roughen highly polished surfaces prior to joining.

Many manufactured materials are available. Model railroad supplies in "O" gauge and "HO" gauge correspond to ¼" and ⅛" to 1'–0" scale, respectively.

*Wood*

In our model, the basic material is basswood, which has many characteristics of the more commonly known balsa wood; it is soft and easy to cut, but is more durable and holds to scale tolerances longer than balsa wood. The student may use balsa, pine, marine, or aviation plywood or whatever material is available in his area.

The following commercially produced materials may assist the student in making a superior model. However, even manufactured materials require work to enhance their appearance. The adventurous modeler may develop his own simulations using available materials. (See Chapter 5 for alternate methods of coloring, etc.)

*Structural Shapes*

I-Beams, channels, tees, columns, · squares, and tubes are available in plastic, basswood, and metal in a large assortment of sizes.

*Exterior Siding*

Three-dimensional siding is available in plastic that allows flexibility in application and custom coloring. Brick, cement block, clapboard, and several stone surfaces may be purchased in both ⅛″ and ¼″ to 1′–0″ scale. Brick, cement block, clapboard, board and batten, and poured concrete simulations are available in basswood. This material is produced in various thickness as well as scale sizes. A large variety of printed paper surfaces that simulate most masonry materials in use are available from many hobby shops, Small Sales Co., and from Architectural Models, San Francisco.

*Roofing*

Shake shingle roofing may be purchased in basswood, in ¼″ to 1′–0″ scale only. Asphalt shingles are available in three-dimensional plastic and printed paper.

*Interior Paneling*

Wood veneers, ideal for paneling interiors, are available at some hobby stores and many lumber dealers. Do not purchase wood veneers with large grain.

*Interior Decoration*

Cloth and vinyl with contact adhesive backing are ideal for rugs, flooring, kitchen and bathroom trim, and some furniture applications. These materials can be purchased in a large variety of colors at most department stores.

*Landscaping*

Hobby shops and many architectural supply stores offer a very large variety of trees and shrubs. (Refer to Chapter 7 on landscaping for a comprehensive discussion of available materials.)

*Furniture*

Machine tools, office furniture and fixtures, and most commercial equipment can be purchased in plastic or metal. These materials will sometimes be adaptable for use in the model home.

*Chapter 3*

## *SELECTING A PROJECT*

If there were another way to say it, we would, but there isn't; so here it is: Take some advice. PLAN this project. Remember that the most important factor in determining the success of your project is not the house you have chosen to build, but the person building it.

Under a general heading of "Self-Considerations" you will need to consider the following aspects of the task:

Outline of self-considerations:

I.   Planning
    A. Carefully chosen house plans.
    B. Time and place to work.
    C. Execution of details.
    D. Sequence of jobs.

II.  Scale Accuracy
    A. Attention to plan dimensions.
    B. Precision measurements.
       1. Use of architect's scale.
       2. Use of square.

      3. Sharpness of pencil points, etc.

      4. Cross-checking for perpendicularity.

III. Materials

    A. Experimentation before using.

    B. "Flexible response."

    C. Standard materials.

    D. Outside materials.

IV. Tools

    A. Adequate for needs.

    B. Care and maintenance.

It is not practical for a beginning modeler to design and build a house in one year. He may design one the first year, and construct it the next year. The beginner should work from plans he finds in a book or magazine. In this chapter we shall consider all the items outlined above, for they all will bear on construction, but principally we are concerned with a properly chosen plan. There are three initial steps.

1. List your preliminary choices, which should be based on criteria of:
   a. simplicity of design
   b. abundance of dimensions
   c. extent of structural detail
   d. extent of decorative detail
   e. appeal
   f. your ability
2. Eliminate any plans that do not meet the above criteria.
3. Become intimately familiar with the plan you have chosen. Now is the time to change your mind, not later.

If the plan you have chosen does not include much decorative detail, your next decision involves the color scheme for the complete interior of the house. The colors of all rooms must be planned before interior construction can proceed. All interior walls will be finished and surfaced before they are placed in the interior shell of the house. A partition wall between dining room and kitchen, for example, will very likely be papered with different colors, on opposite sides because of the kitchen's nearness to two rooms. Door moldings should be in place after wall color is applied because door moldings in this case will divide the two colors of the two rooms. In addition, rugs and other floor coverings should be in place before interior walls are inserted because they, too, would become color boundary problems in the door areas. Interior construction will be considered in more detail in Chapter 4.

## FINDING PLANS

Perhaps your model can be made from a house you have admired in your neighborhood or elsewhere. Ask the owner for the name of the architect or builder or both. Your interest in his house will probably be a compliment to his mortgaged vanity, and if you find the architect and builder equally vain about their work, you may obtain a set of blueprints. Plans from these sources are ideal.

If you admire a house currently offered for sale, contact the realtor, particularly the agent or sales person whose name (usually) appears on the "for sale" sign, and ask where plans may be obtained. In this case, the interior of the house will be, or can be opened for your inspection so that you may note the color scheme and sidestep any doubts in that area.

## SCALE AND DIMENSION

As you have probably learned, the universal scale for house plans drawn by an architect is $\frac{1}{4}''$ to $1'-0''$. Detail enlargements drawn to a scale of $1''$ to $1'-0''$ should not concern you, but you will need all *four* outside *elevations* of the house, plan views of *all* floors, and all interior dimensions. It is necessary, if the house has a pitched roof of more than two pitches, to have a plan view of the roof as well.

Plans found in popular magazines, such as *Life*, frequently are thumbnail plans adapted by a magazine staff artist to specialized publication needs. Often these plans are redrawn by an artist to be reproduced at scales of $\frac{1}{16}''$ to $1'-0''$, or smaller. To allow certain original features to be seen in the reduced scale drawing, the artist will broaden and "heavy up" certain features, such as interior walls, and thus destroy scale accuracy. He will probably "round off" interior dimensions as well, so that, for example, a living room that is originally dimensioned 12′–5″ × 16′–6″ will be newly dimensioned to 12′ × 17′. In this example, you will find little overall lost space, but had the room been re-dimensioned 12′ × 16′, there would have been too great a distortion. Lost space in this example amounts to 11.6 square feet, or, if we "round off" that figure, 12 square feet of lost space in one room. One can only ask, in these cases, where the termites are.

To begin construction of the model house, you will need normal ¼″ to 1′–0″ scale plans of the house you have chosen. If smaller-scale *fully* dimensioned plans of that house are available, you must draw your own floor plans to, at least, ¼″ scale. Again, the right work sequence will save you much time, because the simplest way to make a pattern from which floors for the model may be cut, is to trace the floor outline directly from the floor plan through carbon paper onto the floor material, which will be ¼″ marine grade plywood.

The roof requires your attention. You must know the angles of the junctions of the various roof planes and you should make sure that the roof is one continuous piece so that it may be quickly lifted from the model for inspection of the interior access. For the architect, a house in model form is a structure as well as a design to be pondered over. The miniature can either finalize a design conception or became a legitimate reason for rejection of major design features. The roof must be lifted from the model dozens of times in order for the model to be useful. Therefore, paradoxically, the roof must be the most strongly constructed piece of the model.

The model house builder should try in every way to be faithful to the scale of his plans, as would the architect himself, but the model builder must also be aware of sensible limits in his attempts to achieve scale accuracy. Rafters, joists, and studs will not usually be shown in ¼″ scale models as their quantity and small size would detract from the purpose of a student's scale model. Large, experienced architectural and engineering firms normally use small models to help solve planning, arrangement, and structural problems. The student, however, *does* have structural problems to consider; he must not only make the roof strong enough to withstand repeated handling, he must also make the underlying structure strong enough to support the roof even when it is clumsily replaced.

The student who has progressed far enough in his planning to choose a design, find plans, and begin construction planning, may sense a conflict of purpose or even have trouble justifying the existence of scale houses. If the result of his efforts is to be a prize-winning model house, he will see that the house must be an excellent *model*, in the craftsman's sense of the word, as well as being an excellent miniature. At this point we begin to see the necessity for a source of standard materials and tools. The student must also consider possible areas in which to work, and the time budget—the amount of time each day that he can spend on the project.

Any two scale model houses regardless of design, require nearly the same amount of time to build. We have chosen a plan that includes typical design and construction problems that will be explained through the course of this book. Other plans may be interpreted, or adapted from the model we have built.

We have chosen an orthodox, middle-income suburban type of design. It is a split-level, four-bedroom conventional plan, a design, in short, one can live with. It includes features that thousands of architects have imagined, drawn, and rendered thousands of times. And, this design is easy to render in scale form for the beginning modeler. On pages 19–20, the plans for this house are reproduced.

Be prepared to devote at least *200* hours to the house. Do not take this figure lightly. With this book as a guide you are going to do the job in the simplest, quickest way, but you will have to learn new techniques, and you will undoubtedly make mistakes in execution, which is another way of saying you will learn new techniques. Try to allow yourself a regular weekly period of, say, twenty-five hours of work, which will result in a completed model in two months. Three hours a week night, and ten hours a weekend is a simple schedule to set up. Try to follow it.

*Chapter   4*

# *BUILDING A SCALE MODEL HOME*

In this chapter we shall proceed step by step through the construction of a scale model house, selected because it incorporates most aspects of home construction and should prepare the student to construct any model home. The house is a split level which allows for the illustration of basement, ranch-style, and two-story construction. Its hip roof is the type most difficult to construct. We have not attempted to construct a home that the average student could not build; rather, this house illustrates the basic structure—the fundamentals of model home construction.

## *A.   LOWER-LEVEL CONSTRUCTION*

CHOOSE A PLAN. STUDY IT. CHOOSE AN INTERIOR COLOR.
TRANSFER THE OUTLINE TO PLYWOOD FLOOR PIECE. CUT
THE EXTERIOR, THEN THE INTERIOR WALL. CUT THE WINDOW
AND DOOR OPENINGS. CHECK AGAINST PLAN. COVER THE WALLS.
MAKE THE FLOOR TEMPLATE, THEN THE COVERING. GLUE
THE WALLS IN PLACE. MAKE AND SET THE DOOR MOLDINGS.

Procedure:

1. Choose a plan with complete dimensions.
2. Draw the wall outlines (through carbon paper) onto the plywood.
3. Cut the walls. Use a miter box.
4. Cut out the window and door openings.
5. Check the wall pieces against plan.
6. Cover the walls with colored paper. Trim.
7. Cut the floor templates from adhesive paper. Dye the rug material, let dry, cut to size, and attach to the template. Attach the template to floors.
8. Glue the walls into place in sequence.
9. Cut the frames from channel pieces. Check the fit. Paint, if desired. Glue in place.

   In this section, you shall learn the basic considerations and structural techniques involved in building the first unit of a typical model home, and before starting construction, you should decide specifically how the walls and floors of the home will be decorated. Naturally, you will want to choose materials that will give good scale effects of color and texture. The colors of walls and floors should harmonize within the room and between adjoining rooms. Repeated designs, if used, especially for wallpaper, should be chosen on a basis of scale fidelity of size of pattern elements in the design used. Fleur-de-lys designs are fairly common, but the individual elements in a fleur-de-lys type of pattern will more than likely be disproportionately large. As a general rule, don't use a large pattern. Remember the scale in which you are working. An inch-high design element will be four scale feet high on a wall, and a raised, flocked design will bulge several scale inches from the wall. With unpatterned materials, the essence of the problem of reducing the size to modeling scale is one of texture. A scale surface must always be finer in texture than the real one. Naturally, these points are only basics. Details of interior decoration will be treated more extensively later in this chapter.
   Next, we shall undertake the framing of the first floor in a typical model home. We shall use the example plan shown. Until

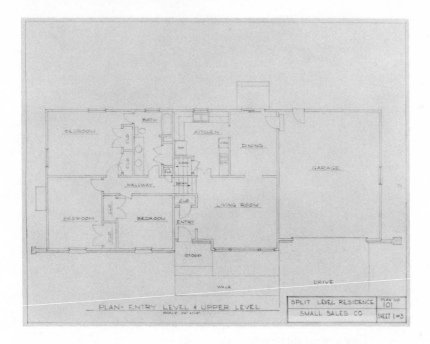

*Figure 4–1. Floor plans for model house to be constructed in text.*

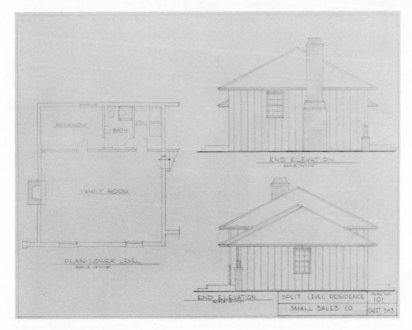

*Figure 4–1. continued*

it is complete, we shall deal solely with the first, or bottom, floor in the model. Until this floor is framed, nothing additional should be built. Here, framing consists of cutting and installing the walls, but not of finishing the windows and doors.

Observe the two plan views, "Plan—Lower Level," and "Plan—Entry Level & Upper Level." The view "Plan—Entry Level & Upper Level" is the floor plan area of the home, or the area the home occupies on its "lot." This area should be traced onto the "A" grade side of a piece of A-C grade ¼" plywood. The tracing should be done as follows:

1. Tape (with masking tape) sufficient carbon paper together to cover the entire floor plan of the home on the A grade side of the plywood. Be sure to keep wrinkles out of the carbon paper.
2. With thumbtacks or with map pins, fasten one edge of the plan onto the plywood over the carbon paper. It is difficult to tape the plan to the plywood, since the plan has the larger area.
3. Smooth the plan over the plywood by using the metal straight-

edge to scrape lightly over the plan away from the attached end. With the plan smooth, fasten the other end to the plywood.

4. Trace firmly and carefully only the outline of the floor plan. Trace the stairway marked "Down." Use the straightedge and a stylus that will not mark the plan. The flat side of a ballpoint pen that will not write (as used in the figure) or a bobby pin may be held against the straightedge. Make a light pencil cross mark across each line you trace to be sure you have traced all pertinent lines.

5. Place a sheet of tracing paper over the entire "Plan—Lower Level." Trace all the walls (inside and outside), all the door and window openings, the fireplace, and the stairway. Make sure this tracing is accurate. Check that the tracing has not shifted slightly during your work.

6. Superimpose the tracing over the plan you have previously traced onto the plywood. Align outside wall lines and pin your tracing over the blueprint. You may wonder if the tracing is just extra work, but it is necessary in this case because the blueprint paper is sufficiently opaque to make seeing through it nearly impossible. The objective here is to superimpose, on the single sheet of plywood, in precise alignment, both floor plans of the home. Therefore the outline of the *full* floor area may be ascertained from one floor plan, the Plan—Lower

*Figure 4–2. Tracing floor plan to plywood base.*

Level, and details of the *lowest* floor area, or Plan—Lower
Level, from the other.

7. Trace firmly and carefully, with straightedge and a pointed
   object, everything you drew on the tracing, cross marking
   lines as you go.

*Figure 4–3. Tracing floor plan to plywood base.*

8. When you are done, remove the tracing, plan, and carbon
   paper.

Now that the lower-level floor plan has been traced onto the
plywood and scale-checked against the plan, you are ready to
begin cutting the exterior walls for that area of the house. Since
the plan indicates concrete exterior walls of 9″ thickness on three
sides of the lower level, $\frac{3}{16}$″ basswood will be used. A standard
ceiling height of 8′ requires basswood walls 2″ high to be cut
from a basswood sheet 2″ wide.

The basswood available to you may be planed and ripped at a lumber yard on machinery with scoring too rough for scale use. However, you will find that the basswood conforms to stated scale thickness and width, and minor surface irregularities, due to the familiar arc patterns left on the wood by the motion of the circular saw, may be removed by light sanding. These irregularities are of no consequence on interior walls, where the basswood will be covered by colored paper or veneer. Do not assume that the ends of the 2″ basswood sheets are square with the length. Before using, trim both ends of *all* basswood sheets in the miter box (Fig. 4–4A). Check these ends with the square for straightness and squareness. Make a habit of checking every cut in the same way, and refer (back) to "Tools and Materials," page 5, for proper use of the miter box.

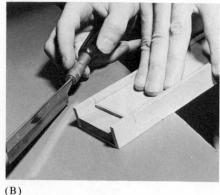

(A)                              (B)

*Figure 4–4. (A) Using a miter box to square wood. (B) Marking the exterior wall—using the square.*

Start cutting the exterior walls for the west, lower level of the home. For the east, north, and west walls, use the basswood described above, ³⁄₁₆″ × 2″. Start with the north wall. Measure the outside-to-outside distance between the east and west walls that join the north wall. You will find a dimension of 7¼₆″. We shall consider this the maximum wall length needed to enclose the lower level on the north side of the home. Note that the floor plan of the lower level indicates that the north wall of that area runs along directly on top of the north wall running the length of the entire home. We shall treat the lower level as a construction unit by itself, so that the north wall will be cut at the corner of the west wall of the utility room and joined to the remainder of the north wall later.

*Figure 4–5. Marking the exterior wall—using the square.*

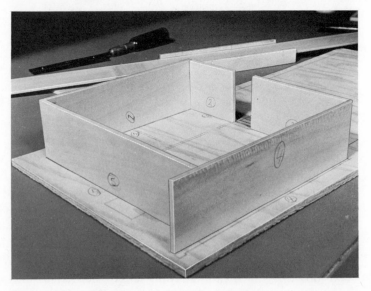

*Figure 4–6. Fitting the exterior wall on the base.*

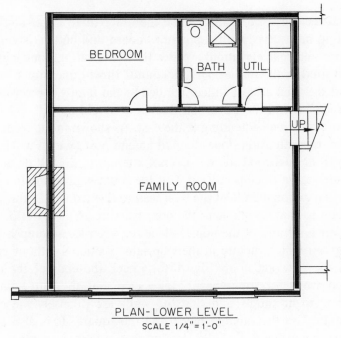

PLAN-LOWER LEVEL
SCALE 1/4"= 1'-0"

*Figure 4–7. Plan. Lower Level.*

Elmer's glue, or "Glue-All," is an excellent adhesive for most wood-to-wood joinery in the model. With this glue, we can use simple butt joints at each corner—the squared end of one wall joining the flat side of the next. Cut the north wall so that it will receive and make these joints with the east and west walls. Check the ends for straightness and squareness. Remember that you are now committed for scale reference to the floor outline on the plywood floor itself. The length of the north wall should be $6\frac{7}{8}''$, which equals $7\frac{1}{16}''$ minus one adjoining wall thickness for the butt joint. Remember to *line* wall material cuts with a sharp pencil point and a square before beginning to saw. This will help to insure the precision of your cut. Then, cut the west wall in two pieces, as indicated. Notice that the stairway from the kitchen into the family room divides the west wall so that the stairway entrance into the family room has no lintel, or transom. Stairway construction will be shown more completely in Chapter 5.

Keep in mind that each wall, or piece of wall, will be cut so that it receives a butt joint at one end and makes one at the other (Fig. 4–6). Go on to the lower-level south wall. Notice that this wall receives brick siding while the other three lower-level walls are to be covered with capped or "board and batten" siding (see front and rear elevations). Since the brick siding (or facing) on the south wall will be $\frac{1}{32}''$ thick, and "three-dimensional" plastic and the thickness of veneer applied to the family room walls will be $\frac{1}{32}''$ thick, the basswood thickness should be $\frac{1}{8}''$. Notice the short wing wall extending to the east. As shown in the front elevation, this extension slopes toward an end post (which will be built up from basswood strips). Do not attempt to do this detail work at this stage of construction. Cut the south wall to the full length shown on the plan. Cut the west wall to size from $\frac{3}{16}''$ thick basswood so that it completes the box structure of the exterior of the lower level unit of the home. Place the five pieces comprising the exterior wall structure in their upright position (without gluing) on the plywood floor (Fig. 4–6). Check the ends of the assembled walls for squareness. Make sure that the butt joints are going to fit snugly and that the walls are precisely the correct length. Use the sanding block and the square. It is also a good idea to number each wall piece, marking the same number on the plywood floor at the proper location of that piece and numbering the locations on the plans for final assembly references. This will key all wall pieces to their positions on the plan. You need not erase the pencil marks since they will be covered with other materials. The next step will be to cut lower-level interior walls from $\frac{1}{8}''$-thick basswood.

Proceed to cut the two short walls that divide the bathroom from the utility room, and the bedroom from the bathroom. These walls, are, of course, the same length, and their door openings correspond exactly in position and size. After these walls are cut and squared, cut the long wall that will separate the family room from the other rooms on this level; pay particular attention to the fit of this wall to the exterior wall piece with which it will join at the stairway up to the kitchen. Notice that the two short walls you have cut determine that the long interior wall is parallel to the north exterior wall. Once again, every piece must be cut to fit the floor plan you have drawn on the plywood sheet.

After ascertaining that the interior wall pieces are true to the plan, number them in sequence with the exterior wall pieces, and assemble the lower-level to check once again for squareness and closeness of joints. Do not hesitate to cut a new wall piece if you find the one on hand has become too short from sanding or imprecise measurement. Notice that it is not yet time to glue any pieces in place.

Windows and doorways are your next consideration. Measure door widths from the plan and, with a sharp pencil, locate the door openings on each corresponding wall piece by laying the wall piece on its precise plan position before marking. Line the sides of each door opening onto wall pieces with the square and a sharp pencil. Line the top of each door opening by assuming a scale door height of 6'–9", or $1\,^{11}\!/_{16}$" and mark this dimension on each side of each door outline. Connect the two marks with the straightedge.

After the door outlines are complete, set the Dremel saw table to its horizontal, or "0 degree" setting (refer back to "Tools and Techniques"), and cut the door openings in the long interior wall you have marked "8", using the cutting sequence shown (Fig. 4–8). Cut slightly more than one pencil line thickness to the *outside* of the door outline since the door moldings will occupy roughly that much space in the door openings. Next, cut the door openings in the two shorter walls.

The door moldings will be cut from $^3\!/_{16}$" basswood channels and measured from the door openings (Fig. 4–9A). They should be made by mitering an end of the channel, inserting the mitered end into the door opening, and marking and cutting the

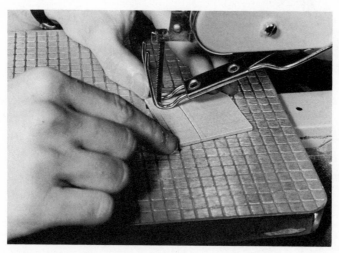

*Figure 4–8. Using the Dremel jig-saw for door cut.*

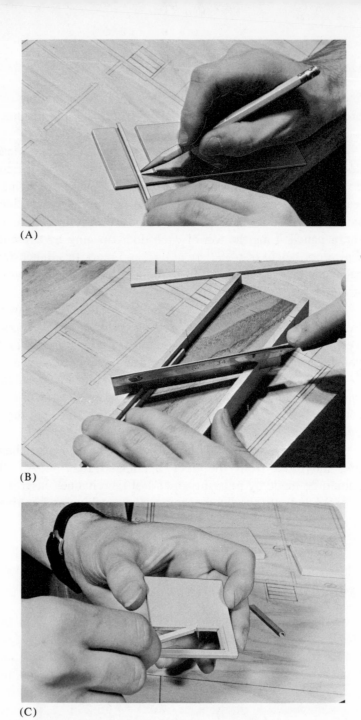

(A)

(B)

(C)

*Figure 4–9. Measuring cutting and trimming channel to trim door opening.*

28

*Figure 4–10. Molded plastic window and door opening. "Inside" cut for window is easily made with jig-saw.*

channel at the length marked off by the bottom of the wall, as shown in (Figure 4–9B). The top piece of door molding must be measured and cut very carefully since this piece must make a neat miter with the other two molding pieces. The window openings will receive a basswood angle molding, but the procedure for measuring and cutting is still the same as for the channel shape. To make crisp, neat miters, it is necessary to place these rather thin basswood pieces snugly against one side of the miter box and saw with light, even strokes of the razor saw. Here again, do not hesitate to cut a new piece of molding if you happen to cut one piece too short.

The window openings will be traced directly from the outline of the plastic window itself. Take care to align the window with the square before marking off the window outline onto the basswood. The plastic windows will, of course, be set into the outside of the wall (Fig. 4–10). Cover the exposed part of the window opening that remains inside with molding. A more complete discussion on the making and setting of windows and doors follows later in this chapter. Windows will not actually be installed until exterior siding is applied.

After cutting the door and window openings with their corresponding moldings, review the color scheme you have chosen for this part of the house. If it is still satisfactory, the next step will be the application of color and finish to the interior walls. Use the "Color-Match" paper to paper the interior walls, but handle the paper with clean hands since it smudges easily. The application of color and trim to the interior walls and the interior side of the exterior walls must be complete before any of these walls may be glued in place. Do this  interior work carefully. The only advice that can be given about the choice of color is: Use common sense and avoid harsh colors (or harsh combinations). Bear in mind that your model will ultimately be displayed so that the colors in all the rooms will be visible at the same time. Colors such as heliotrope and international rescue orange will tend to clash with other more muted colors so that the overall color impression will be dissonant. In a situation of visual discomfort, much fine detail work can be obscured. Therefore, choose harmonizing colors, preferably tints and shades of one color. (For a better understanding of color harmony, consult *Color Science* and *Color Primer* by Ostwald and Jacobsen.)

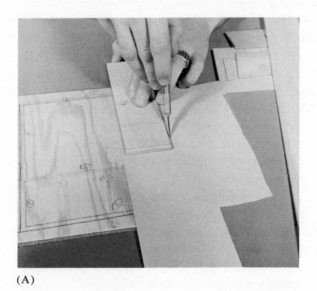

(A)

*Figure 4–11. Procedure for installing color match
paper to interior walls.*

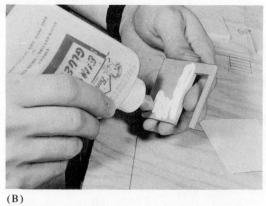

(B)

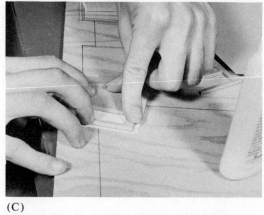

(C)

(D)

*Figure 4–11. continued*

(E)

*Figure 4–11. continued*

Remove dust from sanding or cutting with a tack cloth. Then follow these steps for the easiest way to apply Color-Match paper to the walls, and the easiest, neatest way to achieve a neat interior in the model home:

1. Make sure you know which colors go where.
2. Make sure you apply the color evenly with no bumps or wrinkles.
3. Make sure you trim all edges with a sharp knife and straight-edge.
4. Make sure that the square and miter box are used for all interior trimming.
5. Make sure that you have done all of the above.

Illustration 4–11 shows the best way to apply the Color-Match paper. Onto each wall piece to be papered, smooth over a sufficient amount of glue to entirely cover the piece. Use the first finger of one hand to spread the glue, while keeping the other hand clean to smooth out the paper. Cut rectangular pieces of Color-Match paper slightly larger than, but the *approximate* size of, each piece to be covered. After the glue is applied and spread evenly, and before it becomes tacky, lay the piece of

Color-Match paper, colored side down, on a *smooth, flat, clean* surface, and press the wall piece firmly onto the paper. Use the straightedge and X-Acto knife to trim each piece. When applying pressure to smooth the paper after covering the second side of a wall piece, use a clean sheet of typing paper between your fingers and the wall piece to protect against smudging. Perspiration from your fingers will leave marks that you cannot erase.

Covering for the family room walls presents a slightly different approach to interior finishing. We have chosen $\frac{1}{32}''$-thick scribed basswood veneer for this room. You will not find veneer application necessarily easier than paper application, but a survey of student-built model homes shows a rather widespread use of veneer. Some models are almost entirely decorated in veneer and the effect is drab. Do not be tempted. In one's home, the proper place for this material is a room for casual use, such as a den, a boy's bedroom, or a family room. Remember that you are trying to build a reasonable miniature of a habitable home.

The scribed veneer sheet used here is $\frac{1}{32}''$ thick by $3\frac{1}{2}''$ wide; the scribe marks run the length of the sheet. Since it is desirable that the scribe marks run vertically on the walls, the veneer sheet must be cut into a number of panels sufficient to cover the four walls of the family room. Each panel should be the height of the wall that it will cover (2″) by the width of the veneer sheet ($3\frac{1}{2}''$).

*Figure 4–12. Cutting and installing interior veneer panels.*

To stain or paint the veneered walls of the family room so that all panels will be of uniform stain or color, it is a good idea to paint the entire veneer sheet before cutting it into panels. For a rich, brown stain, Pactra flat enamel in "roof brown" is advisable. Paint the thin top edge of each panel, for the tops will be visible each time the upper-level unit of the home is removed.

Starting with a corner, you will be able to cover the family room walls by attaching one full-sized panel at a time until you reach a corner at which point you will cut another panel to size and then start the adjoining wall.

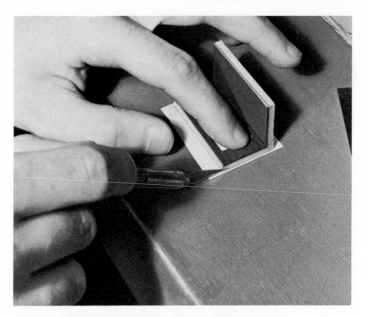

*Figure 4–13. Cutting and installing interior veneer panels.*

The next logical construction step is covering the floor areas to be enclosed by the walls that are now covered and trimmed. This involves the following considerations:

1. Choice of floor covering material.
2. Coloring of the material chosen.
3. Means of attachment.
4. Method of cutting to size.

A very good rug material for the scale of this model is called "velveteen." It can be purchased at any yard goods store. A yard of white velveteen is more than enough rug material for the entire house. Each rug should be dyed. Virtually any color desirable may be achieved by the use of the primary colors of dye (with the addition of water-soluble black ink to darken a color when desired). Instructions for using the dye may be found on the box.

Rugs and other floor coverings (such as simulated linoleum) can best be attached by a commercially obtainable adhesive paper that comes in 11″ × 14″ sheets. This double-sided adhesive paper is called "Redi-mount," and can be purchased at a plastic supply store. It should be trimmed to the exact size and shape of the floor area of each room and marked "top" on the appropriate side. This is important! You will use only the top *adhesive* side of the paper. What will be the bottom side has been found to be a poor adhesive to plywood.

After a rug has been trimmed and attached to the Redi-mount floor template, the assembly should be *glued* to the plywood floor with Elmer's white glue. The protective coating for the bottom of the Redi-mount should *not* be removed before gluing, (Figs. 4–14A–F). In this model home, we chose a velveteen rug for the small bedroom, and used the top protective coating of the Redi-mount itself for the floor covering in the bathroom, utility room, and family room. The velveteen rug was dyed with Rit dye and thoroughly *dried* before attaching it to the Redimount. Velveteen should be dried naturally and not rolled or wrung dry.

Rit dye dissolves readily in hot water. The dye in solution should then be strained (to remove any possible large dye granules that would create spots). A discarded nylon stocking makes a good strainer. Do *not* wrinkle the velveteen while submerging in dye.

After rugs and other floor coverings are ready to be glued to the floor, the next step will be gluing in place those walls now prepared and trimmed and then gluing down floor coverings. Alternate the gluing of walls and floor coverings as you proceed. Start with the exterior wall marked "1." Apply glue evenly to the wall outline on the floor; spread the glue carefully so that the entire outline is covered. Do the same to the bottom of the wall piece (Figs. 4–14G–I), being extremely careful to keep glue

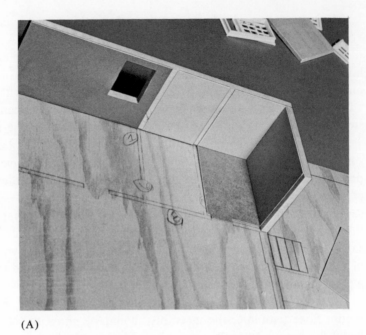

(A)

*Figure 4–14. (A) Redi-Mount cut for carpet installation.*

from contact with the wall paper. Press the wall onto its place on
the floor. Apply glue to the floor outline of the wall marked "2,"
to the butt joint end of that wall, and to the bottom of that wall
as well. Place the two walls in their place on the floor, pressing
downward gently (4–14G). Check to make sure that no beads of
glue have oozed from any of the joints. Glue down the floor covering for the utility room. Glue down the two interior walls
marked "6" and "7," using the same technique as above; next,
glue in place the floor covering for the bathroom. Glue the interior
wall marked "8," joining it to the other walls in place, checking
to make sure that the assembly is precisely aligned with the floor
plan. Next, glue down the bedroom rug. Make sure that no glue
is visible. Once extraneous glue has dried, it is far more difficult
to remove than if done immediately after the glue is applied.
The result of the above work can be seen in Fig. 4–15A. Notice
that the door frame channels are in place only where floor coverings have been applied. These door moldings can be attached at
any time after the floor covering is in place.

(B)  (C)

(D)

*Figure 4–14. (B, C, D) Dyeing carpet material.*

The next step, then, is to cover appropriate areas of walls marked "3," "4," "5," and "8" with painted veneer pieces. Do this using C-clamps and veneer pieces in order to distribute pressure over the entire glue surface (Fig. 4–15B). Cutouts in the veneer will be made at the locations of the two doors in the wall marked "8" and the fireplace. When the veneer is applied, a template for the floor must be cut. In our model, the template itself (Redi-mount) with top cover in place resembled miniature tile or vinyl floor covering sufficiently that it was used without change.

After covering the family room walls with veneer, glue the walls in place on the plywood floor (Fig. 4–16).

(E)

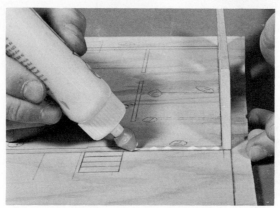

(F)

(G)

38

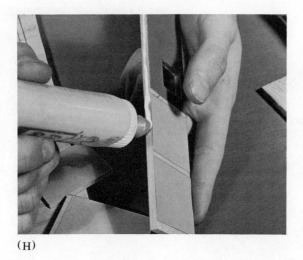

(H)

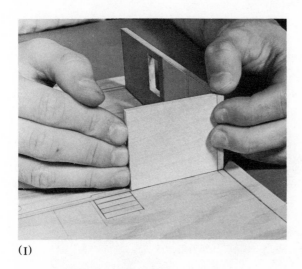

(I)

*Figure 4–14. (E, F) Attaching carpet material to Redi-Mount. (G, H, I) Gluing the exterior walls to the base.*

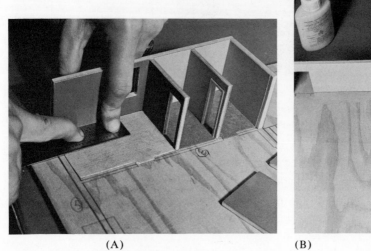 

(A)                                          (B)

*Figure 4–15. (A) Carpeting bedroom floor. (B) Use of C-clamp when gluing exterior walls.*

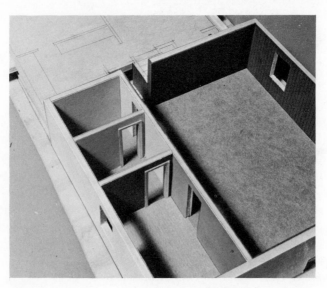

*Figure 4–16. Lower level interior completed.*

## B. *PLATFORMING TO ENTRY LEVEL*

PIECES ARE NAILED TOGETHER AFTER FITTING, AND EDGES
OF UPPER PLYWOOD PIECE ARE COVERED WITH BASSWOOD
STRIP. GARAGE FOUNDATION IS SET IN PLACE.

Outline of Procedure:

1. Any scrap pieces of plywood may be used to achieve correct elevation. Plywood is used to minimize warping.
2. Draw mid-elevation plan on top piece of plywood before attachment to lower scrap pieces. Note stairway cutout and clearance needed for stairway construction.
3. Cut $\frac{3}{16}''$ inside of the plan outline of mid-elevation, exterior walls in order to allow for the trim strip ($\frac{3}{16}'' \times \frac{1}{4}''$) to cover the sawed edge of the plywood. The garage foundation is $\frac{3}{16}'' \times \frac{1}{4}''$ basswood. The garage floor is ground elevation, while the mid-elevation floor is one scale foot or $\frac{1}{4}''$ above this level. A $\frac{3}{16}'' \times \frac{1}{4}''$ strip absorbs any height deficit of exterior walls around the garage area.
4. The ground elevation piece of plywood should extend several inches beyond the foundation line for ease in mounting styrofoam at a later time.
5. Attach all the platform's components to original $\frac{1}{4}''$ plywood floor piece to which lower elevation framing is mounted.

The next step after surfacing the last basswood walls is building the elevation from lower level to entry level—the elevation that includes the kitchen, living room, and dining room. This platforming may be done with scrap pieces of $\frac{1}{4}''$ plywood (Fig. 4–17A). Notice that any pieces of approximate floor plan size may be used except the top piece—the top surface of which will be the actual floor of the entry level. Each successive platforming piece is check-fitted to the plan outline as well as checked against possible warpage. Make sure that the top floor piece is cut $\frac{3}{16}''$ *less* than the mid-elevation, floor plan outline (the reason will be explained shortly) and has a smooth surface suitable for the mounting of floor coverings as in the lower elevation.

(A)

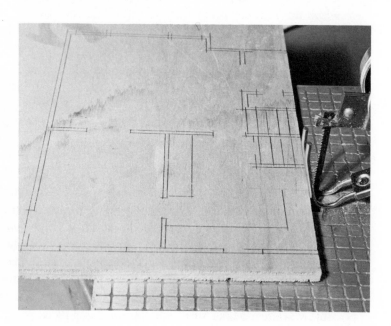

(B)

*Figure 4–17. Platforming to entry level*

42

(C)

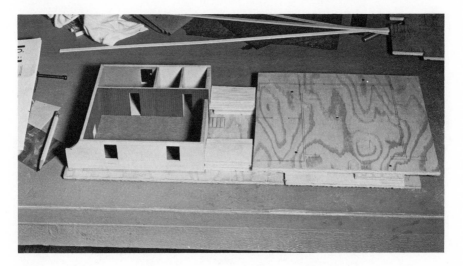

(D)

*Figure 4–17. continued*

(A)

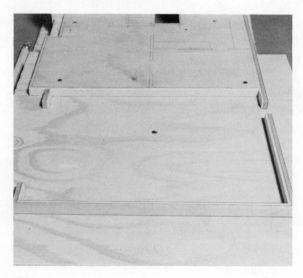

(B)

*Figure 4–18. Garage foundation.*

44

(C)

*Figure 4–18. continued*

When cutting the floor plan or top piece of plywood, a means must be found of covering the raw plywood edge that will be exposed after the exterior walls are mounted. Observe the entry-level elevation area of the plan. Note that the garage is ground level or "grade" elevation, while the entry-level elevation is slightly higher. As the plan shows, the entry level is at least two "steps" higher than ground level. Notice the step in the garage and the stoop at the front entry. This means that the entry level can be assumed to be about one scale foot higher than grade. A $\frac{3}{16}'' \times \frac{1}{4}''$ strip of basswood is used for the garage foundations (Fig. 4–18A). Note the gaps for the rear garage door and the larger, front garage door (Fig. 4–18B). In order to erect the exterior walls of the entry level and garage area, it is necessary to have a continuous, level run of foundation. Since there is a $\frac{1}{4}''$ deficit of elevation, we have a foundation built up with a $\frac{3}{16}'' \times \frac{1}{4}''$ basswood strip so that 2″-wide basswood sheets may be used for exterior walls. Note that *all* walls in the house can be 2″-high basswood pieces. Take special note of the stairway opening for the stair that descends into the family room. This cutout must be precise and clean, as you will see when you begin work on the stairway.

## C.  STAIRWAY CONSTRUCTION

DETERMINE RISE AND HORIZONTAL MEASUREMENT AND THE
NUMBER OF STEPS FROM PLAN. USE $\frac{1}{8}''$ BASSWOOD. CUT
STRINGERS, TREADS, AND RISERS. GLUE IN STRINGERS,
TREADS, AND RISERS.

Procedure:

1. Draw a careful outline of the stair support (one is needed for each stairway). Draw a triangle; divide the number of stairs and treads into the height and elevation of triangle.
2. Using a vise, clamp both stair supports together and cut as one.
3. Use the flat side of a file for finishing the support area.
4. Stringers are the diagonally placed structural members supporting the treads. Cut the treads slightly wider than stringer cutout support area. Use $\frac{1}{32}''$ basswood.
5. Cut risers to fit.
6. Do a trial fit. Paint, if necessary.
7. Glue in the stringers.
8. Glue in the treads and risers. (Cut the floor covering or floor-covering template before doing this.)

The construction of a typical stairway in a model home or building closely resembles full-scale construction. Riser, treads, and stringers are used (Fig. 4–19G). A crucial step in stairway construction is the determination of stringer angles and cutouts. The stringer profile is drawn from measurements taken from the plan. In this case, the plan shows a short stairway rising from the family room into the kitchen. Note the scale width and length. The first step in drawing a stringer pattern is to cut two pieces of basswood to the plan stairway length. Treads, in order to be authentic, must have "nosing." In a $\frac{1}{4}''$ to $1'–0''$ scale model, stairway nosing should be about $\frac{1}{32}''$.

Observe Figs. 4–19B–C. We have drawn a rectangular area, taking dimensions from the stairway height and length. Next, the rectangle is duplicated. Each is then bisected by a diagonal of the stairway. The lower of these triangles will be

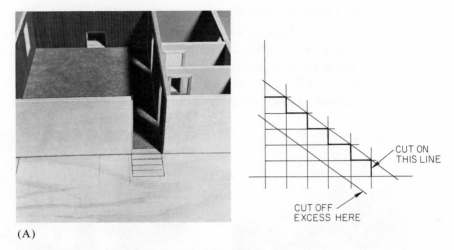

(A)

*Figure 4–19. Stairway construction. Stairway construction, although simple to the experienced model builder, is extremely difficult to the beginner.*

divided equally by vertical lines into the number of steps shown on the plan, which in this case is five. The simplest way to divide an area into equal segments is by using the scale. After dividing the area into the required number of steps, you can see from Fig. 4–19A that the next obvious step is to intersect the diagonal stringer line with horizontal lines corresponding to tread levels. These lines form the actual support faces for the treads. Transfer this diagram to the rectangular piece of basswood and cut another piece of identical size. Clamp both basswood pieces in a vise and cut out the stringer opening (Figs. 4–19D–F). Use the razor saw to cut the openings, but use fine sandpaper around a sanding block or a fine file for smoothing the cut areas. Cut the treads to fit the stringer openings rather than cutting them from measurements taken from the plan; this is done to avoid uneven nosing of the stair treads due to accidental, unequal stringer cuts. Cut risers in the same way using $\frac{1}{32}''$-thick basswood.

After removing the two stringer pieces from the vise, turn them over, refasten them in the vise and cut off the triangular area of excess basswood (Fig. 4–19I). Remove the stringers and insert them into the stairwell for fit (see Fig. 4–19H). While in this case the stair assembly could have been painted, we chose to assemble and glue the stairs in place without surface finishing (other than light sanding) because of our similar unpainted treatment of the frames and moldings elsewhere on the lower level. This is an option, which, if carefully exercised, can reduce work as well as add to the authenticity of the model's finish (e.g., "blonde" stain or simulated ash).

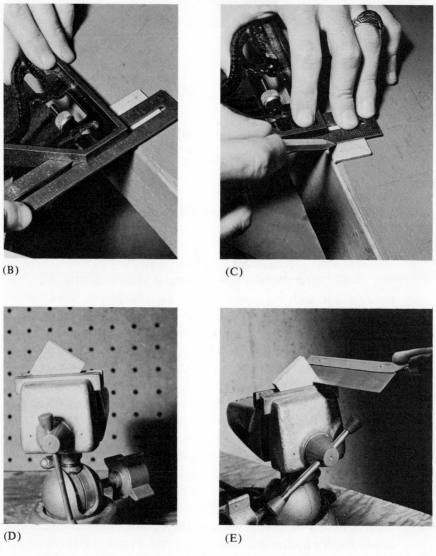

(B)

(C)

(D)

(E)

*Figure 4–19. continued*

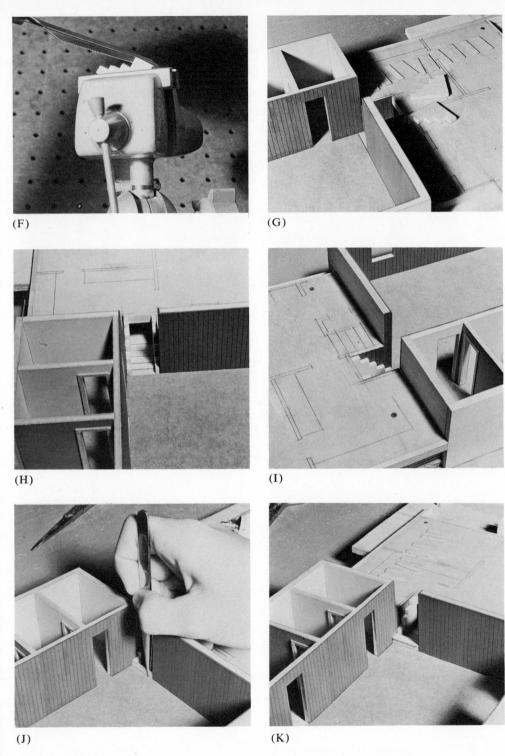

(F)

(G)

(H)

(I)

(J)

(K)

*Figure 4–19. continued*

49

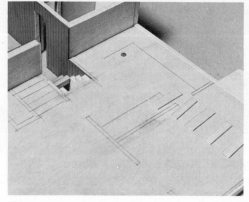

(L)

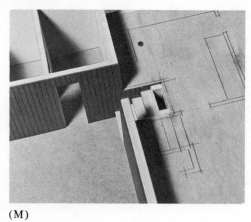

(M)

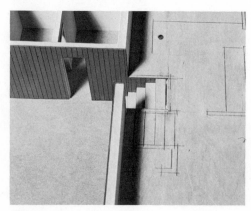

(N)

*Figure 4–19. continued*

## D. *ENTRY-LEVEL CONSTRUCTION*

CHOOSE INTERIOR COLOR SCHEME. CUT EXTERIOR, THEN
INTERIOR WALLS. CUT WINDOW AND DOOR OPENINGS;
CHECK THESE AGAINST PLAN. COVER WALLS. MAKE FLOOR
TEMPLATE, THEN COVERING. GLUE WALLS IN PLACE.
MAKE AND SET DOOR MOLDING.

*Figure 4–20. Constructing exterior walls. Entry level.*

Procedure:

1. Cut the walls.
2. Cut out the window and door openings.
3. Check the wall pieces against the plan.
4. Cover the walls with colored paper. Trim.
5. Cut the floor templates from adhesive paper. Dye the rug material, paint the kitchen floor piece, let dry, cut to size, attach to the template, and attach the template to floors.
6. Cut the door frames from the channel pieces. Check the fit. Paint, if desired. Glue in place.
7. Glue the walls in place in sequence.

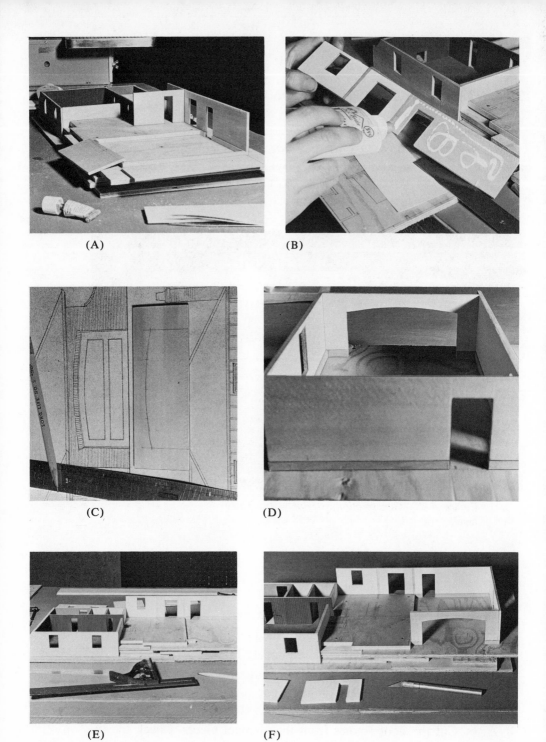

(A)

(B)

(C)

(D)

(E)

(F)

*Figure 4–21. Basically the same procedure as lower level. C & D illustrate the garage door.*

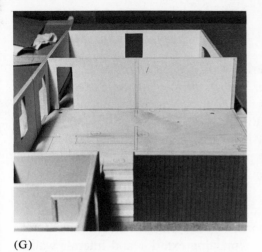

(G)

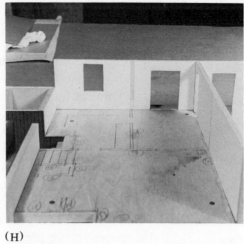

(H)

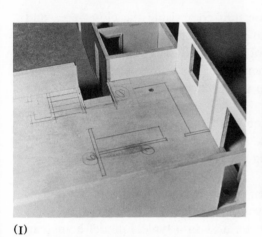

(I)

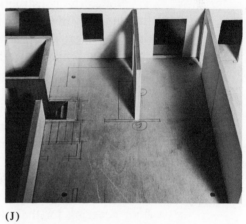

(J)

(K)

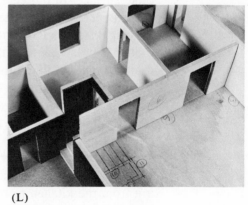

(L)

*Figure 4–21. continued*

Begin cutting the exterior walls for the entry level. Number them as in the lower level. Remember to cut the exterior walls first; then cut the windows and doors. (Notice the unusually wide sliding door between the dining room and the patio area.) The south living room window is made of nine components, three of which are plastic window pieces (Figs. 4–22A–D). Notice that even though this wall is an assembly, butt joints at the lower east wall, which separates the living and dining room area from the garage, are made in the conventional manner. The wall section holding the three living room window pieces can be made from the pieces shown after the remaining exterior and interior walls for the entry level are cut.

Notice the construction unit comprising the closet area and the similarity of this unit to other closet area units in the bedroom or upper level. The walls of these small enclosures are cut to size, covered, and glued together before the unit is glued to the floor. The stairway enclosure in the kitchen area is another such unit (Figs. 4–22E–F).

Pay particular attention to the west walls of the entry level. Together they comprise a "split wall," and the coverings for this wall will acquire a mating wall face on the upper-level exterior wall.

After colors have been chosen, proceed to cover all the interior wall pieces just as you have done for the lower level. The floor covering for the kitchen area in a typical model home can be any desired scale approximation to represent linoleum tile or other surface. In this case, the floor covering is merely a piece of white paper that is splatter-painted black by a spray can held at varying distances (three to five feet) and is attached to the Redimount template as were the "rub" coverings (Fig. 4–22G). The dining room and living room floor coverings, for the sake of convention, should be made of an identical color but not, however, made in one piece. Cut separately and dye the velveteen coverings for these rooms with the same care, or greater, that you exercised earlier.

Notice that the stairway from the living room to the upper level is constructed in exactly the same way as the stairway leading from the kitchen to the lower level. Pay particular attention to the elevation difference between the top tread of this stairway and the edge of the interior wall against which the stairway is constructed. The difference is somewhat less than the thickness of the upper floor. We have chosen not to carpet the stairway because the thickness of the velveteen prohibits sharp folds, and it would be quite impractical to attempt to cover the small treads and risers with individual strips of material. After all the interior walls and floor coverings for the entry level are in place, cut the door moldings in the miter box and install them.

By now you may have wondered about our omission of any discussion of fixtures. While it is clear that the plan shows two rooms—the kitchen, on the entry level, and the bathroom on the upper level, with fixtures of the conventional type (such as, stove, refrigerator, cabinets, and the normal bathroom fixtures)— the construction of these items is dealt with at the end of this chapter, since these fixtures may be installed successfully after the finished walls have been glued to the floor.

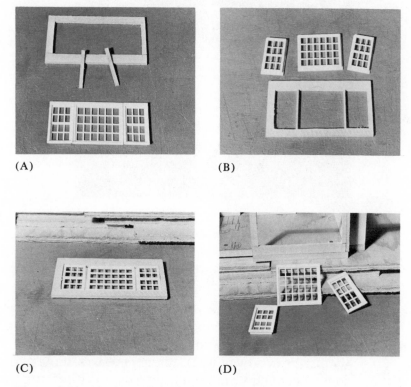

(A)    (B)

(C)    (D)

*Figure 4–22. (A, B, C, D) Constructing a bay window using molded plastic windows. Same effect is possible using wood strips or wire grill.*

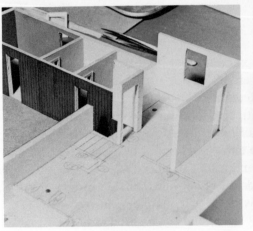
(E)

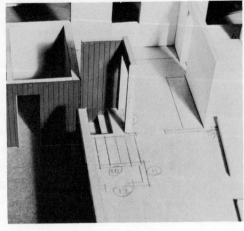
(F)

*Figure 4–22. (E, F) Stairway enclosure. Entry to lower level.*

(G)

*Figure 4–22. (G) Spraying the kitchen floor covering.*

## E. UPPER-LEVEL CONSTRUCTION

CHOOSE INTERIOR COLOR SCHEME. TRANSFER PLAN OUTLINE
TO PLYWOOD FLOOR PIECE. CUT EXTERIOR THEN INTERIOR
WALLS. CUT WINDOW AND DOOR OPENINGS; CHECK
AGAINST PLAN. COVER WALL. MAKE FLOOR TEMPLATE, THEN
COVERING. GLUE WALLS IN PLACE. MAKE AND SET THE DOOR
MOLDINGS.

Procedure:

1. Draw wall outlines (through carbon paper) onto the plywood.
2. Cut the walls.
3. Cut out the window and door openings.
4. Check the wall pieces against the plan.
5. Cover the walls with colored paper. Trim.
6. Cut the floor templates from adhesive paper. Dye the rug material, let dry, cut to size, attach to the template. Attach the template to the floors.
7. Cut the door frames from channel pieces. Check the fit. Paint, if desired. Glue into place.
8. Glue walls in place in sequence.

A problem to be solved during the construction of every architectural model is how to join separate stories and / or the upper story and the roof so that they may be separated and joined in precisely the same location many times without difficulty. There are several ways of joining the upper and lower stories in the model shown here. We have chosen one of the simplest. Small pieces of brass rod are used to fit into mating holes in two matching locations of the exterior walls of both elevations. Small pieces of rod glued into the upper floor fit into mating holes in the top edge of the exterior walls below. Choose a location in which to insert the small rod sections into the floor, drill holes to receive them, then glue the rods in place. After aligning the upper and lower stories vertically, press down lightly and firmly on the upper story so that the two protruding rod ends make slight indentations in the upper edge of the lower-level exterior walls. Use a small hand drill to drill the holes. If the upper section rests unevenly, remove the rods, fill the holes, and begin again. Notice that the east "exterior" wall of the upper-level area receives the additional wall coverings needed to complete the west *interior* walls of the entry level.

By now, you should have no problems in planning and executing the wall construction. One of your main concerns should be keeping all the walls strictly vertical. When you are cutting to size and gluing bedroom-level walls to the floor, the walls *must* be set vertically or your model will acquire a ramshackle quality. The slightest difference between the vertical planes of the first and

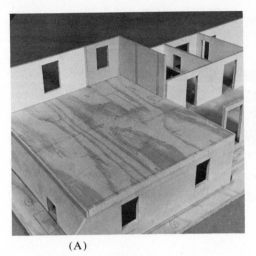

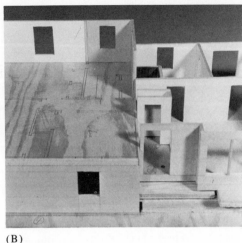

(A)                                    (B)

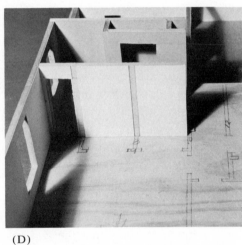

(C)                                    (D)

*Figure 4–23. Sequence of construction—upper level walls and floor covering.*

second stories will be easily detected. Once again, use the square to key the two levels of exterior walls to each other. Observe the wall-cutting sequence.

The color and texture of the wall and floor coverings are, of course, once again, purely a matter of cautious choice. By this time, you may feel an increased awareness for the wholeness of an architectural design and the importance of planning details,

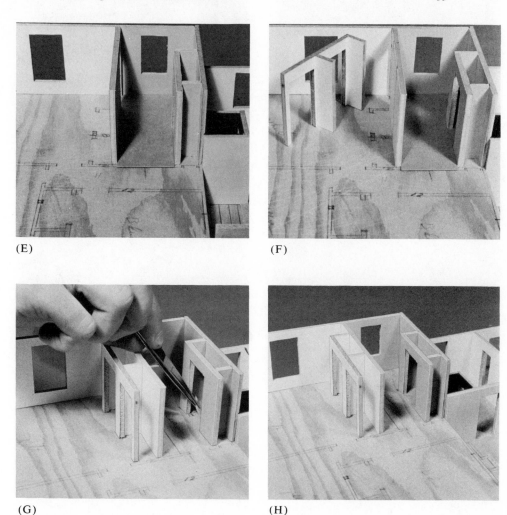

(E)

(F)

(G)

(H)

*Figure 4–23. continued*

even in choosing the wallpaper color. Notice colors used in the
bedroom area. Blue predominates, while the gold carpet con-
tinues from the living room into the hallway. Door frames and
moldings are in harmony with the wallpaper colors.

Remember to construct the closet walls as a unit (refer back
to Section D). Careful execution of these details will have a
cumulative effect that will be rewarding.

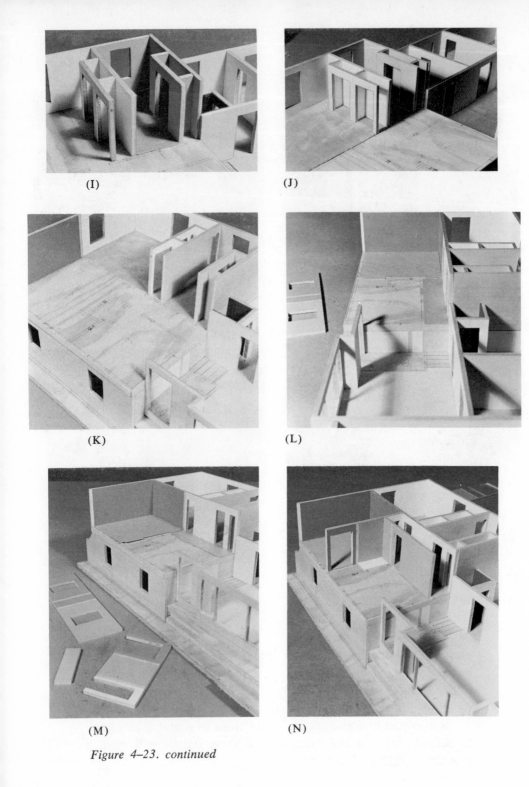

(I)  (J)

(K)  (L)

(M)  (N)

*Figure 4–23. continued*

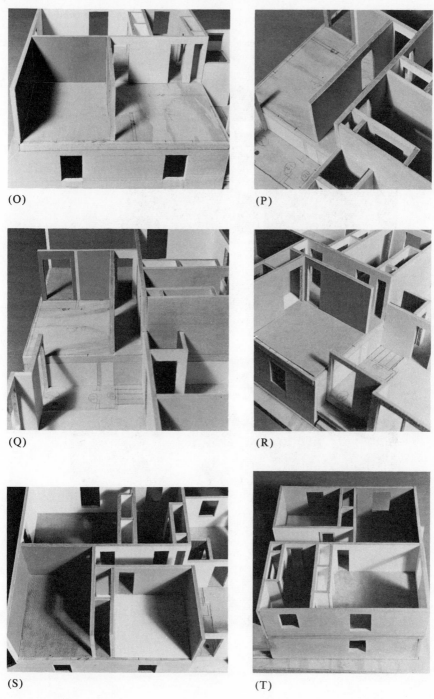

(O)

(P)

(Q)

(R)

(S)

(T)

*Figure 4–23. continued*

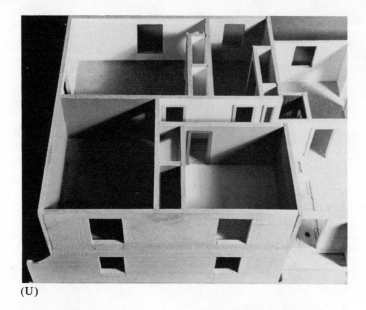

(U)

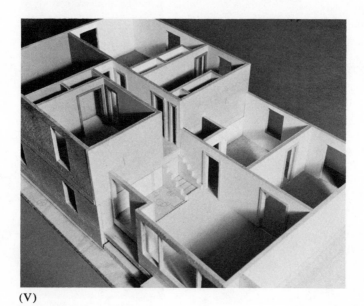

(V)

*Figure 4–23. continued*

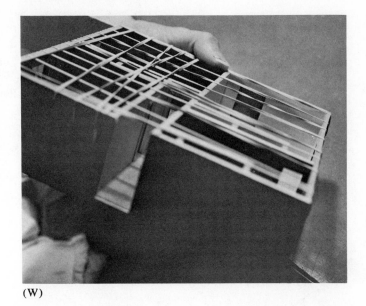

(W)

(X)

*Figure 4–23. continued*

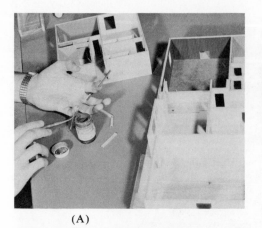

(A)

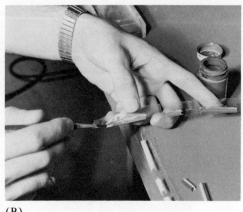

(B)

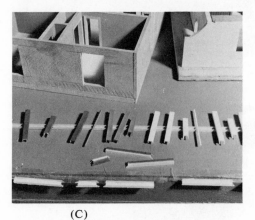

(C)

*Figure 4–24. Painting small trim pieces.*

*Figure 4–25. Installing molded plastic door and frame.*

(A)                                         (B)

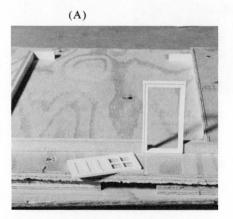

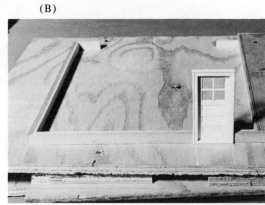

## F. *ROOF CONSTRUCTION*

FROM THE ELEVATION VIEWS OF HOUSE, MEASURE HEIGHT
OF VARIOUS ROOF SECTIONS. USING PLAN DRAW PLAN VIEW OF
ROOF (INCLUDING OVERHANG). DRAW EQUILATERAL
TRIANGLE FOR PYRAMID SECTION ABOVE BATH AND
BEDROOMS, CUT PIECES, AND ASSEMBLE FOR FIT. USING
ABOVE TECHNIQUES, CUT PIECES FOR SECOND SECTION AND
TRIAL FIT. JOIN TWO SECTIONS, PAINT ROOF, INSTALL
FASCIA AND GUTTERS AND PAINT.

Procedures:

1. If you are a beginning model builder, it is best to make a trial roof out of cardboard. Use heavy, grocery box cardboard so that bevels can be fitted.
2. Use available shingled material.
3. Consider the probable life of the model; if short (less than a year), use only basswood sheet. If for indefinite future use, construct a sandwich roof to avoid warpage.
4. Make accurate measurements, straight and accurate beveled cuts. Use adjustable table on jig-saw.
5. Measure the pyramid sections that are symmetrical from elevations and transfer to the plan view the "X" dimension.
6. Cut white cardboard pieces for the bottoms of both roof sections.
7. Cut cardboard trial-roof faces.
8. Cut four pieces of shingled material from cardboard trial templates.
9. Cut on bevel needed. Do final smoothing of bevels with a file, fine rasp, or sandpaper around a sanding block.
10. Assemble the pyramid structure for fit—do not glue.
11. Determine the height and width of the other roof section in the same way as the first. Note the differing widths on the long axis of this section (procedure 5).
12. Treat the hip end of long section (above the garage) as you treated the pyramidal section (procedure 5).
13. Cut additional pieces from drawing based on the elevation and plan-view dimensions.

14. Note that the longer section extends well into the pyramidal section.
15. Glue the long-section pieces together. Use books or other heavy objects as a jig while the glue dries.
16. From the plans, measure the area to be cut from the inside face of the pyramidal section. Cross check the end view against the assembled roof section and cut an opening in the pyramidal section. Also, cut the chimney opening in the opposite face.
17. Glue the pyramidal section together using a jig (procedure 14).
18. Glue the two roof sections together.
19. Finish covering the bottom of the roof with white cardboard.
20. Spray paint the shingles, varying the distance of the nozzle from the board for weathered effects.
21. Add the basswood fascia.
22. Add ⅛″ quarter-round for guttering.
23. Glue in place, then paint the fascia and guttering.

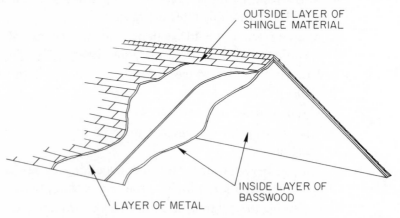

*Figure 4–26. Sandwich Roof construction.*

Before attempting the roof construction, it is a good idea to construct a trial roof from cardboard or another cheap, disposable material. You may have concluded (and rightly) that the roof is the most troublesome, major component of the house. Many model home builders spoil an otherwise presentable model by a slipshod construction of the roof. The roof is the single most obvious component of the assembled house; unless removed, it dominates the view.

## Trial Roofs

There are several types of roof structure for model homes. We are concerned here with the type that uses a prescored basswood sheet (with the shingle texture stamped on). If you think your model has proceeded well enough that you may wish to keep it for later use, you should construct a "sandwich" roof to avoid warping. This type of roof utilizes a sheet of galvanized metal between the surface material of scored, shingled basswood and another, later-to-be-hidden layer of basswood. In the construction of this model house, however, we have limited ourselves to the more typical roof construction method. The finished roof resulting from this method will be sufficient for almost all student purposes.

It is always advisable to make a trial roof. The main purpose of trial roofs is to provide exact patterns from which you will cut the final roof sections. Cardboard is cheap. Do not hesitate to make a second, even a third, trial roof if problems occur.

Here are the steps in computing the size and shape of roof sections:

1. Observe, on the plans, the four-sided pyramid roof over the bedrooms or upper level of the house. Measure the height from the apex to the base of the pyramidal form. Measure the base of the pyramid. (This should be done by subtracting both gutters from roof width in plans.) Draw a rectangle to the base dimensions of the pyramid, taking care not to include the gutters in the measurement. Then cut a piece of white cardboard to this shape. Do not confuse this piece with the disposable box cardboard used in the pitched faces of the trial roof. The white cardboard will be a permanent component of the roof, the underside of the roof, as well as the ceiling of the bedrooms.

2. Cut a piece of ¼″ × ¼″ basswood to the height of the pyramid subtracting the thicknesses of the ceiling cardboard and the ceiling beam (to be hidden and glued to the white cardboard). Also allow for bevels at the top. This will support the first triangular face of the real roof.

3. Figure the actual size of the triangular roof faces by referring to the plan elevations; looking at the house from the front, measure the peak of the pyramidal section to the chimney end of the front elevation. This dimension is the true length/altitude of the triangular roof face shown in the end elevation. This dimension and the base dimension of the pyramidal section on the end elevation (minus gutters) are the true length and height of this end roof section.

4. Repeat procedures 2 and 3 for the other faces of the pyramid roof sections.

5. Cut four pieces of heavy box cardboard, which will have two underside bevels, and one exterior bevel to glue guttering to. Degrees of bevels are determined by trial fitting on the Dremel saw (Fig. 4–27).

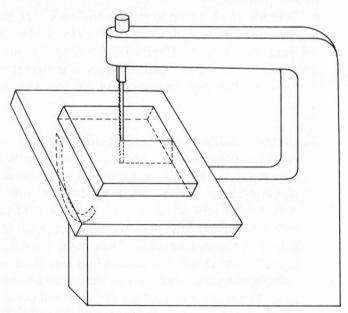

*Figure 4–27. Beveling with jig-saw.*

6. Glue three of the box cardboard pieces to a duplicate, temporary cardboard base. This trial base will be discarded; do not yet use the real base. Books or other heavy objects will form a jig to hold the four pieces together while the glue sets. Leave one triangular section unglued for easy disassembly of trial section. If at this point the trial roof presents no problems, go on to the long roof section covering the rest of the house.

7. Construct the trial longer section before completing the real pyramid section. Determine the height and width of the other longer hip-roof section by directly measuring from the plan elevations. Treat the hip end of this section as though you were again constructing the pyramid. Cut the bottom pieces of white cardboard and at least three ¼″ × ¼″ supports. Remember that all pieces are to be beveled; none of them join another at a right angle.

Notice the irregular shape of the extension of the long axis of the second roof section (Figs. 4–28A–B). This exists solely as a means of attachment to the pyramid section and it will be hidden. Therefore a cutout is necessary in the pyramid section: hence, the one unglued triangular face. The pattern for the roof joint cutout may be obtained from the plans in the same way as the triangular faces for the pyramid were obtained (Fig. 4–28C). Notice that the bevel of the cutout is an interior bevel.

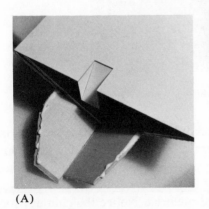

(A)  (B)

*Figure 4–28. (A) Illustrating a "Sandwich Roof." (B) Extension of longer roof section into pyramid section.*

(C)

*Figure 4–28. (C) Pyramid Section cut out.*

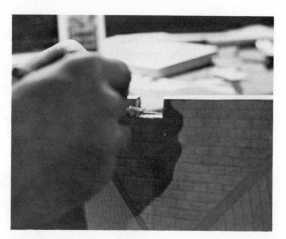

*Figure 4–29. Chimney cut out.*

When you have successfully completed both sections of your trial roof, use your patterns or even the dismantled trial-roof faces to cut the material for the real roof. Be careful to make accurate measurements, and allow for differences in thickness between the trial material and the real material. Notice the chimney location. This can be cut out after the real roof is glued together. Obtain measurements for the chimney cutout from the plans (Fig. 4–29).

Follow the same construction procedure as outlined for the trial roof, using the real, shingled material. Notice that Fig. 4–30 shows details of the stairwell ceiling. After you have completed the roof sections, the next step is to apply angle molding to simulate roof cap and fascia. These can be cut and fitted to the completed roof with Elmer's glue. Notice Fig. 4–31 showing rubber bands that hold fascia trim. Next, glue on the cap trim (Fig. 4–32). Then paint the roof the desired color; in the model a flat brown, Pactra enamel spray was used. Prevent paint from getting on the fascia and the underside of the roof by using mask-

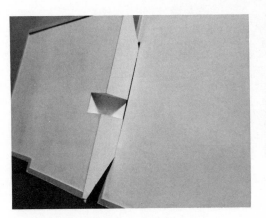

*Figure 4–30. Ceiling stairwell.*

*Figure 4–31. Rubber bands holding fascia while glue dries thoroughly.*

*Figure 4–32. Gluing cap trim.*

*Figure 4–33. Installing guttering.*

*Figure 4–34. Flashing installed.*

ing tape and newspaper guards. After painting, go back and install the gutters (Fig. 4–33), using ⅛″-quarter-round molding. Then lay a piece of copper wire in the roof valley to simulate flashing or metal draining (Fig. 4–34).

NOTE. This roof holds itself in position by the chimney cutout and the split level. Simpler, one-sectional roofs may require pins for positioning as in our second story.

*Chimney Construction*

Build the chimney from the bottom up. Form a hollow chamber the height of the first story according to dimensions from the front elevation. Then fit in the second "step" of hollow structure, and finally the third. Take special care that the chimney is perpendicular to each floor as the roof and third stories must match snugly. Apply simulated brick veneer, trim, and paint.

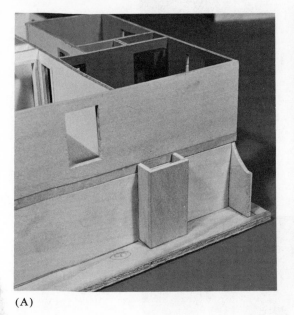

(A)

(B)

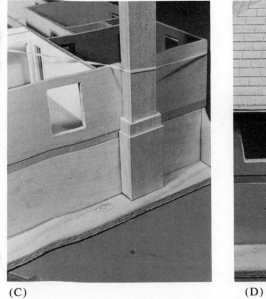

(C)

(D)

*Figure 4–35. Construction of the chimney.*

(E)

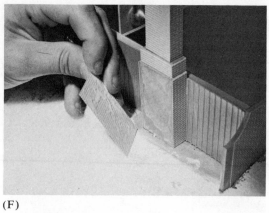

(F)

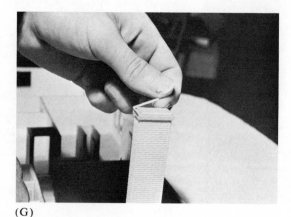

(G)

*Figure 4–35. continued*

**74**

(H)

(I)

(J)

*Figure 4–35. continued*

## G.  MOUNTING THE MODEL

CUT PLYWOOD BASE TO OVERALL DISPLAY SIZE. LOCATE
HOUSE ON PLOT PLAN AND GLUE HOUSE TO BASE. BUILD UP
LANDSCAPE TO DESIRED CONTOURS WITH PLASTIC FOAM.
FILL SMALL, IRREGULAR AREAS WITH PLASTER; LET DRY.
CUT PLYWOOD SIDES OF DISPLAY; STAIN AND ATTACH TO BASE.

Procedures:

1. Mounting the nearly complete model on heavy plywood to give the model its landscape location is the reversal of the design sequence done for the purpose of ease of handling the model during the hours of construction. The bottom "slab" of the house should not be nailed to the display base until all the exterior and interior walls are glued in place. The plot plan can be drawn any time during construction.
2. Obtain, cut to size, and glue down styrofoam blocks to render earth fill where needed. Use small styrofoam scraps for awkward, hard-to-fill areas. However, some irregular areas are best filled after finishing procedure 3.
3. Carve (or sand) contours into landscape with a sharp steak knife, electric carving knife or "Model Maker."
4. Cut strips of ½" thick plywood to cover the sides of the styrofoam.
5. Use plaster to fill in all cracks, seams between styrofoam blocks, and other gaps.
6. Attach the sides.

The sequence of mounting and landscaping the model home is purposefully the reverse of the sequence found in actual home building. The reason is that for ease of handling the model must be held until the very last stages of construction. However, the reversal of the procedure can still be instructive.

Normally, the architect deals with a lot that has boundaries defined by a legal survey. These boundaries usually enclose an area so that the architect has a field within which he may plot the final structure. With most model homes, the student can see that the concept of legal, hence artistically unpleasant, landscaping boundaries are not pertinent. Therefore, the modeler is at liberty to do something that the architect cannot. He can design the land to conform to the design of the house. This is not entirely a bogus design situation, since in practice the architect may specify extensive modifications to an existing site in order to accommodate an architectural scheme. The modeler must realize that the house and its lot are to be designed in harmony with each other.

The model home should be virtually complete before mounting on the display board, the size and shape of which will be determined by the student's own common sense. Most model homes are mounted on a square display board. There seems to be no reason for this other than the anonymity of the square. Most lots are *not* square. However, it is a good idea, unless you are dealing with a specific house design and lot, to use the rectangular, if not square, display format.

A 30″ × 30″ piece of ½″- or ¾″-thick plywood is ideal for the display board. This converts into a 120′ × 120′ lot, which is probably a nice, suburban, statistical norm.

Once you have decided on a location and an approximate range of the landscape contour, nail the house to the display board with several sturdy nails.

(A)

*Figure 4–36. (A–K) Sequence for mounting the model to base with basic site preparation.*

(B)

(C)

*Figure 4–36. continued*

78

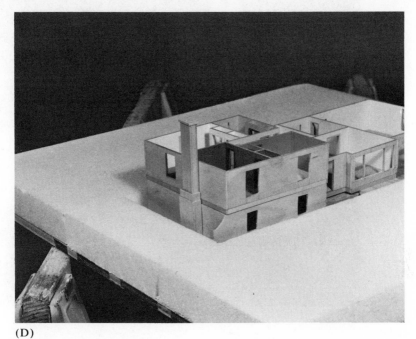

(D)

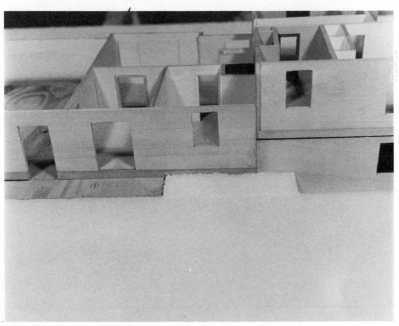

(E)

*Figure 4–36. continued*

**79**

(F)

(G)

*Figure 4–36. continued*

*80*

(H)

(I)

*Figure 4–36. continued*

*81*

(J)

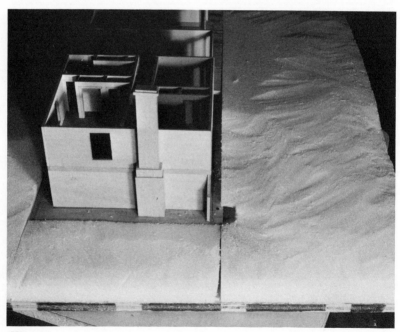

(K)

*Figure 4–36. continued*

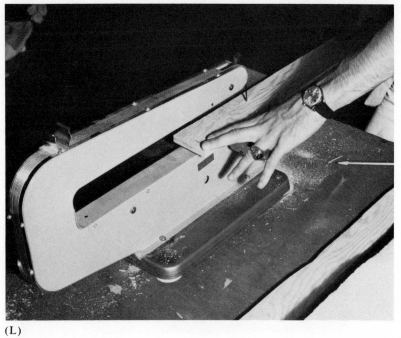

(L)

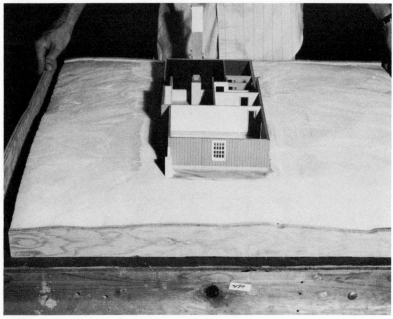

(M)

*Figure 4–36. (L–N) Framing completed base.*

**83**

(N)

*Figure 4–36. continued*

## H. SIDING WITH WINDOWS AND EXTERIOR DOOR FRAMES/FIXTURES

USE MANUFACTURED SIDING MATERIALS; CUT PIECES TO SIZE, AND THEN PAINT.
GLUE SIDING PIECES TO EXTERIOR WALLS. FINISH REMAINING SMALL STRUCTURES AND
COVER WITH SCALE SIDING AND BRICK.

Procedures:

1. Trim excess plaster from the edges around the foundation and the uncovered exterior walls.
2. Obtain required amount of board and batten scale siding and three-dimensional scale brick and cut enough board and batten pieces (of 3″ width) to cover the exterior walls of the upper-elevation section.
3. Place the siding pieces carefully in location and trace window openings (with X-Acto Knife). Cut the window openings.
4. Paint the siding pieces.

5. Glue the siding pieces to the upper-elevation section. Use C-clamps over a protective piece of scrap basswood, or cardboard; use rubber bands, if necessary.

6. Locate the upper elevation in its place and cut the board and batten siding pieces for the lower elevation so that the battens line up vertically with those of the upper elevation.

7. Cut the window and door cutouts (as in procedure 3); paint and glue in place. Clamp with C-clamps.

8. Cut the required pieces of plastic scale brick to fit the front of the lower elevation.

9. Glue to the exterior walls and brush on paint.

The model home is now nearly complete. At this stage, all structural elements should be glued in place and the house be fastened securely to its display board. The landscape fill should only need sanding to make it ready for applying grass and trees, etc.

You should now cover the exterior walls, and install the windows and doors to complete the structure.

Before painting and applying the siding, however, make sure that all excess plaster is sanded smooth and that the grade slopes smoothly from the house to the edge of the display area. You should apply grass (flocking) to the wet, painted landscape surface only after all the siding, window, and door work is done. However, it is a good idea to complete all rough finishing of the plaster/styrofoam fill next to the house in order to lessen the possibility of damaging the house.

From the elevation views of our model home, we can see two different siding applications, both of which are traditional. One is a normal brick facing which is rendered by means of ¼" to 1'–0" scale plastic sheets with three-dimensional brick patterns stamped on. The other material is a board and batten (capped) siding also available in textured (basswood) sheets conforming to model home scale. We shall apply the board and batten siding first since its area coverage is more extensive. As with the basswood veneer used early in interior construction, the board and batten siding comes in 3½"-wide sheets, the vertical batten element running the length of the sheet. Once again, we can apply an earlier technique. As in veneer application, we apply the siding

(A)

(B)

*Figure 4–37. Installing board and batten exterior siding.*

(starting at a corner) and continue with 3½″ segments until we have finished an area. The siding should be painted in the same way as the veneer: i.e., the sheet should be painted first, and then cut. Observe the upper- and lower-level elevations of the house. The seam between the upper-level exterior walls and the lower-level exterior walls is a critical joint because the batten strips

(C)

(D)

*Figure 4–37. continued*

should give the appearance of vertical continuity from the ground to roof, or for a run of two storeys. Therefore, you will have to cover the upper-level exterior walls first, then match identically the batten patterns to cover the lower-level exterior walls. The siding application allows you to close any minute gaps between the levels.

(E)

*Figure 4–37. continued*

Remember that the plastic windows must fit snugly against the siding. This requires cutting small pieces away from the battens immediately above and below each window in order to make the window fit. Take your time doing this and be sure to align the windows vertically. After all siding pieces are cut to fit the walls and window openings, paint them and allow them to dry thoroughly before gluing them in place. For this model home, we chose a warm gray enamel and painted the siding segments twice. Some touchup painting, however, was done after the siding was in place.

Siding application can be a fairly lengthy job. Needless to say, it is a very critical job and will determine the quality of appearance of the finished model.

Brick siding can be painted after application to exterior walls. (See page 102 for a tip on coloring masonry.) Notice the wing wall and the chimney areas. The wing wall was built from basswood strips, then carefully covered with brick facing cut to size. Here again, great care (straight cuts to exact size) give scale validity to the siding materials represented. It is not enough merely to cover a surface. The corner seams must be nearly invisible, particularly in the case of the brick chimney.

Notice the discrepancy between the brick arch over the large garage door and its actual execution in the model shown here.

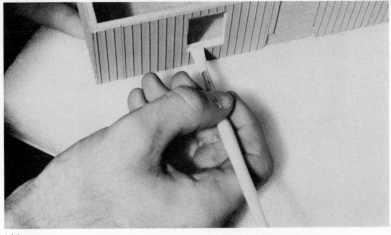

(A)

(B)

*Figure 4–38. (A–C) Mounting molded plastic window.*

This is a good example of compromise in scale accuracy. The tediousness, effort, and chance for mistakes in rendering this brick arch were not worth the effect. Similarly, shutters were not used, although they are shown. Also notice that the garage door is executed differently. The model builder here felt that the horizontal lines representing seams, where folds would occur in the garage door, were more accurate than the lines shown on the plan. If you look closely, you will notice further exterior departures from the original plans. We feel that slavish devotion to all details in a set of plans would betray a lack of invention which every model builder should avoid.

(C)

(D)

(E)

Figure 4–38. (D, E) Installing molded plastic door.

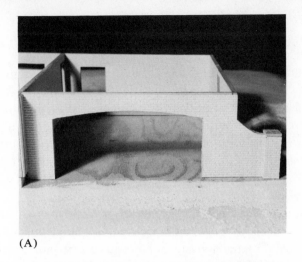

(A)

(B)

*Figure 4–39. (A) Garage door arch. (B) Garage door completed.*

## 1. EXTERIOR PAINTING AND LANDSCAPING

You have arrived at what may be the most important stage of model home construction, for now, you need to create an environment for the nearly complete model; and while, as was remarked earlier, the sequence you have followed establishing the house on its lot is the reverse of normal architectural planning, you may still gain some insight into the architect's problems. Remember that you have chosen a plan of a house to be situated on an actual piece of ground with all its unique qualities of soil, elevation, drainage, light and shade, building-line limitations, and possible restriction from utility lines. While it is impossible to simulate all these factors in the model home display, it is yet instructive to consider them while you are landscaping the model. Attention to realistic requirements such as these may determine the winner of a contest. Your final choice of a location for the model on the display board was probably motivated by a consideration of the above factors.

Now you may proceed to enhance the land on which the house rests. Already, while building up the actual bulk of the "earth" surrounding the house, you have given a certain character to its topographical features. Now, with the final painting of the exterior of the house, you will complete the model (exclusive of furniture) for most student display purposes. Should this model be for commercial or professional use, you will have specific design factors to contend with.

You have previously painted the siding and roof. The detailed finishing of the house involves planning, choice of material, and cutting the pavement material for the front walk, patio, and driveway. Also, the stoop must be installed at the en-

(A)

*Figure 4–40. (A, B) Marking and laying patio.*
*(C) Finished driveway and walk.*

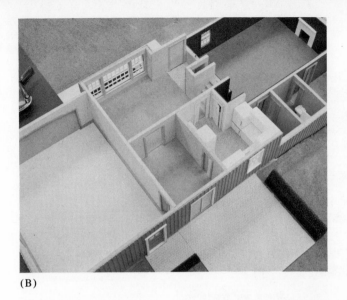

(B)

(C)

*Figure 4–40. continued*

trance to the home. The pavement material can be, and in the case of the model shown here is, a fine grain sandpaper cut to the pattern of the front walk and drive (Fig. 4–40C). The patio is made from the plastic brick sheet (Figs. 4–40A–B). Notice the exposed foundation at the rear of the house, particularly in the garage and kitchen areas. This should be painted with the same "concrete" gray that you will use later to paint the interior, garage area foundation (Fig. 4–41).

*Figure 4–41. Stoop and front walk.*

Construct the front door stoop from basswood pieces. Paint the plastic front door. Remember that the front garage door differs from the plan in that the modeler in this case felt that the garage door should display the seams. The outline of the door should be traced from the plan, cut slightly higher than plan dimensions, and then sanded down to fit. The small edges of the front garage door jamb and arch can simply be painted since the thickness of the garage door will cover all but a small fraction of their surfaces.

It is a good idea to remember that the house plans available to a modeler may not always show small detail items which, if rendered in the model, will help to make a convincing miniature house. Such omissions vary in importance. For example, two items not shown in the model house pictured throughout this chapter are roof vents and exterior lights. Most homes of the type scale modeled and pictured here have lamp posts by the front walkway, outdoor, wall-mounted lights near the front door, garage lights, etc. All homes need roof vents to equalize air pressure in plumbing drains. These are optional features which may be constructed (e.g., roof vents may be made from small-diameter brass tubing). All these items help to make an outstanding model and, additionally, help the modeler as a potential architect or craftsman to gain a clear picture of an architectural structure as a design that is complete only when all its components are present.

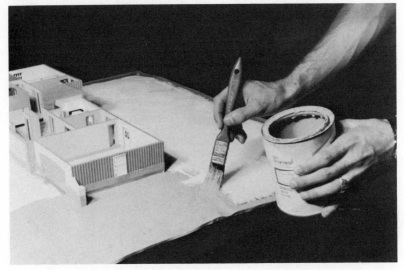

(A)

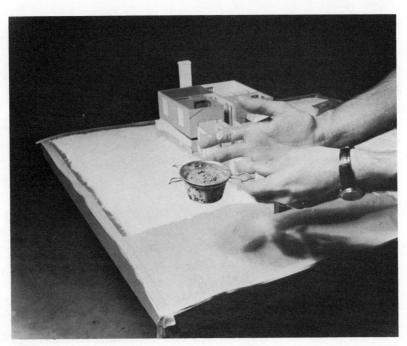

(B)

*Figure 4–42. Painting and flocking yard area.*

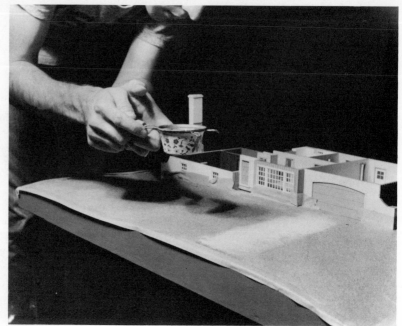

(C)

(D)

*Figure 4–42. continued*

96

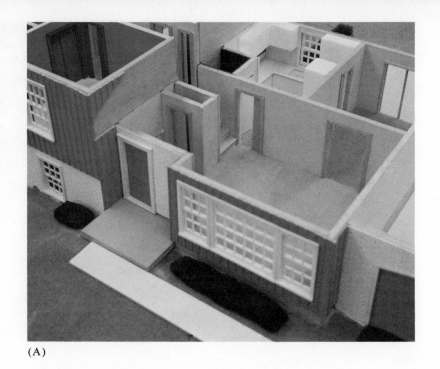

(A)

(B)

*Figure 4–43. The completed model home.*

97

(C)

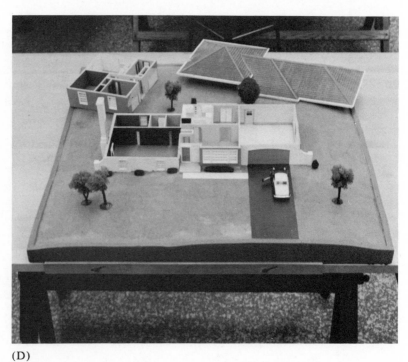

(D)

*Figure 4–43. continued*

**98**

(E)

(F)

*Figure 4–43. continued*

**99**

We shall limit our discussion of the application of grass, set-ting of trees, etc. There is no point in our describing the aesthetic arrangements of trees, and other landscaping features, such as rock gardens, streams, and fountains. These embellishments will become a pleasant challenge to the model builder's inventiveness.

You may cover the yard around the model home in the fol-lowing manner: Choose a house paint (either latex or oil base, preferably the former) of a convincing green. Using masking tape, mask off the lower inch or so of foundation and siding of the house. The height of the masking should be determined by your tendency to spill paint. Also, mask off the top edges of the plywood pieces that form the edge of the display. When painting the exterior foundation, do not worry about paint spilling onto the "yard." Apply paint in about a foot-wide swath and sprinkle flocking (preferably through a fruit juice strainer) onto the wet paint. Sprinkle a surplus of flocking to make sure that all wet paint will be covered. Proceed around the house, painting, then applying flocking so that the flocking is applied while the paint is wet. Wait until the paint is absolutely dry, then with a vacuum cleaner, get rid of the excess flocking.

Trees may then be installed at the desired locations. As you can see, paint was not applied inside the walk and driveway areas for obvious reasons. After the paint is dry, mask off with a non-adhesive covering (several pieces of typing paper will do) the areas of the walk and drive and apply glue to the bottom side of the sandpaper coverings and the styrofoam/plaster areas on which they will fit. Remove the masking paper and press the sandpaper pieces down, using weights if necessary.

When you have completed the nine sections of this chapter, you have completed all essential features of a model home.

*Chapter  5*

*ALTERNATE BUILDING METHODS*

The steps shown in Chapter 4 will apply to most model homes and will help the student build a home of his own. This chapter outlines some of the other methods available. Remember that the basic construction steps remain the same regardless of the student's design.

## EXTERIOR SIDING MATERIALS

Chapter 2 listed some of the materials available for exterior siding on the model. Here we will compare the merits of various materials.

### Three-Dimensional Plastic Siding

Plastic sidings, primarily masonry, are easy to work with. They may be cut with scissors or a knife blade, and they adapt to curved surfaces. This material may be colored with crayon, or most paints. Enamel should be used for the raised colored surfaces. When the enamel dries, use a white or gray water-base paint to fill the mortar joints, and then wipe the surface clean with a damp cloth, leaving the mortar joints filled (Fig. 5–1). The student should experiment on small pieces of any material to obtain the desired effect prior to finishing a large section of material.

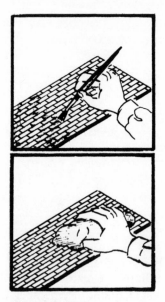

*Figure 5–1. Paint three-dimensional siding.*

### Printed Paper

The principal advantage of paper is that it is very easy to apply to the model. It is easily cut and can be affixed to most surfaces. Since the paper is precolored, the student must be careful in matching pieces when several sections must be used to insure continuity of the pattern.

### Basswood

Basswood siding in clapboard, board and batten, or vertical scribing will be used on most homes. It must be cut with a razor saw or coping saw and may be stained or painted. We recommend spray painting prior to gluing to the exterior walls.

Basswood masonry designs should be painted like plastic siding. Here, again, experimentation is recommended.

## Home-Made Siding

The student will find an outlet for his imagination if he chooses to produce his own sidings rather than use the manufactured materials. He should realize that brick siding, for example, need not look exactly like brick under a microscope. It need only simulate brick.

The modeler can produce brick, block, and other sidings on balsa or basswood by scratching the wood with a blade, using the metal straightedge. He can give it the same finish as a manufactured product.

The adventurous student may use real stone, aquarium rocks, or sand to form his own siding. Into a form filled with epoxy glue, you can drop some of these materials to produce a beautiful masonry siding. The same method may be used for patio and fireplace construction.

## ROOFING

Many of the suggestions for manufactured siding materials also apply to roofing. With the exception of the $\frac{3}{16}''$ basswood shake shingle used in Chapter 4, roofing materials that merely cover the constructed roof may be made of plywood, basswood, or plastic. Constructing the roof is usually the most difficult phase of modeling because the roof pattern must be continuous despite the various angles of the roof valleys and crests. If possible, each section of the roof should be made with one continuous piece of material since it is difficult to conceal joints in the roof. Methods of roof construction include:

## Asphalt Roofing

The best asphalt roofing available is three-dimensional plastic. Like the printed paper material, it is easily cut and glued, but its three-dimensional effect adds a great deal to the roof, which is after all, the viewer's first impression of the model.

*Shake Shingle*

The ³⁄₁₆" shake shingle manufactured by the Small Sales Company is a superior roofing. It needs no backing material and is extremely realistic. It may be left natural or stained. However, one disadvantage is that it is rather difficult to cut and fit, therefore, the modeler may waste a large amount of material before he has the perfect roof.

With patience, the student can also build a shake shingle roof with wood strips that have been scored. The strips will fit better if leveled with a planer.

*Flat Roofs*

Gravel and tar roofs may be simulated by use of fine-grained sandpaper or by painting the roof and sprinkling sand or bird gravel on the roof while it is still tacky.

*Tile Roofs*

Tile roofs are difficult for the student to make. A number of materials—e.g., styrofoam, plaster of paris, paper, and plastic straws—may simulate tile. However, the final results will depend largely on the skill of the model maker. There has been a cardboard tile on the market that is very acceptable and has a good three-dimensional effect. Painted paper is also available, but here again, the advantages of a third dimension are lost.

## INTERIOR WALL COVERING AND FLOORING

Care should be given in interior color selection as explained in Chapter 4. Avoid "loud" colors; favor pastels. Also avoid using too many different colors. Other surfacings available are listed below.

*Paneled Walls*

Wood veneers and thin sheets of brick, mahogany, and other woods may be purchased and are excellent for paneling. Avoid large-grained woods that have a tendency to distort the scale.

Also available are contact papers (adhesive-backed papers) with various wood-grain finishes.

## Wallpaper

A few commercial wallpapers should be suitable for your model. However, you must take care to avoid patterns that would be completely out of scale. Plain or textured papers are best, and contact paper is easy to install.

## Carpeting

Cloth with adhesive backing can be found that is ideal for carpets and some furniture applications. Velvet or velveteen has no distracting pattern. Avoid thick cloth that has a tendency to dominate the room and in which the legs of your scale furniture "sink" to "1'."

Another material for use on carpets and furniture covering is flocking. Paint the area to be covered the same or a similar color as the flocking selected, then sprinkle flocking over the area while paint is tacky. After the paint completely dries, use a vacuum sweeper to pick up excess. The excess can be saved for reuse or retouchnig.

## Wood Flooring

Vertically scribed basswood is ideal for wood planking. It is available in various widths and takes stain. Plain wood can be scored with a blade and metal straightedge.

## Tile Flooring

Vinyl material, in a variety of colors and styles, simulate kitchen and bathroom floors and trim. These materials can readily be found with adhesive backing.

## Doors and Windows

Plastic windows and doors simplified the construction of our sample model. You can easily make doors from wood paneling, with no unusual problems. Windows, on the other hand, offer a variety of possibilities to modelers. Here are a few suggestions:

1. Use clear plastic mounted in flange for floor-to-ceiling window-walls. Also, use door track or wooden channel molding. Remember that most door track and flange has a groove that is only ⅟₃₂″ thick regardless of the size of the piece.
2. Small windows can also be framed as above. Panes may be illustrated by small strips of wood glued to the plastic. A diamond window pattern may be produced by using screen wire in the window frame diagonally (Fig. 5–2).

*Figure 5–2. Window using wire screen.*

## USE OF PLASTICS

The professional model builders use a large amount of plastic in their models because it is relatively easy for them to use and it makes the finished model extremely strong. Since a complete discussion of how to use plastics would require several volumes, we shall not attempt to cover that material completely in this book.

Plastics require caution, because they differ from wood in several respects. Plastic requires rather potent "glue," ethyline di chloride, which heat-fuses rather than glues the pieces to be joined. Some softer pieces may be bonded with acetone base adhesives. Plastic may not adhere well to wood. Harder plastics must be cut with a fine-toothed saw or be scored and broken like glass. Softer plastics may be cut with a knife. Unlike glass, plexiglass will not break. Brittle plastics will bend over the heat of a butane torch or boiling water. You must experiment for exactness. Finally, ethyline di chloride and acetones may be applied by hypodermic syringe, and must be used in very sparing amounts.

In most cases, the beginner should avoid plastics until he masters basic techniques with wood. Only an advanced craftsman can use plastic with a minimum of waste.

## USE OF METALS

Metals now available include sheets and rods of aluminum and brass in various gauges or thicknesses. The larger the gauge number, the thinner is the sheet or rod. The Dremel tool cuts and finishes metal for such uses as roof lining, structural columns, or simulated flashing in roof valleys.

Metals are useful for the imaginative beginner as well as for the experienced designer who relies on them for structural analysis and experimentation.

In the hopes of prolonging the life of the model, many builders laminate roof surfacing to a thin sheet of tin. This, in turn, is undercoated with a material similar to the top surface, preventing warping and providing finish for open-beam decor.

SOLDERING TIP.   Roughen the two surfaces lightly; clean and apply flux. Use rosin-core solder also until your soldering judgment develops. Experiment on scraps before attempting finer joints.

## MISCELLANEOUS BUILDING TIPS

The following tips not only illustrate the building methods shown, but may stimulate the student to develop his own special techniques.

LOUVER.   No model home is complete without louvers in the eaves. Here the louver is made by cutting a plastic shutter in half. (Figure 5–3.)

CUPOLA.   A cupola may be made from a wood block and shingled with cardboard or plastic roofing which is very easily worked. For the finishing touch, add a map pin to the top. (Figure 5–3.)

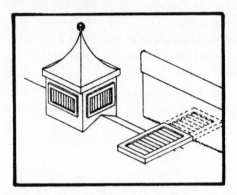

*Figure 5–3. Louver and cupola.*

WALL.   Corrugated metal sheets can be made into an attractive wall section. Walls may be laminated over wood or framed with flange or door track. Corrugated and waffle patterns in clear plastic are also available. (Figure 5–4.)

*Figure 5–4. Corrugated metal wall.*

GUTTERING. Guttering is necessary for the complete model home. Use of quarter-round in the appropriate size is effective for this purpose. (Figure 5–5.)

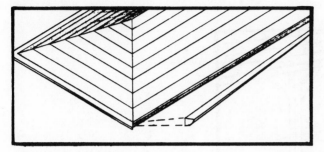

*Figure 5–5. Guttering.*

GARAGE DOORS. Garage doors of any size and shape may be constructed of ¹⁄₁₆″ clear plastic or basswood sheets as the back panel. Patterns may be of basswood strips that are ¹⁄₃₂″ thick and any width desired. The drawing at the left of Fig. 5–6 illustrates how easy it is to convert single garage doors into double doors. Simply place one door into the miter box and trim the molding running down the left-hand side. Next, place your second door in the miter box and trim the molding running down the right-hand side. Simply glue both doors together for a double garage door effect. (Figure 5–6.)

*Figure 5–6. Double garage doors.*

PORCH POSTS.   Posts for front porches and support brackets and trim for roof can be constructed of basswood strips. The porch can be made from basswood sheets and painted gray to simulate concrete. (Figure 5–7.)

*Figure 5–7. Porch posts.*

GABLES.   There are many ways to construct gabled ends on model houses. The one shown in Fig. 5–9 is made by scalloping the ends of scribed sheathing. Other methods are to use lap siding horizontally or use capped siding in the vertical position. (Figure 5–9.)

The specially cut trim may be carved or cut from thin strips of basswood.

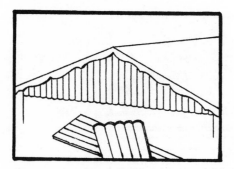

*Figure 5–8. Gables.*

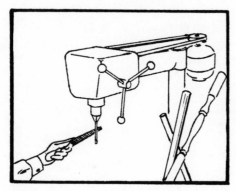

*Figure 5–9. Miniature lathe.*

MINIATURE LATHE. Special model shapes, porch posts, railings, pillars, etc. may be made very simply. Place the dowel selected into a drill press and, using a small finish file as a lathe tool, turn to the desired shape. (Figure 5–9.)

## Chapter 6

# *FURNITURE AND FIXTURES*

The modeler may design very imaginative furnishings on his own. Several well-tested methods can be adapted to your special purposes with little trouble. From the crudest furniture carved from soap to the most involved and elaborate plaster molding, no factor demands more thought than scale. A perfectly finished table will be very unattractive if the thickness of the top contradicts the scale of the house.

Unfortunately, scale household furniture is not readily available, but commercial styles of model furniture are available. Some of these mass-produced items may be adapted for your home by the judicious use of a knife, a paint brush, or flocking. Almost anything for use in an office or factory is available in plastic or lead, and many of the tables or chairs require only minor alterations to convert from institution to home. *Architectural Graphic Standards* is a very good book to use for furniture and fixture sizes.

An alternative material to the traditional balsa and basswood is high-density styrofoam, which can be cut very precisely with a Model Maker, an electrically heated wire blade and stand. High-density styrofoam has a very smooth appearance, almost no texture, and is almost pure white. It may be sawed, carved, and painted.

Combinations of materials will often solve minor construction problems: Heated wire will fuse into styrofoam, metal sheeting will reinforce contact veneer or cardboard. Wood dowel can be combined with plastic or metal as well by use of epoxy or acetone adhesive. Use metal or plastic for strength, and wood or paper for texture or color.

Whatever you can improvise will add to the appeal of your finished model. Here are several ideas you can adapt for your own use.

*Sinks*

You can make a round sink from the commercially available rectangular sink. Daub a bit of plaster of paris into the rectangle, let it set a few minutes, then shape into corners with your finger. After the plaster of paris dries, fill shallows and carve excess. Add a faucet made of an end of a paper clip embedded in the wall.

*Bed*

1. Cover foam or wood block with very fine, tightly woven material, placing cotton at one end to simulate pillows.
2. If the bedspread does not hang in small enough folds or drapes, then remove the spread, carve drape-like grooves, and paint a slightly darker tone than you want. While paint is still wet, wipe lighter colored flocking into it, leaving grooves and ridges to simulate the vertical folds of material.

*Coffee Table*

Use veneer, no thicker than $\frac{1}{16}''$, and add small dowels for legs.

*Top Curtains*

Do not use real fabric as the folds will be too large. Use paper, pleated. Austrian tissue is available in almost any color from your local artist supply store.

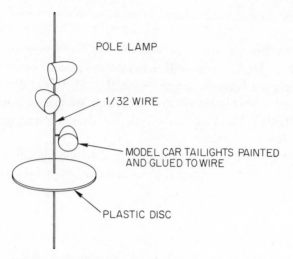

POLE LAMP

1/32 WIRE

MODEL CAR TAILIGHTS PAINTED
AND GLUED TO WIRE

PLASTIC DISC

*Figure 6–1. Construction of lamp pole.*

## Pole Lamp

1. Place a ⅟₃₂″ wire in floor.
2. Glue model car tail lights to a ⅟₃₂″ wire.
3. Add a round piece of veneer with center hole for table.
4. Fix into floor. The ceiling will fit over the top end of the wire for removal, but the pole will not be permanently attached to the ceiling. (Figure 6–1.)

## Modern Fireplace Chimney

Use a ⅜″ tube for stack, plastic or metal funnel for hood (if metal, fill seam and paint), and metal vertical edge on bottom of up-turned funnel. The chimney can also be carved from wood or styrofoam.

## Spiral Staircase

Rough-cut .040 brass sheeting for match pattern, then stack and clamp together. File to shape and drill hole through all steps at once. Solder each to ⅟₁₆″ brass pole, and then epoxy on railing of ⅟₃₂″ brass wire.

MODERN FIREPLACE

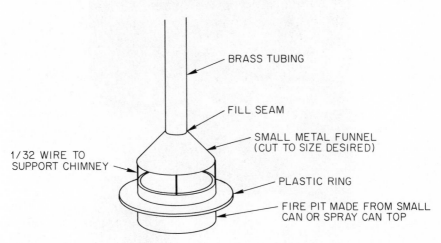

BRASS TUBING

FILL SEAM

SMALL METAL FUNNEL
(CUT TO SIZE DESIRED)

1/32 WIRE TO
SUPPORT CHIMNEY

PLASTIC RING

FIRE PIT MADE FROM SMALL
CAN OR SPRAY CAN TOP

*Figure 6–2. Modern fireplace.*

SPIRAL STAIRWAY

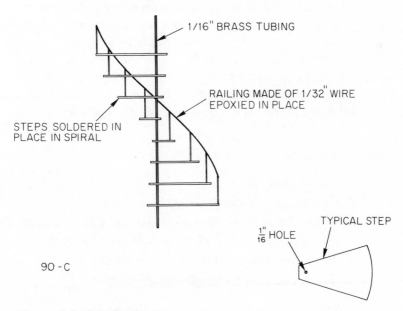

1/16" BRASS TUBING

RAILING MADE OF 1/32" WIRE
EPOXIED IN PLACE

STEPS SOLDERED IN
PLACE IN SPIRAL

90 - C

TYPICAL STEP

$\frac{1}{16}$" HOLE

*Figure 6–3. Spiral stairway.*

*Figure 6–4*

*Wall Decor*

Pictures cut from magazines such as *Better Homes and Gardens* may be used, with caution, to decorate interiors. Beware of the subject, and consider color harmony with interior walls. Only the smallest pictures will be successful; Find an article dealing with a decor similar to that of your model, then look for a head-on shot of a wall with pictures, but check the scale carefully. Interior decorators are usually glad to help students.

*Furniture Upholstery*

1. Carve from balsa.
2. Paint a hue slightly darker than desired.
3. While the paint is still tacky, dust on lighter colored flocking (or spray from Velvet Spray adhesive bottle).
4. Press plenty of flocking into the wet paint.
5. Brush when dry for good scale simulation.

This method avoids rug-plush or velvety look by varying the direction of the nap and emphasizing contours and depth.

*Furniture*

For items to duplicate:

1. Make wood jig with pins at structural joints and extremities.
2. Stretch wire over frame.
3. Solder, tie, or glue.
4. Remove from jig.

(A)

(B)

*Figure 6–5*

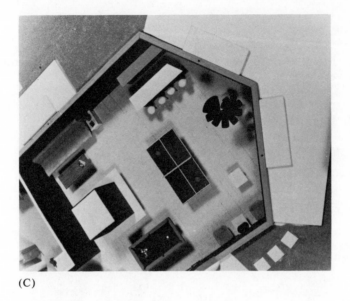

(C)

(D)

*Figure 6–5. continued*

CARVING TIP. When carving crumbly materials, follow the mason's method. Cut in from the edge, not toward the edge.

### Decorative Roof Cornices

For interior or exterior fancy moldings at the ceiling; use a ¼″ strip of cardboard along which you have cut equally spaced tabs. Then cut ¹⁄₁₆″ off at every other tab. Now the cornices may be glued at ⅛″ from the wall, every other tab forming a regularly patterned indentation.

### Plaster Casting

If you wish to duplicate a structural ornament or piece of furniture that has few projections, but requires tedious work for exact replication, consider using the readily available brush-on rubber solution that will form a mold for plaster casting.

1. Form your original of soap, wood, plaster, or metal.
2. Then brush on the first light coating of rubber solution.
3. When this coat is *completely* dry, apply a second coat.
4. Repeat the process until the original has four to six coats, evenly distributed.
5. Now peel the dried rubber mold from the original, trim it, and begin pouring the plaster casts. If your item to duplicate is very intricate, then cut the dried rubber mold apart, and cast the item in two portions. You can use anything for the original, as it will not be destroyed by the rubber. Cuts may be repaired with rubber cement. The molding process requires some skill; therefore, a little practice may pay off before you attempt to cast intricate furnishings or ornamental elements.

Many hobby shops manufacture their own rubber solution; one particular manufacturer is Bersted.

## Chapter 7

## MOUNTING, LANDSCAPING AND
## PHOTOGRAPHING THE MODEL

Once the house has all interior walls in place, easy access can be had for contouring the plastic foam, papier mache or cardboard terrain. Apart from a few ground rules, any number of innovations can neatly customize your model's appearance.

The ground should slope away from the house for the scale equivalent of several yards, and, if extreme contours are planned, thought must be given to natural drainage flow. For the purpose of reproducing an actual plot, some tasteful exaggeration of vertical scale will better indicate the existing slope.

Too much landscaping enthusiasm can obscure a model; all contouring and plants should enhance, but not detract from, the model. For instance. if many *trees* are planned, but they threaten to block the view of the model, you may wish to alter the scale, making the trees smaller than life, or you may wish to construct the trees from bare wire alone—giving the suggestion of many full trees without blocking the eye-level view of the house's elevation.

*MOUNTING AND LANDSCAPING THE MODEL*

Four basic materials (and their use) can be quickly discussed for forming the contours around the model:

1. Styrofoam.
2. Papier mache.
3. Screen and plaster of paris, or wood fibre plaster.
4. Cardboard.

Probably the most modern and simple method is the use of styrofoam. The plastic is cut, sculptured roughly, then glued into position. Next the seams and texture are filled in with plaster of paris.

Papier mache, while it utilizes the cheapest materials, is not the simplest nor quickest method. Once the surface is dry and hard, it may be difficult to place the shrubs without danger of bursting through the surface.

Screen wire and plaster of paris make a strong but very heavy landscape. However, the wet plaster simulates the scale of actual terrain very realistically. Vinegar slows the rate of drying. Experiment for proportions.

The layered cardboard landscape might best be used with a contemporary house design. Many architects leave the raw edges of the cardboard layers untrimmed and unfilled, thus pointing up the completeness of detail in the house itself.


*Construction of Trees*

Trees and shrubs can be constructed from any of these materials, or from others, depending on the modeler's necessity and invention:

1. Dried field weeds, such as goldenrod, trimmed down to scale.
2. Lichen, particularly the ends of the growth.
3. Frame work of bare wire to suggest outline of foliage.
4. Electrical conduit splayed apart at the top.
5. A ping-pong ball on a wire or stick (ultracontemporary).

When placing the lichen on the branches, keep a can of hair-spray handy. This will dry quickly and give reasonable assurance that the foliage will not fall apart. The scent will not last very long.

### Simulation of Grass

Grass may be simulated by means of flocking, sawdust, or even textured surfacing of the styrofoam, plaster, or cardboard. Flocking produces the most even results and can be easily mastered.

1. Choose a color that will not be too conspicuous and detract from the color on the model's exterior. You may wish to mix browns, grays, and greens experimentally to find the ideal blend for your model.
2. Apply adhesive either by quickly brushing on an even coating of white glue, or facing the exposed elevations of the house and then spraying an even coat of adhesive. (Some builders prefer to use colored latex paint instead of glue.)
3. Now, using a screen box or a sieve, dust on a light even coat of the flocking. Before adding more flocking, check for any areas where glue either has not adhered, or where too much glue has been applied.
4. Complete dusting of flocking, making sure that more than enough to stick to the adhesive has been dusted uniformly. Once adhesive is dry, blow off excess and store for reuse, or for touchup before displaying: brush it on problem areas without applying new glue.

Sawdust may be applied in much the same manner, and it may be dyed to the exact color desired. However, it is often more effective to mix the flocking or sawdust colors, perhaps even slightly altering the blend in shaded areas of the landscapes or in garden areas. If you use white glue instead of paint, expect it to brown slightly in a few months.

### Paths and Roadways

Paths and roadways present no problem, and may be surfaced before or after they are fixed in the landscape. Flocking, sawdust, emery paper of 400-grade coarseness, or even plain construction paper can serve as surfacing materials. Most sandpaper should not be used, as its large grain tends to destroy the scale of the project. Another problem with sandpaper is its color, which does not replicate normal drive or path surfacings. Before surfacing the landscape, you may wish to try "pouring" plaster of paris into actual molds just as concrete is laid. Then smooth over with a stick, and groove the plaster of paris for simulated expansion joints. If you use balsa, be sure to fill its natural pores before painting.

## Pools and Ponds

Pools and ponds are a temptation to the model builder, but beginners should avoid anything with running water. Very good simulation of swimming pools, streams, and natural ponds can be easily achieved with the simplest of materials. One method that entails some work, but gives the illusion of depth involves four steps:

1. Sink a shallow box into the terrain.
2. Paint the bottom a light-medium blue, and gradually paint the sides lighter toward the top edges.
3. Cover the sunken, painted box with a light green piece of glass or plastic. This surface might well be stippled or rippled, so as to let the light through, but slightly distort the view of corners and edges in the sunken box.
4. Apply grass, earth, rocks or foliage up to and beyond the edges of the sunken box, thereby completely hiding the top edges.

A simpler method involves a clear piece of plastic or glass, which again should be rippled or stippled. This is placed flush over a painted pattern designed to represent either a natural pond or an artificial pool and fountain. Camouflage the edges.

If the motion of a fountain cannot be represented, use very small lengths of plastic wire that will bend naturally to reflect light just as the moving water in a fountain's jet does.

A rectangular swimming pool looks best, as the more imaginative abstract shapes appear a little too artificial, destroying the scale illusion. For swimming pools, most likely you want the inside corners of the sunken box to show. Therefore, once the sunken box is painted a very light blue or white, you can cover it with light-blue acetate on glass. The glass will support the acetate and light blue color will replicate the clean water. Plastic sheeting also comes in colors, and if available, would serve well.

*Originality*

In landscaping, as in other elements of detail, the most important rule to remember is that an original method may enhance the model more than the most skillfully executed traditional method. Many imaginative details of landscaping can accent an uninteresting corner of your plot. Experimentation and advice will indicate whether an idea is too unique and detracts rather than enhances the model.

Weeds and other growth in your own neighborhood may lend themselves very well to miniature shrubbery with a little alteration. Goldenrod, for example, can be trimmed to form very delicate branch structures. If the plant is dry, it may be either dipped in dye or sprayed. After the color is dry, be sure to spray the plant with plastic or shellac to help prolong its strength.

Intricate-appearing rock gardens can be quickly assembled from smooth pebbles either in their natural form or painted. These may be glued to a plaster, wooden, or cardboard backing to offset a garden with an entry-way or walkway.

If your contouring is to include drops, rises, or split-level construction, you may want to consider building a retaining wall as part of a garden, beside a walk or drive, or to border a backyard patio. Probably this can be constructed separately from the contour, and then be situated for final touchups.

More ambitious students may wish to include small streams in an inconspicuous corner of their lots, perhaps even with small waterfalls which could be simulated by using quick-hardening epoxy resin.

Another unique idea for the corner of a larger lot is a simulated vegetable garden.

For all outdoor surfaces, try to avoid the solid, untextured single color. Instead, spatter lightly with a slightly varying hue of the base color. This will help provide the natural look in color as well as in texture.

One ingenious teacher of drafting led his class in a group exercise in landscaping. Each student was assigned one detail of planning and executing an entire public park complete with wooded areas, ponds, shelters, roads and paths, recreational facilities, and a variety of realistically scaled shrubs. Using such an exercise to acquaint the beginner with the materials and methods of model building, might help him to avoid many kinds of errors when he begins the painstaking construction of his own house.

## PHOTOGRAPHY

Once your model is finished, and you have invested so much time, energy, and even a little bit of yourself in it, you may wish to photograph the model. Just as the construction itself differs from full-scale construction, so the photographing of a model requires certain adjustments.

The amateur photographer will be most successful in the open air, photographing the model against a natural background with natural, evenly distributed broad daylight. Normally, you should focus on a near level with the first story of the house, and you should angle the model slightly to avoid a two-dimensional effect. After all, you have built in three dimensions, so show them off in your photograph.

In a studio, keep all obstructions away from the path of artificial floodlighting, as the smallest shadows will be hideously exaggerated. You may wish to construct or borrow a simulated cloud backdrop using no fine lines or harsh contrasts. Black and white shots will be more likely to simulate the appearance of a real house.

Make sure that the shadows do not dominate the photograph, and especially that shadows do not fall toward the camera lens. Always avoid double shadows, or conflicting light sources, to maintain realism.

*Chapter 8*

*MODELS IN SCHOOL AND INDUSTRY*

Figure 8–1. Student's model house. Scale ¼" = 1'. This model by Arthur Elliott, Jr. was a first place winner in the Greater Kansas City Model Home Contest. The detail of the interior is shown in Chapter 6.

Figure 8–1. continued

*Figure 8–1. continued*

129

Figure 8–1. continued

Figure 8–2. Harry S. Truman Sports Complex. Scale 1" = 25'. Model of cardboard used in extensive drive for public funds. Kivett and Myers, Project Architect; Charles Deaton, Architect, Design Associate; Bryant Architectural Models, builder; photo by Paul S. Kivett.

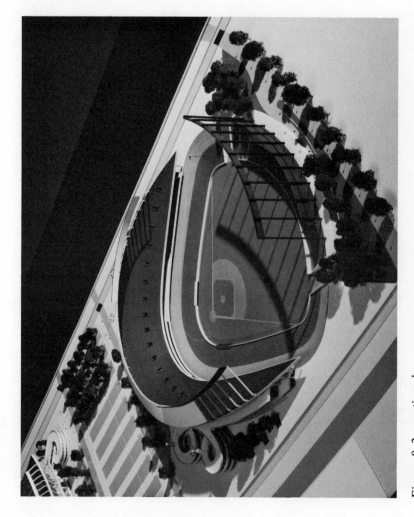

*Figure 8–2. continued*

*Figure 8–2. continued*

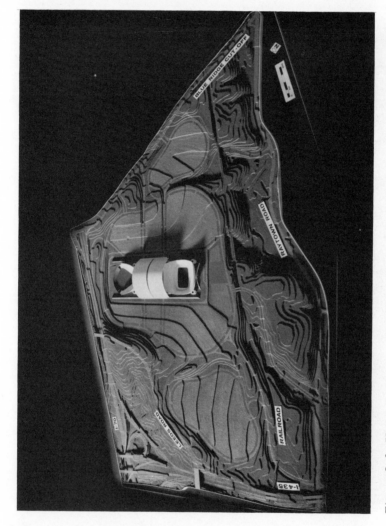

*Figure 8–3. Harry S. Truman Sports Complex. Scale 1:150. Site study used for planning roads and site preparation. Credits same as Fig. 8–2.*

*Figure 8–4. Kansas City International Airport. Scale ½" = 1'. Scale interior reflecting how functional the design could be in the terminal. The photographic technique is exceptional. Kivett and Myers, Architects; Burns & McDonnell Engineering Company, Engineers; model by the architects; photo by Paul S. Kivett.*

Figure 8–5. *Fernbank Science Center. Scale ⅛" = 1'. In order to duplicate the stone requested by the architect the builder created a mold for a three-dimensional siding of paper. The imaginative model builder will find that any material can be simulated. Toombs, Amisano & Wells, Architects; Bryant Architectural Models, model builder; photo by Hayes Photo.*

*Figure 8–6. School Floor Plan, Swanton, Vermont. Scale $\frac{1}{16}$" = 1'. Model illustrates on practical use for models: arranging space use and traffic flow. Shaver & Co., Architects; Bryant Architectural Models, model builder; photo by Hayes Photo.*

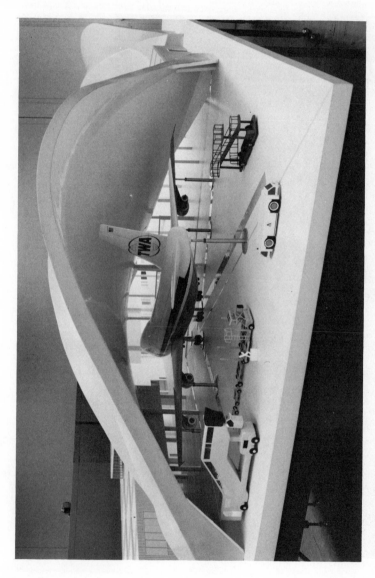

*Figure 8–7. TWA Overhaul Facility. Scale 1:150. Model used to illustrate new hangar design. Aero-Shell, Dutten Biggs, Architects; Bryant Architectural Models, builder; photo by the architects.*

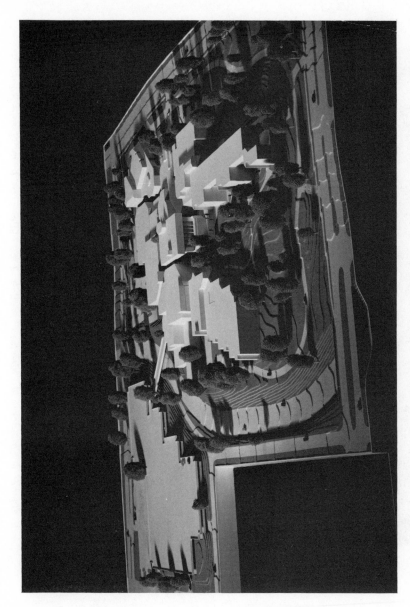

*Figure 8–8. Penn Valley Junior College. Scale 1:100. Model of plastic and wood to assist in location of buildings on existing site. Marshall & Brown, Architects; Bryant Architectural Models, builder; photo by Hayes Photo.*

Figure 8–9. Embarcadero Center, San Francisco. Scale 1" = 50'. Model used to determine how proposed new structures would appear alongside existing buildings. Special problems are encountered when trying to show details at such a small scale. Project by Caldwell, Banker & Company; Architectural Models, Inc., builder; photo by Gerald Ratto.

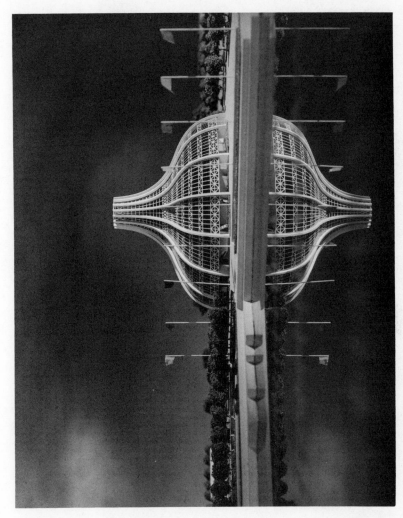

*Figure 8–10. Cultural/Convention Complex. Scale 1" = 50'. Small model used to stimulate public interest in community project. This is probably one of the most common uses for architectural models. Skidmore, Owings & Merrill, Architects; Architectural Models, Inc., builders; photo by Gerald Ratto.*

*Figure 8-11. Ontario Motor Stadium. Scale 1" = 20'. Model to promote facility in Ontario, California. Note how real the photograph appears. Benham-Kite and Associates, Inc., Architects; Architectural Models, Inc., builders; Linesch & Reynolds, Landscape Architects; photo by Gerald Ratto.*

142

*Figure 8–12. Stanford Children's Convalescent Hospital, Palo Alto, California. Scale 1" = 30'. Model primarily noteworthy for beautiful roofing and landscape effects. Stone, Marracinni & Patterson, Architects; Jack Stafford, Landscape Architect; Architectural Models, Inc., builders; photo by Gerald Ratto.*

*Figure 8–13. Washingotn, D.C. Capitol Mall Master Plan. Scale 1" = 100'. This photograph shows only a portion of the complete model. Note that the builder used detail on the more famous buildings to make the model more recognizable. Skidmore, Owings & Merrill, Architects; Architectural Models, Inc., builders; photo by Dwain Faubion.*

*Figure 8–14. San Francisco International Market Center. Scale 1" = 50'. The detail of the site is the highlight of this model. The project is shown in detail while the existing structures are roughed-in for effect only. Wurster, Bernardi & Emmons, Architects, Lawrence Halprin & Associates, Landscape Architects; Architectural Models, Inc., builders; photo by Gerald Ratto.*

145

*Figure 8–15. Radium Aggregate Plant, Pleasanton, California. Scale ³⁄₁₆″ = 1′. This model was built to clarify the complex drawings. This is one of the most practical uses for model building. Models of this type are also used to familiarize personnel with the plant layout. Kaiser Engineers, Engineers; Architectural Models, Inc., builders; photo by Gerald Ratto.*

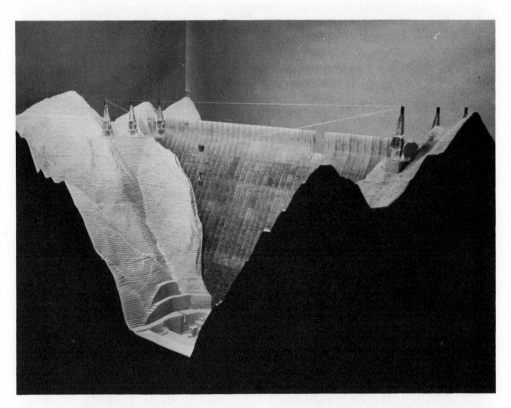

*Figure 8–16. Dworshak Dam Working Model. Horizontal Scale 1" = 40'. Vertical Scale 1" = 20'. This actual working model was used by Dworshak Dam Constructors to calculate their pouring schedule when constructing this facility. Architectural Models, Inc., builders; photo by Joseph Rapley.*

*Figure 8–17. Santa Clara Library. Scale 1" = 8'. Model used to study interior lighting. Edward D. Stone, Architect; Architectural Models, Inc., builders; photo by Karl H. Riek.*

*Figure 8–18. Stanislaus State College Master Plan. Scale 1" = 80'. Model used for extensive landscaping project. Reid & Tarics, Architects; Architectural Models, Inc., builders; photo by Dwain Faubion.*

*Figure 8–19. Ardway Building, Kaiser Center, Oakland. Scale 1" = 16'. Model to illustrate ability of new and old architecture to blend together. Skidmore, Owings & Merrill, Architects; Architectural Models, Inc., builders; photo by Jeremiah Bragstad.*

# GLOSSARY

ANGLE MOLDING. (Sometimes called "angle.") Molding designed to cover a corner joint inside or outside. Its cross section forms an "L."

APEX. The top, summit, or cap.

BALSA. Light, easy to carve wood; more shrinkage and warp than basswood.

BASEBOARD. Wood molding running around base of walls.

BASSWOOD. Light, easy to carve, kiln dried, cuts fine, light blond, receives glue well.

BEVEL. The slant or slope of a line or surface when not at right angles with another line or surface.

BEVEL JOINT. A miter joint, especially when two pieces meet at other than a right angle.

BOARD AND BATTEN. Board siding with thin strip to cover seams.

CROSS HATCHING. Texture or surfacing in which lines are scored first parallel from left to right, then from to top bottom, forming a fine checkerboard effect.

*151*

DOOR JAMB.   Side of the opening to door or window against which the door or sash abuts.

EAVES.   Overhang; the part of the roof, and attic, which extends beyond the exterior wall of the house.

ELEVATION OF A BUILDING.   A view of one face, left to right, top to bottom. A normal structure has four elevations, called N, S, E, and W elevations.

FASCIA.   Plank used for trim; vertical facing beneath outer edge of roof or interior facing of window opening.

FLASHING.   The metal lining of a valley in a roof, usually running into a drain and downspout. Use a wire or copper foil under layered shingle.

FLEXIBLE RESPONSE.   Willingness to modify and adapt.

FLOCK(ING).   Dust-like particles of textile for simulation of carpet, grass, and material. Used with paint or glue.

FLUE (OF A CHIMNEY).   The actual air-channel for conducting the smoke from the fireplace.

HIP ROOF.   Roof with sloping ends and sides.

I-BEAM.   Structual beam with cross section in the shape of an "I."

INSIDE CUT.   A cut that begins in the center of a piece of material, but does not reach the edges of the piece (as for a window).

JIG.   Open frame or pattern to hold items for reproducing, gluing, or drilling.

LAP SIDING.   Stacked horizontally with tilt to deflect rain.

LICHEN (*LIKN*). (ALSO SPELLED LYCHEN.).   Dried plant complex of algae and fungus that can be painted to simulate foliage.

MITER BOX.   A wooden form for precision cutting of angles, usually perpendicular angles and 45-degree angles. (Also MITER: A kind of joint, as in the common picture frame.)

NOSING.   Projection of the stair tread over the riser.

PERPENDICULARITY.   A perpendicular line or plane.

PITCH (ROOF).   The steepness of the roof, or stairs, commonly stated in the degee of inclination, referred to as "steep." Rise/run is pitch.

REPLICATE.   To make an exact (scale) replica see (SIMULATE).

RISE.   Vertical measurement between two stair treads. Rise of roof; height.

RISER.   Stairway vertical plank between treads. Tread: flat part. Overhang: nose.

RUN.   The distance from one end of the roof to the other. The distance between end supports.

SILL.   Door or window beam across bottom of door or window frame. Threshhold.

SIMULATE.   To approximate the original, representing the basics, or the feeling of the original. (See REPLICATE.)

SPATIAL THINKING.   Mental manipulation of sizes, shapes, and areas.

STRINGER.   One of the sloping sides of a stair, supporting the treads and risers.

TEES.   Pieces of molding with a cross section that forms a "T." Used for structural model.

TEMPLATE.   A die used to shape or scrape curved or angled surfaces. A patterned structure for repetitive marking, or for duplicating.

THUMBNAIL SKETCH.   Often a very small-scale sketch with unreliable accuracy.

TONGUE AND GROOVE.   Siding or boards fitted with small grooves on one side, and extended tongues on the other, thereby fitting together.

TRANSOM.   Opening over a door or window; also the supporting beam. Also door or window head.

TRUE.   To make exactly accurate.

VENEER.   A thin layer of wood used as a covering layer of material for a wall.

# INDEX